IMAGES
of America

LINVILLE GORGE WILDERNESS AREA

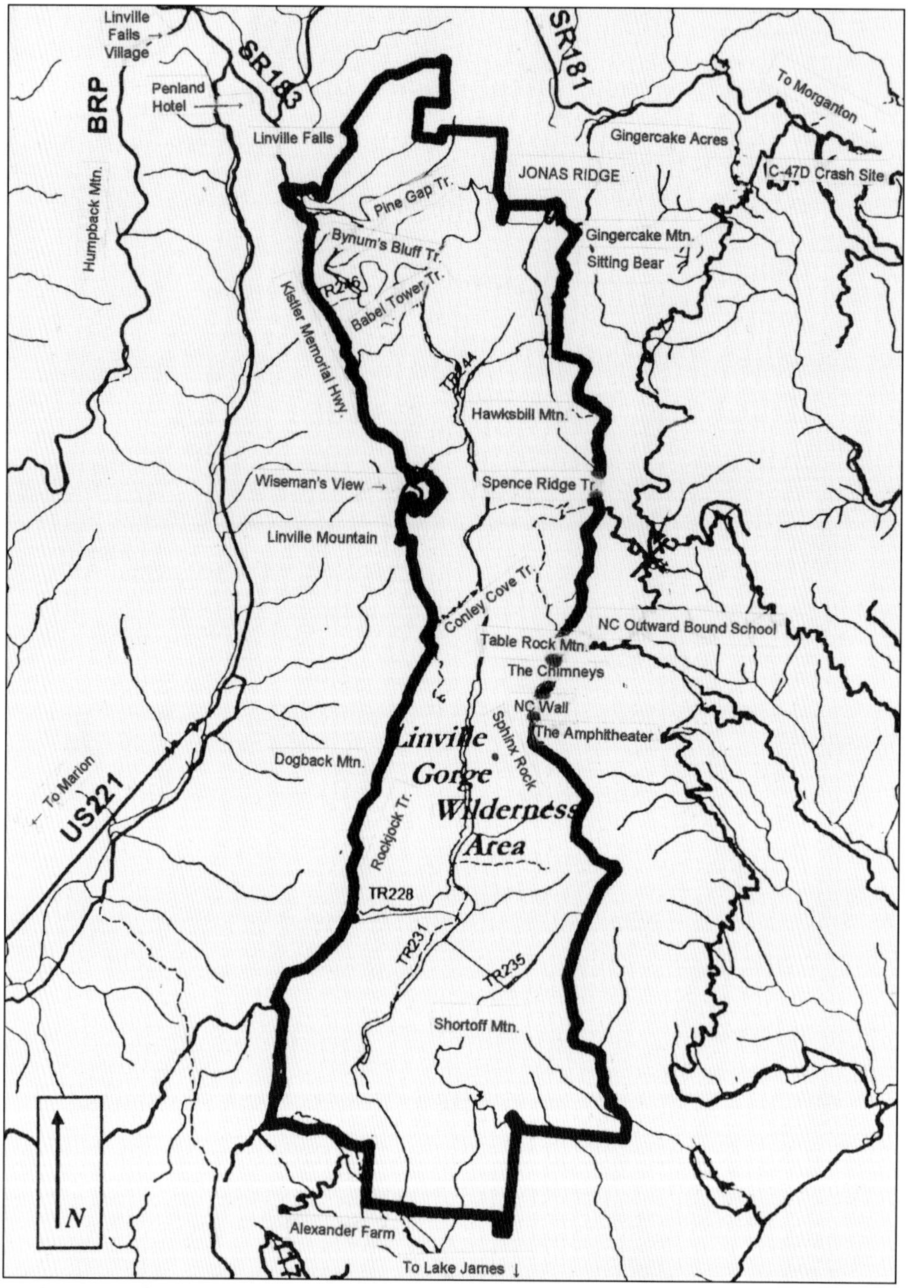

Map of Linville Gorge Wilderness Area. This map indicates the locations of key natural and man-made features in this book. (Courtesy of the author.)

On the Cover: Linville Falls resident Frank W. Bicknell recorded this outing to the summit of Hawksbill Mountain on April 24, 1909. From left to right, the party includes Mrs. Read, Molly Franklin, Henry Franklin, Mabel Hyams, and Jessie Bicknell (perched on the "bill" of Hawksbill). Behind the group, Table Rock Mountain appears on the left; across the gorge and to the right appears Dogback Mountain. (Courtesy of the North Carolina Office of Archives and History.)

IMAGES
of America

LINVILLE GORGE WILDERNESS AREA

Christopher Blake

ARCADIA
PUBLISHING

ISBN 978-0-7385-6851-5

Published by Arcadia Publishing
Charleston, South Carolina

Printed in the United States of America

Library of Congress Catalog Card Number: 2008935045

For all general information contact Arcadia Publishing at:
Telephone 843-853-2070
Fax 843-853-0044
E-mail sales@arcadiapublishing.com
For customer service and orders:
Toll-Free 1-888-313-2665

Visit us on the Internet at www.arcadiapublishing.com

For Peter H. Blake (1953–2008)
and Allen Hyde and Bob Underwood, pathfinders.

CONTENTS

ACKNOWLEDGMENTS

This collection of photographs of the Linville Gorge Wilderness Area builds largely on a foundation of professional and amateur pictures taken from the early 1870s onward and now preserved in the archives of universities and state departments of cultural resources. Perhaps a quarter of the images in this book were provided by friends, by small informal groups, or by the author. Sources are indicated in the captions for each individual photograph.

The institutions to which I am indebted are the following: for the Rufus Morgan and Bayard T. Wootten photographs, the North Carolina and Southern Historical Collections of the Wilson Library at the University of North Carolina at Chapel Hill; for the Frank W. Bicknell photographs, the North Carolina Office of Archives and History, Raleigh, North Carolina; for the D. R. Beeson, James A. Goforth, and William Cary Hattan pictures, the Archives of Appalachia at the Sherrard Library of East Tennessee State University in Johnson City, Tennessee; for the Albert "Dutch" Roth images, the University of Tennessee Libraries, Knoxville, Tennessee; for the National Park Service photographs, the Blue Ridge Parkway Archives in Asheville, North Carolina; for the U.S. Forest Service pictures, the Grandfather Ranger District Headquarters in Nebo, North Carolina; for the Marion A. Wright photograph, Winthrop University, Rock Hill, South Carolina; for the John D. Rockefeller Jr. portrait, the Library of Congress in Washington, DC; for George Masa's pictures, Pack Memorial Library in Asheville, North Carolina; and, for help with an outmoded laptop, a hearty thanks goes to Barbara and Larry of Interlink in Newland, North Carolina.

Local contributions include images from the collection of Friends of Linville Gorge, an informal non-profit group dedicated to increasing the public awareness of this unique wilderness area by publications, hikes, mushroom forays, and maintenance of the Devil's Hole Trail; I include photographs from Allen Hyde, Mike Fischesser, Brad Sanzenbacher, Forest Dula, Carl Fleming, C. Lewis Paschall, and Leroi Rose. Once again, my debts, personal and editorial, to Dorothy H. Watson might fill a gorge.

For current information on the Linville Gorge Wilderness Area visit:

http://groups.yahoo.com/group/linvillegorge/

Linville Gorge Discussion Group was founded on May 25, 2003, by owner and moderator Bob Underwood and has a membership (as of winter 2008) of over 400. The group offers online forums, trail data, photograph galleries, topographical maps, and GPS data.

www.linvillegorge.net.

Linville Gorge Data is a sister site to the Linville Gorge Discussion Group and is owned and moderated by Ken Crump. The site contains collections of GPS waypoints, sites, and maps, as well as member forums and photographs.

INTRODUCTION

How often have visitors to the Linville Gorge stared with awe into the wilderness canyon below them from Wiseman's View or Table Rock Mountain and recalled Longfellow's line, "This is the forest primeval," or mused with wonder, "why it's just the way the Indians left it." So well has the U.S. Forest Service managed the natural beauty of this 12,000-plus-acre tract in the Pisgah National Forest that evidence of human activity there is slight. Yet the Linville Gorge Wilderness Area is far from being the unblemished nature preserve that romantic sightseers might weave fantasies about. In fact, irony dwells in the fact that this rugged gorge, while indeed a stand of virgin, unlogged forest, has a rich and varied background of settlement, agriculture, development, speculation, murder and mayhem, and especially of recreational use. The Linville Gorge has also made its appeal to culture, attracting novelists, painters, balladeers, and particularly landscape photographers. Such visitors have interpreted the wilderness in the light of their own distinctive perspectives on the place. It is with the visual record of the wilderness that this book is concerned.

The history of Linville Gorge is not something concluded in the remote past. The wilderness is in a ceaseless state of change and not—as some might think—pretty much the same year after year. Natural forces, such as storm, flood, lightning strikes, and geological action, all work dynamic transformations on the area. Hurricanes Frances and Katrina, for example, formed new channels far downstream on the Linville River, while scouring the riverbanks of all vegetation for 8 to 10 feet up the gorge side. Forest fires caused by lightning strikes have devastated large areas at the Linville Gorge's southern end. Great boulder fields on the slopes all around the canyon are gradually moving downhill toward the river in what Linville Gorge trail guide author Allen Hyde calls "slow-motion rockslides." And, most daunting of all, the stands of native hemlock are rapidly dying off from the predations of an invasive insect, the hemlock wooly adelgid, changing the deep green robes of the ridges and peaks to the ghastly silvery sheen of dead timber. Humankind, of course, continues to have a negative impact on the Linville Gorge. The waters of the Linville River have been polluted near their sources to the north, and the water is not potable. Untended campfires cause their share of forest fires. The popularity of the wilderness means increasing use by a growing recreation population whose impact increases year by year. Yet there is a positive side to human activity here; new facilities have been constructed so as to blend in with the surroundings. The footbridge spanning the Linville River at Spence Ridge Trail and the migrating bird viewing platform near Pinnacle Rock are two examples of conscientious design. U.S. Forest Service administrators limit the number of campers allowed in the wilderness during the months of highest use. Adopt-a-Trail volunteer crews trim vegetation, maintain rainwater runoff ditches, and haul out litter. Conservancy groups purchase additional land for the Linville Gorge.

A large share of the Linville Gorge's history has been made by government organizations. Two of these are federal agencies charged with the management of the area: the National Park Service (of the nation's Department of the Interior), which oversees the Linville Falls Recreation Area, and the U.S. Forest Service (of the Department of Agriculture), which tends to the wilderness gorge below the Linville Falls. Their ongoing legacy is one of preservation and protection.

The pictorial record of the wilderness area ought to be framed with a brief history of the place, including what we know of it eons before man came on the scene. Visible evidence of its origins lies readily to hand, all over the Linville Gorge. The Linville Gorge was formed during a period of continental collision 300 million years ago. The collisions created great folds and fault lines, heaving up the Appalachian chain. Then came periods of separation and gradual erosion through weathering and the action of river water. Typical of the geology of the Linville Gorge is the presence of older rock atop much younger rock.

The history of Native American presence in the Linville Gorge is enigmatic. The first human visitors to the Catawba River Valley to the south of the gorge arrived some 12,000 years ago. Burke County abounds with archeological sites of these Paleo-Indian settlers who flourished in the rich game lands of the area's forests, rivers, and creeks. Artifacts reveal substantial and continuous hunting and fishing in the Catawba Valley from the late Pleistocene all the way to the Colonial period. Most of this activity was centered in the fertile river valleys at the foot of the Blue Ridge. There is no evidence of permanent Native American settlement in and around Linville Gorge. Popular legend settles the Cherokees in the gorge, naming Table Rock Mountain as their "mystic altar, or *Attacoa*." Most likely, the Linville Gorge was used simply as a seasonal hunting ground. Cherokee presence in the area is attested by their word for the place, *Eeseeoh*, meaning "river of many cliffs." A tradition has descended that the area around the Linville Gorge remained neutral, open for all Native American food gathering. What makes this unlikely is the fact that the Cherokee considered the Catawba, who were living east of the Blue Ridge, as a perennial enemy. During the period of intense political rivalry between France and England, efforts were made by both governments to pacify the indigenous peoples of the mountains by signing treaties, opening trade routes, and building forts. The 1740s–1750s saw numerous abuses by white traders and fierce retaliatory attacks by Native Americans. In 1756, North Carolina moved to protect the Catawbas from the Cherokees by erecting a stockade near present-day Old Fort. The 1760s saw the flaring up of bitter conflicts between the Native Americans and the English. In 1760, a number (perhaps as many as 24) of English traders were murdered, the Cherokee besieged Fort Prince George, and settlements along the Yadkin and Catawba Rivers came under attack. When the French and Indian War ended in 1763, Colonial representatives met with Native American leaders to sign a peace treaty. A royal proclamation prohibited whites from settling or even venturing into the lands west of the Blue Ridge chain. It was this agreement that William Linville violated, when, in 1766, he led a hunting party along the river that now bears his name.

In July 1766, North Carolina's royal governor William Tryon wrote to his superintendent of Indian Affairs, John Stuart, that he had learned that William Linville, his son, and a John Williams had been ambushed by an unknown tribe of Native Americans in the first week of July. Williams alone had escaped to his settlement with injuries and had since died. Tryon leaves it unclear where the attack occurred and to which settlement the wounded man fled. It is likely that Daniel Boone accompanied the search party that recovered the Linville's bodies in or near the gorge. By 1777, all the Native Americans had been run out of the area by militia commanded by Waightstill Avery and General Rutherford, and henceforth the gorge, river, and falls bore Linville's name. With the natives driven out of the area and their lands ceded by the Treaty of the Long Island of the Holston River in June 1777, the settlement of the Blue Ridge began in earnest.

European settlement concentrated on the areas suitable for farming, that is, at the Linville Gorge's northern end along the Linville River and on Jonas Ridge and at the rich alluvial plain to the south, near Shortoff Mountain. Early ownership of acreage in and around the Linville Gorge is a hopelessly muddled issue due to a Civil War attack on the Burke County courthouse by Stoneman's Raiders in 1865, a futile act, which destroyed most early records by fire. Many early land grants were those deeded to veterans of the Revolutionary War, who typically received parcels of one square mile (640 acres). Land tended to end up in the hands of a few individuals. William Ervin, for example, owned most of the Linville Gorge in 1833, holding 397 of those square-mile grants. Col. Isaac T. Avery claimed some of the same land, for the grants often overlapped. George Walton, interested in the area's iron deposits, also laid a claim. Samuel Alexander received a government grant for 150 acres lying at the bottom of the Linville Gorge in 1777. Samuel Franklin and his two sons (David and Lawson) entered grants for 1,200 acres of the land and, along with J. G. Wiseman, left their mark as working residents of the place—not absentee owners, as were Ervin, Avery, and others. Grants issued to William and Robert Tate in 1795 included most of Linville Mountain. A persistent story of a lost lead mine in Linville Gorge finds support in the Charles McDowell grant of 1805, which records a "furnis and led mine."

The early 19th century saw the growth of small communities around the "grand canyon of the east" and its dawning popularity as a destination for travel writers. Near the waterfalls, the community of Linville Falls sprang up as a small farming settlement. To the east, Jonas Ridge, named for Jonas Braswell who died of exposure nearby, lay on the route to Morganton in the Carolina piedmont. At the bottom of the Linville Gorge, the Paddy's Creek settlement was founded near Linville Cove, above present-day Lake James. Before the coming of the railroad, these were fairly isolated places, yet most of them were well within a day's ride of each other. The famous French botanist Andre Michaux visited the Linville Gorge in September 1794 gathering plant specimens for the royal nurseries back home. In the spring of 1816, botanist Thomas Nuttall discovered the small golden-flowered shrub known as "mountain golden heather" (*Hudsonia montana*). This highly endangered plant grows only in the wilderness area. Another severely threatened species, Heller's blazing star (*Liatris belleri*) favors the same habitat. Famed University of North Carolina professor Elisha Mitchell came to the area in 1828 to measure mountain elevations and observed Table Rock Mountain in the distance.

Railroads had a significant impact on the history of the Linville Gorge, as two separate systems were operating in the area. In 1909, the Carolina, Clinchfield, and Ohio Railroad (CC&O) completed its first stage, running from Dante, Virginia, to Spartanburg, South Carolina. The CC&O tracks, now part of the CXX system, pass below Linville Gorge then loop their way up Hunicutt Mountain seeking the crest at Altapass. For years, there was a "Linville Falls" depot in the Ashford community below Linville Mountain; however, Linville Falls lies seven miles to the north. The other railroad, the East Tennessee and Western North Carolina (ET&WNC), popularly known as "Tweetsie," like the Clinchfield, passed east from Johnson City but headed northeast to Boone, North Carolina. Besides offering passenger service, the Tweetsie was used for timber hauling. Spur connections to the major logging operation of the W. J. Ritter Company in Pineola meant that forest resources around the northern rim of the Linville Gorge could be exploited. Today massive stumps, sawdust piles, and a complex of old roadbeds amid young growth forest around the head of the Linville Gorge testify to the heavy logging during the early 1900s.

Even before the railroads opened the area to tourism, a series of travel writers such as Henry E. Colton and Charles Lanman passed through on horseback to describe the scenery of the Blue Ridge. Later writers such as Wilbur C. Ziegler, Ben S. Grosscup, and Margaret Morley added praise of large and comfortable hotels to their picturesque descriptions. In his novel *Master of the World* (1903), Jules Verne opens a science-fiction tale on Table Rock Mountain at Linville Gorge that vies with the travel writers in its luxuriant prose.

In 1890, the Morganton Land Improvement Company purchased the area surrounding the falls, hoping to develop it as a summer resort and building a small white-framed cottage overlooking the falls. The venture fell through, however, and, in 1897, the company's real estate holdings were liquidated. Another doomed plan for the falls and gorge included a hydroelectric plant. Fred "Fritz" Hossfeld eventually assumed ownership of the Linville Falls area. His son, Fritz Jr., moved there and managed the property as a tourist attraction with a succession of local men acting as guides. One of this volume's most prolific photographers, F. W. Bicknell and his wife, Jessie, sister to Hossfeld Jr.'s wife, Katie, lived for many years in the cottage at Linville Falls. Upon Fritz Hossfield's death, his sister Giulia Luginbuhl inherited the property. Not interested in holding the land, she put it on the market. A retired Conway, South Carolina, lawyer named Marion C. Wright began a passionate campaign to have the falls area purchased for the American people. He interested Blue Ridge Parkway superintendant Sam Weems in the plan and secured necessary financial backing from John D. Rockefeller Jr. In 1951, Rockefeller donated $92,000 for the 1,200-acre Hossfield tract, thus, ensuring its future preservation as part of the National Park Service system. Below the falls, the wilderness area grew in gradual increments, starting from a 7,500-acre tract purchased for the Pisgah National Forest in 1951. When President Johnson signed the Wilderness Act in 1964, the area became part of the National Wilderness System. In 1984, the North Carolina Wilderness Act increased the area to over 10,000 acres. Groups such as the Foothills Conservancy continue to add acreage to the wilderness area as land comes on the market.

Since the early 1960s, soldiers of the U.S. Army Special Forces stationed at Fort Bragg, North Carolina, have come west to the Linville Gorge to conduct various specialized training exercises. Green Berets laid out some of the first rock climbing routes on the area's cliffs in the 1960s and continue to train in this rugged terrain that is so suitable for small-scale unconventional operations.

In 1967, the North Carolina Outward Bound School launched its famous wilderness education program from a facility at the base of Table Rock Mountain. Challenging students to fulfill their potential and work cooperatively, the school offers training in climbing, rescue work, camping, and other outdoor skills.

Among the organizations and smaller groups currently active in the wilderness area are the Foothills Conservancy of North Carolina, Friends of the Mountains-to-Sea Trail, the Carolina Mountain Club, the Carolina Climbers' Coalition, Friends of Linville Gorge, university biology departments (among them Appalachian State), and an online Yahoo discussion group by Linville Gorge expert Bob Underwood. The nearby Jonas Ridge Fire Department and Burke County EMS teams are regularly called upon for rescue operations in the Linville Gorge since accidents are many and fatalities not uncommon. History continues to be made in Linville Gorge including the first night rescue by Black Hawk helicopter and the filming of the 1992 movie *Last of the Mohicans,* to name two examples.

The problem of organizing the materials in this volume resolved itself with a topographic approach whereby major landscape features determined the book's sections; thus, the Linville Falls, the Linville River, the peaks and cliffs on and around the two walls of the Linville Gorge (from Jonas Ridge southward on the east and Linville Mountain on the west), the forests of the Linville Gorge, and, finally, human presence in the area make up the five chapters of the book. Enter now this fabled wilderness in the company of adventurers clad in gaiters and wool, struggling with bulky, heavy camera equipment and determined to record and share the awesome grandeur of the place.

Please note that the photographers' original captions appear within quotation marks.

One

Linville Falls
"The River Steps Down"

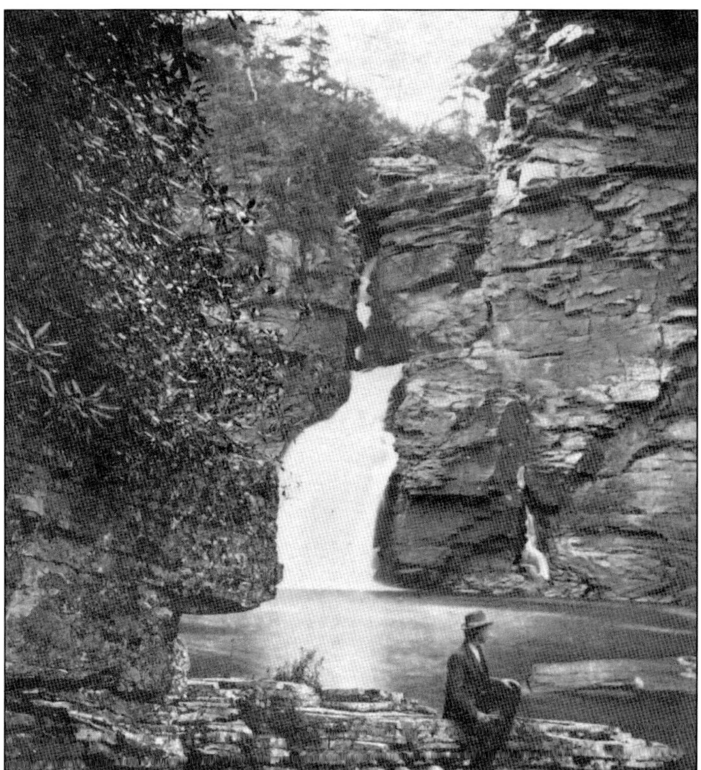

Linville Falls and Plunge Basin, 1873. From its headwaters near Grandfather Mountain, the Linville River flows placidly through Avery County. After entering the Blue Ridge Parkway's Linville Falls Recreation Area at milepost 316.5, it plunges in several dramatic stages to the Linville Gorge, through which it winds for 16 miles before entering Lake James. Rufus Morgan produced stereographic slides of the Linville Falls and Linville Gorge for sale in the early 1870s. (Courtesy of the North Carolina Collection, Wilson Library, University of North Carolina at Chapel Hill.)

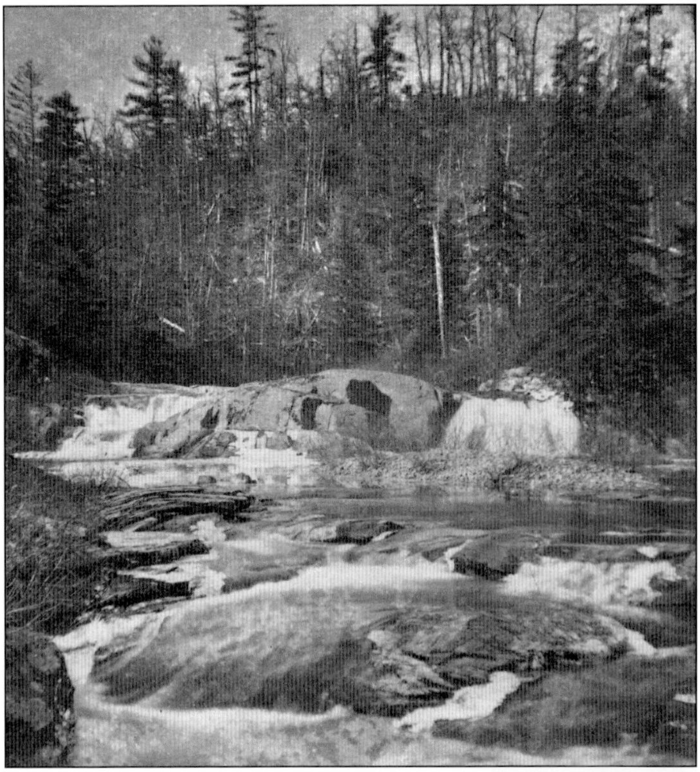

Upper Falls by Rufus Morgan, 1873. First in the series of waterfalls on the Linville River, Upper Falls is a pair of cascades usually separated (at times of normal water level) by a central rock mass. The slope behind the falls appears to have been logged or hit by heavy winds. (Courtesy of the North Carolina Collection, Wilson Library, University of North Carolina at Chapel Hill.)

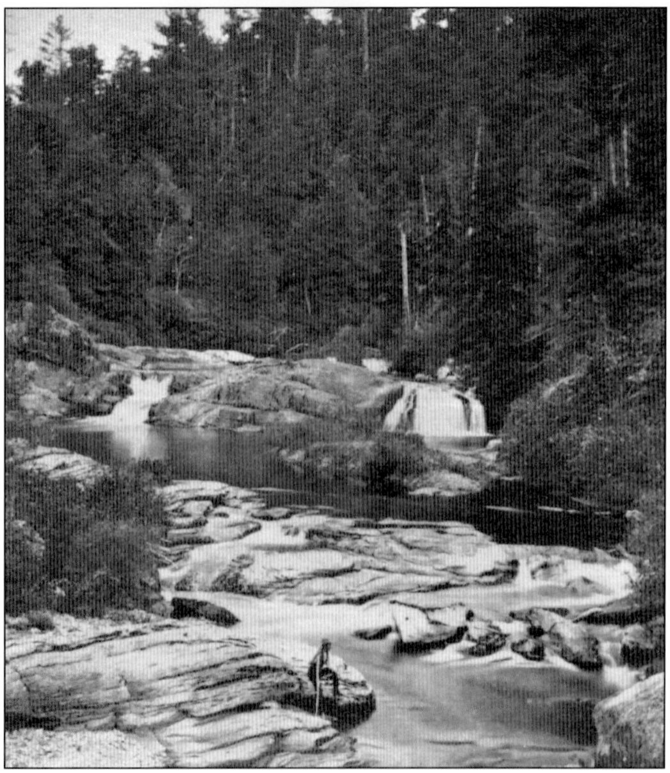

Upper Falls and Seated Figure. Morgan liked to pose unidentified sightseers in his pictures to establish the scale of the landscape features. Behind the seated figure, to the left and out of view, is a noted geological "window," as it's described, evidencing the continental collision that forced up the Blue Ridge chain. Under an overhang, older rock lies atop much younger rock. (Courtesy of the North Carolina Collection, Wilson Library, University of North Carolina at Chapel Hill.)

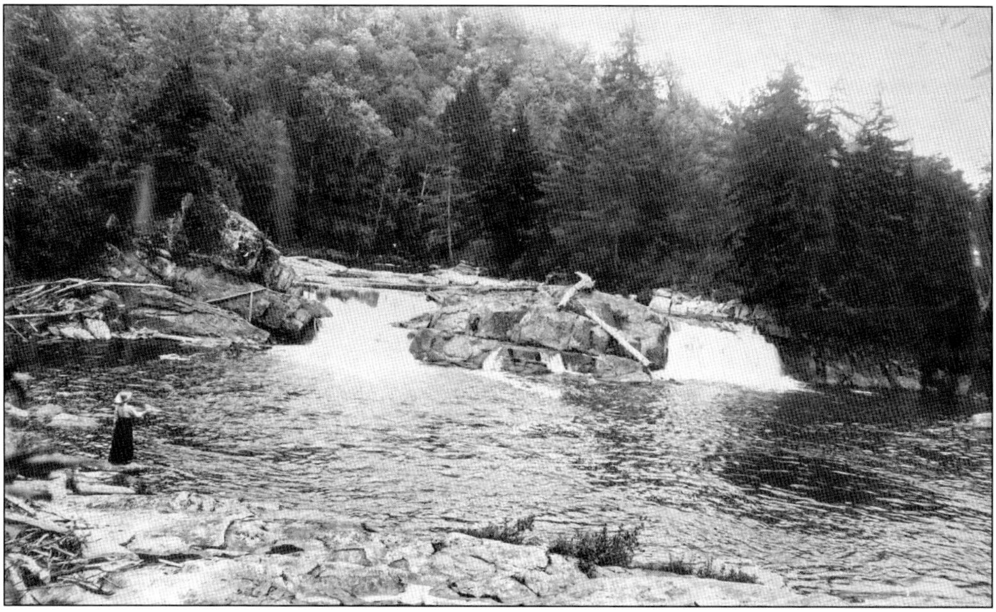

"JESSIE FISHING AT UPPER FALLS, 22 MAY 1908." Both Bicknells were avid fishers; here in a full-length skirt and sun hat, Jessie angles for trout in the pool below Upper Falls. The photograph taken by her husband, Frank, indicates the extent of the timber washed downriver by heavy rains. (Courtesy of the North Carolina State Archives.)

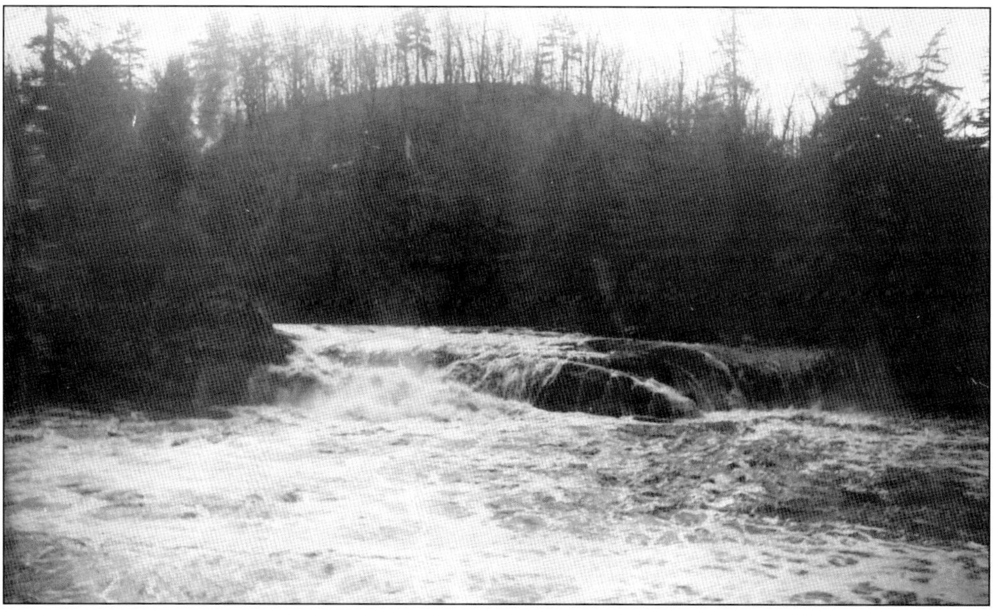

"UPPER FALLS AT HIGH WATER, 13, APRIL 1909." Even higher waters have been known to completely submerge the central rock mass of Upper Falls, which is usually as the result of tropical storms and hurricanes. At the beginning of the 20th century, logging crews cut timber around the north end of the Linville Gorge for sawing and planing at the W. J. Ritter Company mill in Pineola, four-and-a-half miles north. The hill behind the Upper Falls has been cleared, probably for Bicknell's own sawmill upstream on the river. (Courtesy of the North Carolina State Archives.)

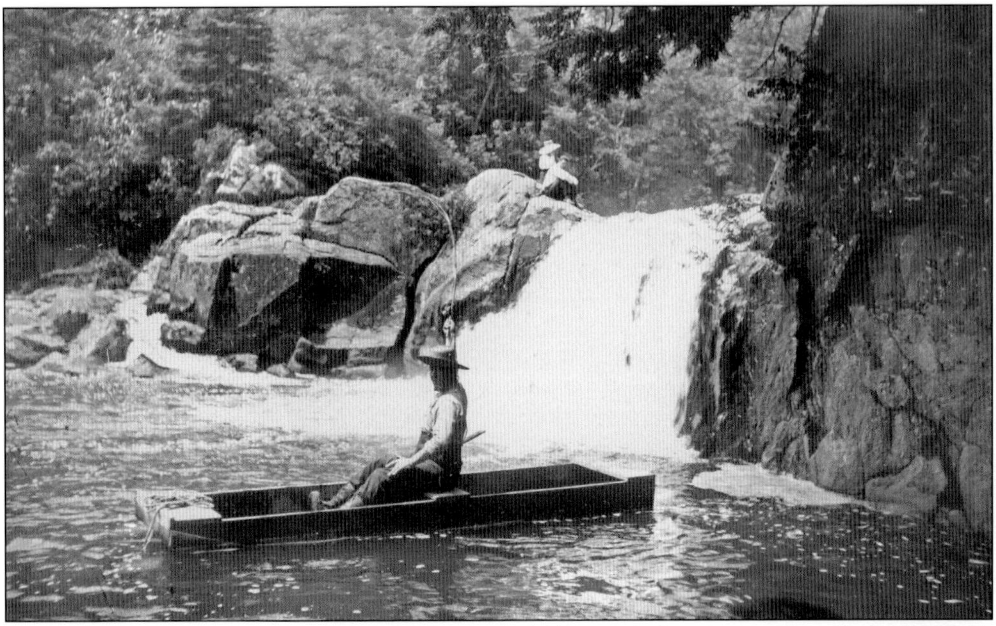

"A Nervous Moment, 1 August 1910." Fritz Hossfeld Jr. might be nervous about losing his catch or about losing the anchor for his skiff and going over the Lower Falls, a few yards downstream. Some people have survived being swept over the Linville Falls though more have died. Above him, sister Eleanor and brother William sit on the central rock. (Courtesy of the North Carolina State Archives.)

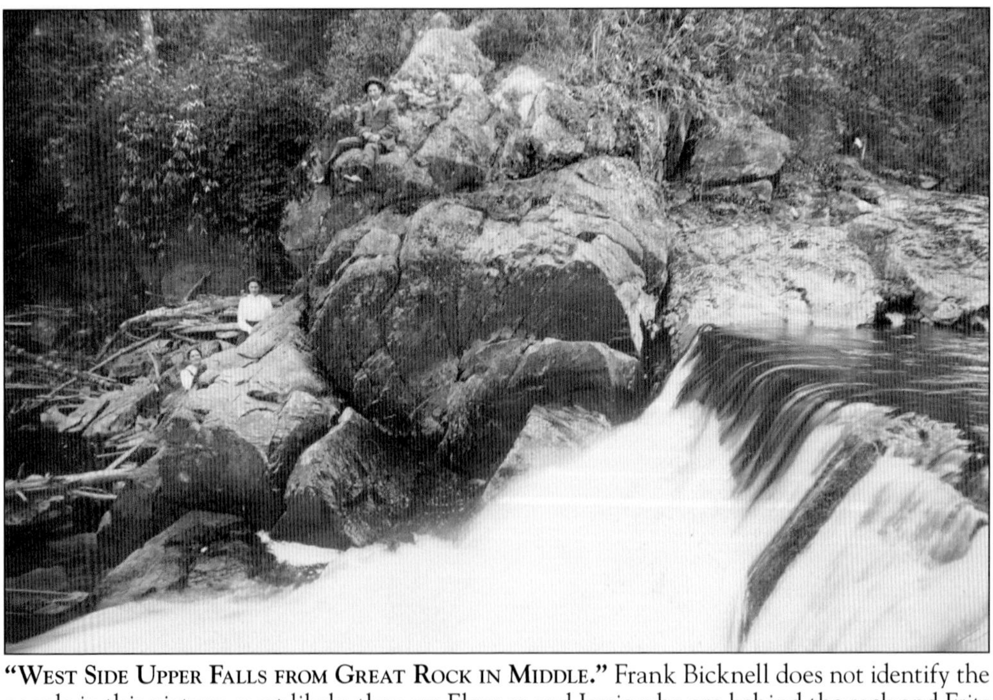

"West Side Upper Falls from Great Rock in Middle." Frank Bicknell does not identify the people in this picture; most likely, they are Eleanor and Jessie who are behind the rock and Fritz Jr. above it. Behind the women can be seen considerable timber carried down by the river at high water. (Courtesy of the North Carolina State Archives.)

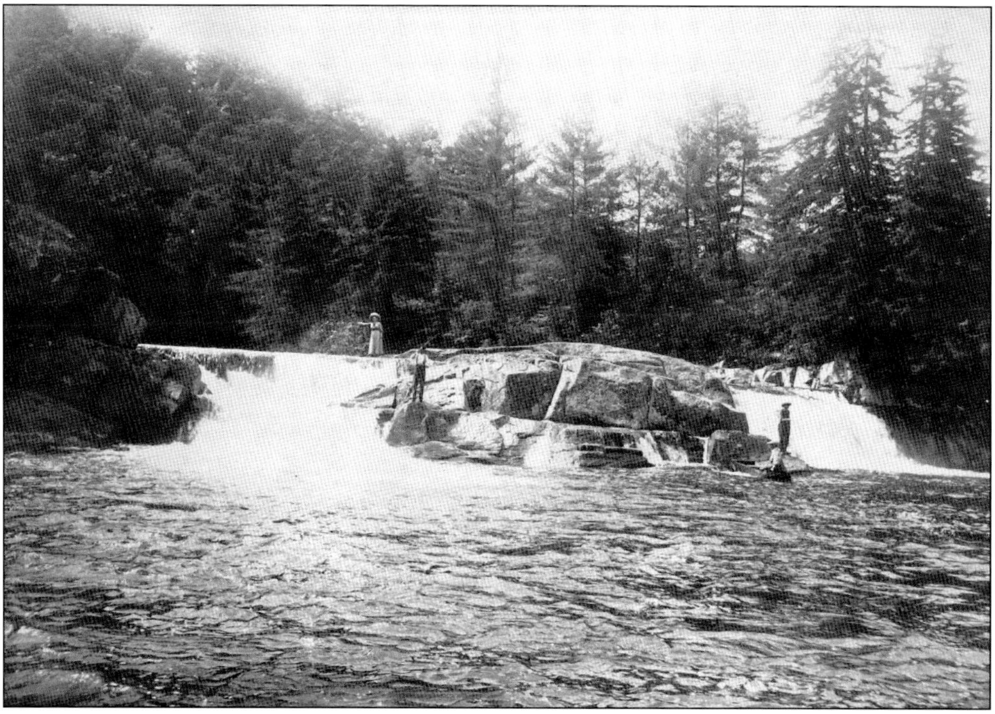

"FISHING AT UPPER FALLS, 24 JUNE 1909." Friends of the Bicknells, Dr. Clark and family, have waded out to the central rock of the Upper Falls. (Courtesy of the North Carolina State Archives.)

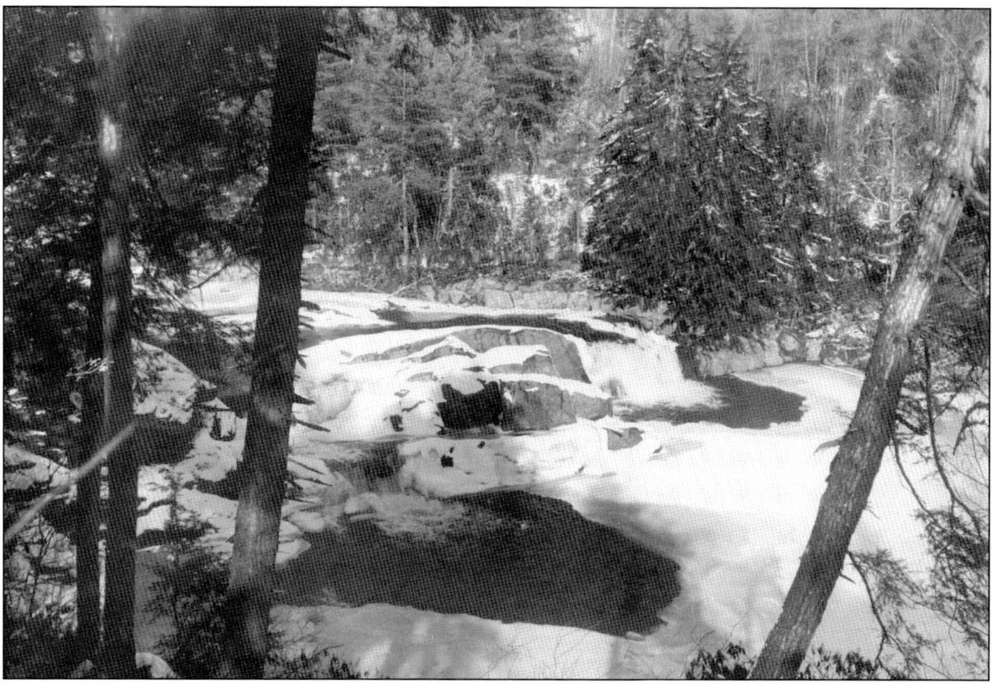

"UPPER FALLS IN ICE AND SNOW, JANUARY 1910." The Linville Falls take on an especially magical quality when viewed after a snowfall. The stillness is broken only by the monotonous rustling of rapids and the deep thunder of the falls. (Courtesy of the North Carolina State Archives.)

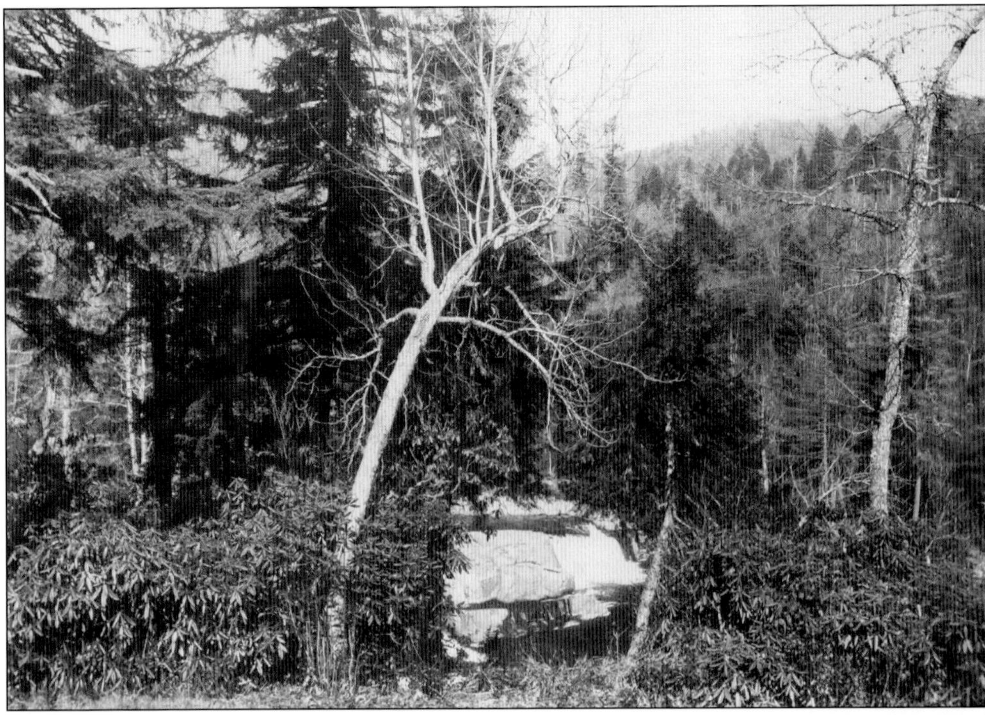

"Upper Falls from Our Porch, October 1901." This photograph taken by Frank Bicknell indicates the near proximity of the cottage to the Linville Falls. The Morganton Land Improvement Company had hoped to deck the cliffs nearby with similar cottages as a resort village. (Courtesy of the North Carolina State Archives.)

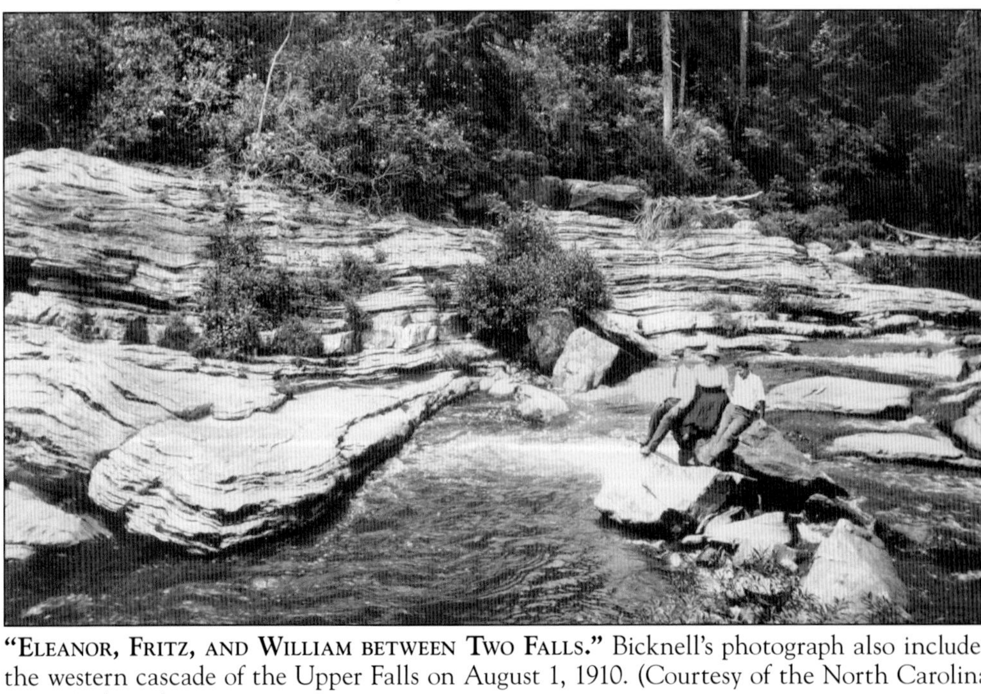

"Eleanor, Fritz, and William between Two Falls." Bicknell's photograph also includes the western cascade of the Upper Falls on August 1, 1910. (Courtesy of the North Carolina State Archives.)

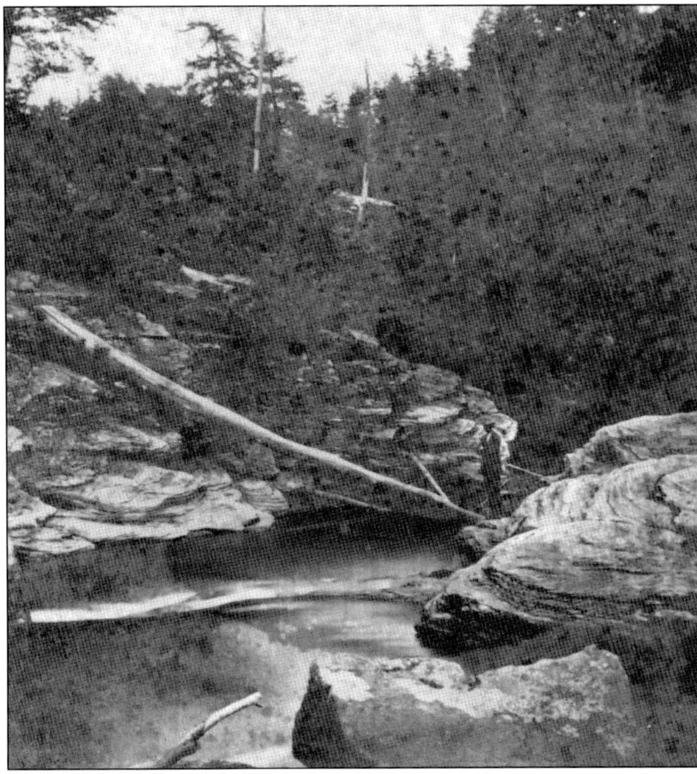

"Beauties of the Linville River." Below the Upper Falls, the Linville River narrows into a channel snaking its way around massive boulders and gathering speed for its final two plummets. Notice the tree trunks jammed in the rocks by high waters. Just behind the man in Morgan's photograph is a gap in the rock through which the Linville River sometimes falls directly, without veering to the right and entering what's commonly referred to as the "window." (Courtesy of the North Carolina Collection, Wilson Library, University of North Carolina at Chapel Hill.)

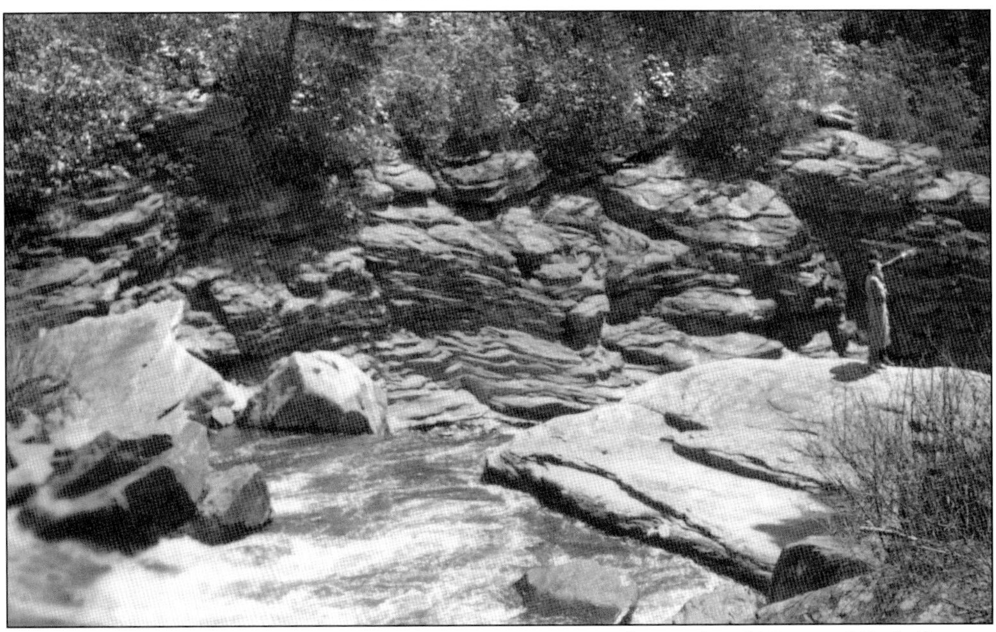

National Park Service Officials at Lower Falls. In this undated National Park Service photograph, two unidentified National Park Service officials regard the cliff tops on the Linville Gorge's western side, which are probably Erwin's View or Chimney View. Notice the folded rock above the river, which is evidence of great geological stresses. (Courtesy of the Blue Ridge Parkway Archives.)

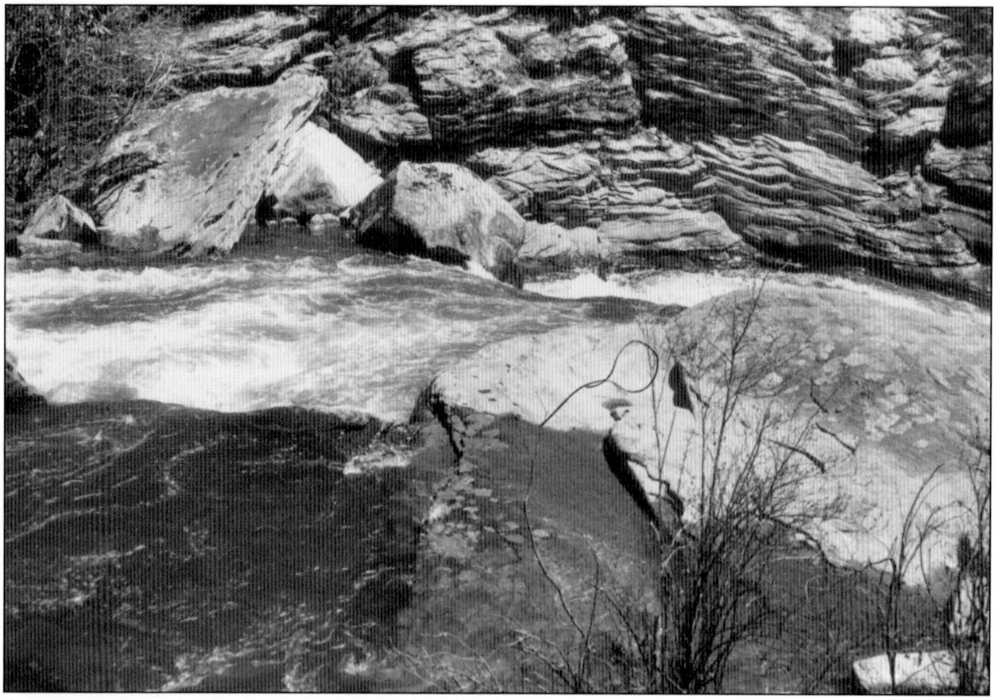

Physical Geography Study. National Park Service photographer C. E. Westveer made this close-up view of the narrow channel above the Lower Falls sometime in the early 1970s. (Courtesy of the Blue Ridge Parkway Archives.)

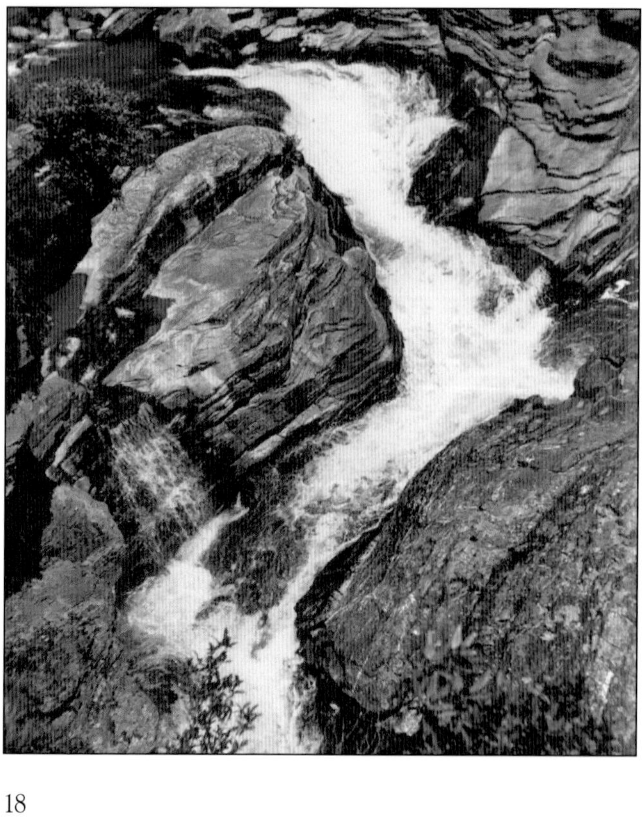

Geology of the Lower Falls. Blue Ridge Parkway supervisory landscape architect Edward H. Abbuehl made this study of the river's course just above the Lower Falls on June 14, 1938. The image is evidence of National Park Service interest in the Linville Falls at an early date, less than three years after the construction of the Blue Ridge Parkway had begun and many years before the land went on the real estate market. (Courtesy of the Blue Ridge Parkway Archives.)

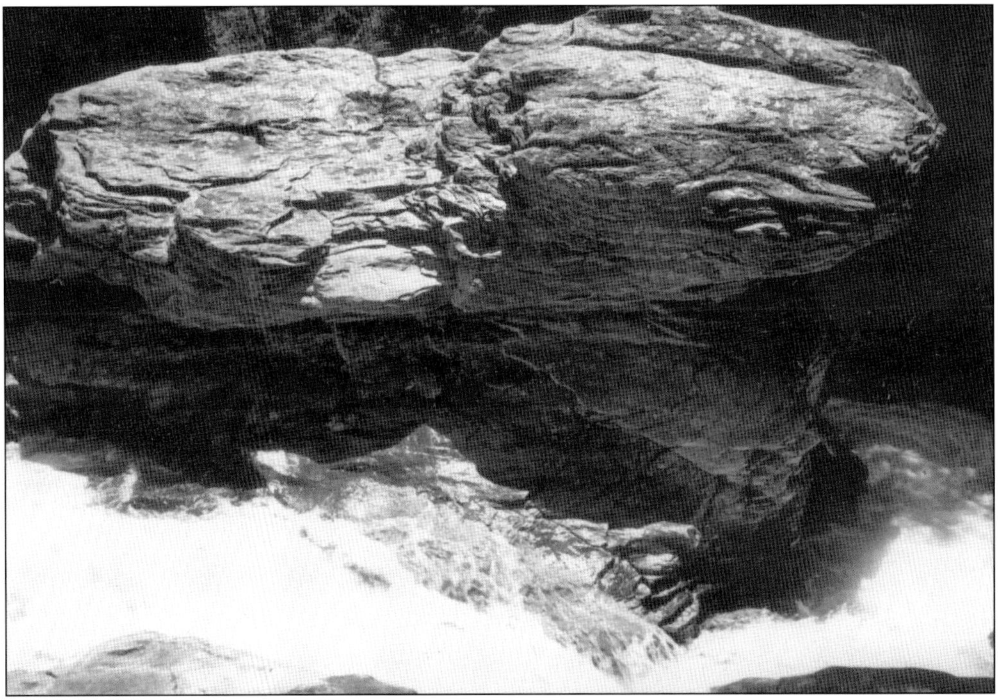

LINVILLE RIVER APPROACHES THE WINDOW. Here the river thunders its way into the chute of the window then makes a sudden turn to the left. When logjams block the window, the river flows through the gap to the left of the prominent boulder above the water. This is another undated picture taken by National Park Service photographer C. E. Westveer. (Courtesy of the Blue Ridge Parkway Archives.)

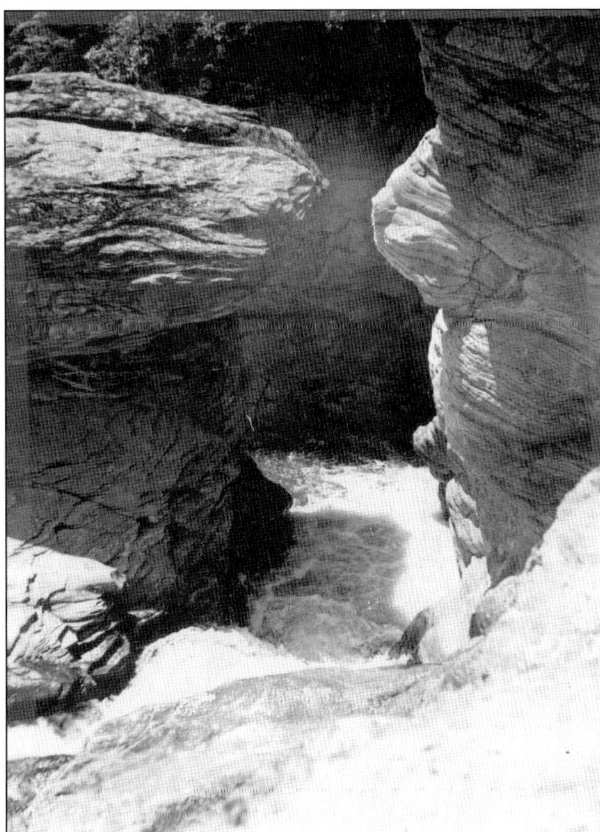

THE WINDOW. Sightseers at the Upper Falls View balcony can look straight down into the window where the river makes its final step into the Linville Gorge. Edward H. Abbuehl took this photograph on June 14, 1938. (Courtesy of the Blue Ridge Parkway Archives.)

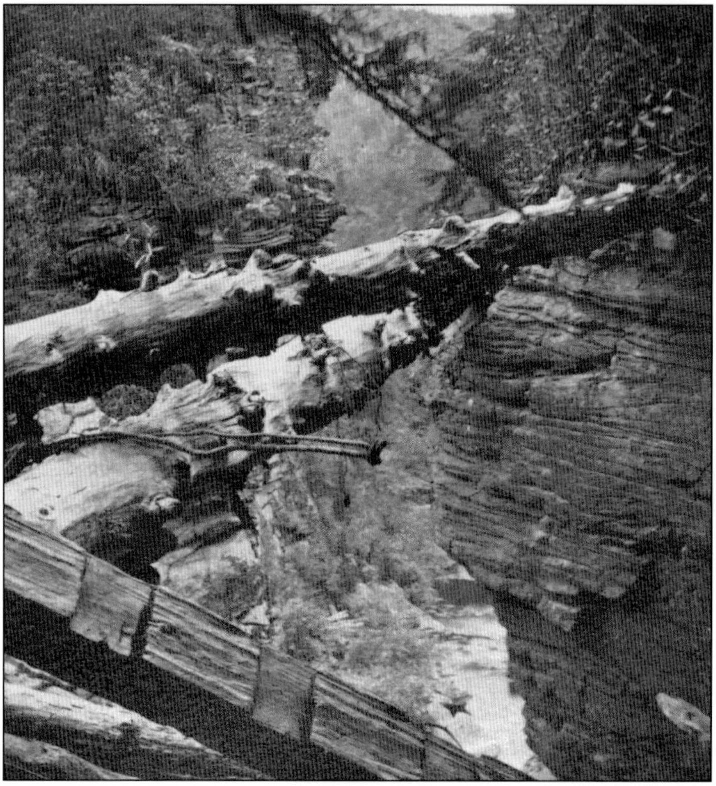

"THE GATEWAY OF THE LINVILLE." Rufus Morgan gives an exact depiction of the flotsam that piles up at the Lower Falls during times of high water. The banks of the Linville River in the Linville Gorge continue to collect debris such as lumber from buildings, signposts, planks, car tires, and other objects. (Courtesy of the North Carolina Collection, Wilson Library, University of North Carolina at Chapel Hill.)

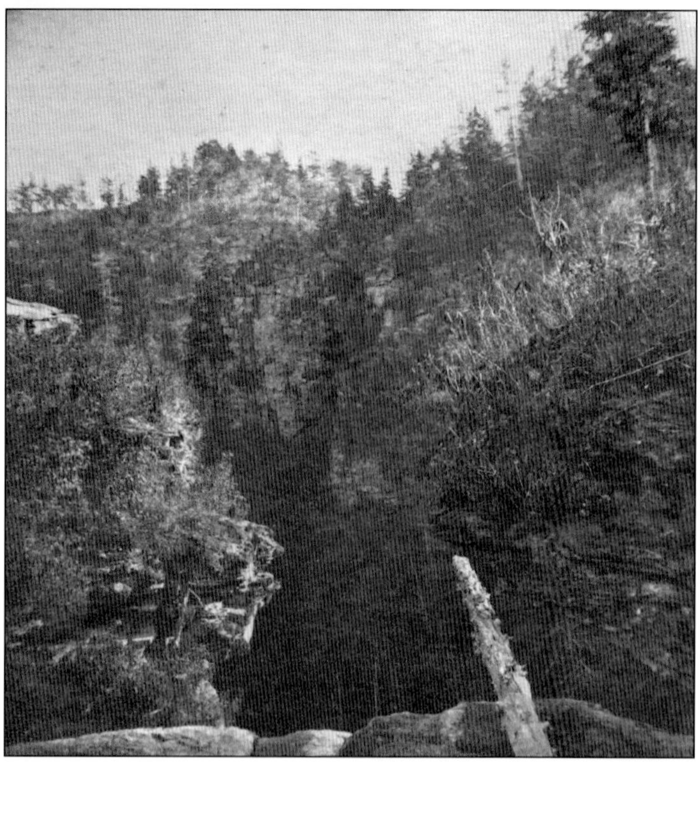

"LOOKING INTO THE GORGE OF THE RIVER FROM THE TOP OF THE FALLS." This is our first view of the Linville Gorge proper so far. The National Park Service has built three rock-walled balconies on the west (right) side of the canyon. From these, one can look north to the waterfall. To the left of the tree trunk lodged atop the big boulder is the narrow gap over which the river sometimes flows at high water. (Courtesy of the North Carolina Collection, Wilson Library, University of North Carolina at Chapel Hill.)

"Linville River from the Top of the Falls." This view by Rufus Morgan depicts the large pool below the Linville Falls, known variously as the "Plunge Basin" or the "Boiling Pot." Again a tree trunk has lodged itself at the top of the Linville Falls. The large square-shaped boulder in the center might have broken away from the Linville Falls. It is a popular viewing point from which to gaze upstream at the cascade. (Courtesy of the North Carolina Collection, Wilson Library, University of North Carolina at Chapel Hill.)

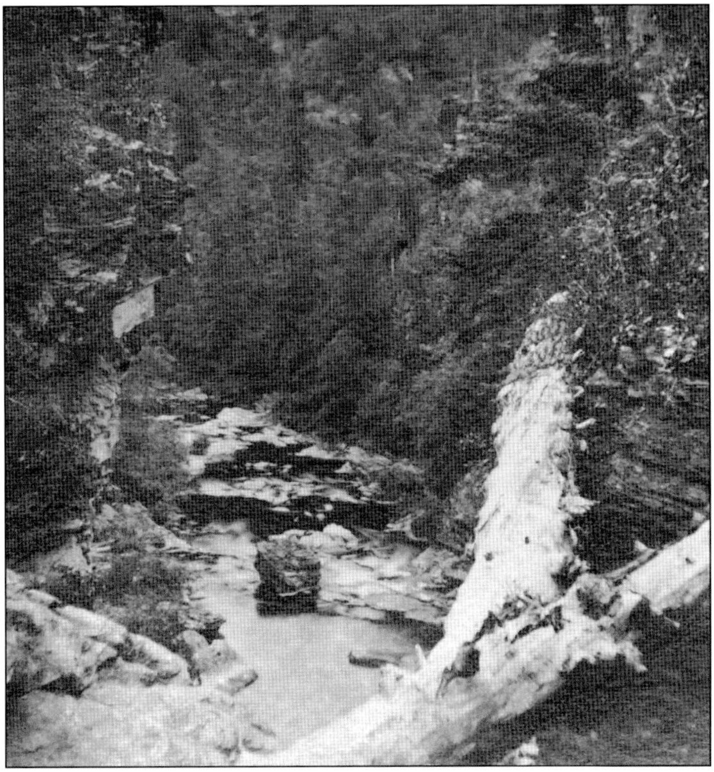

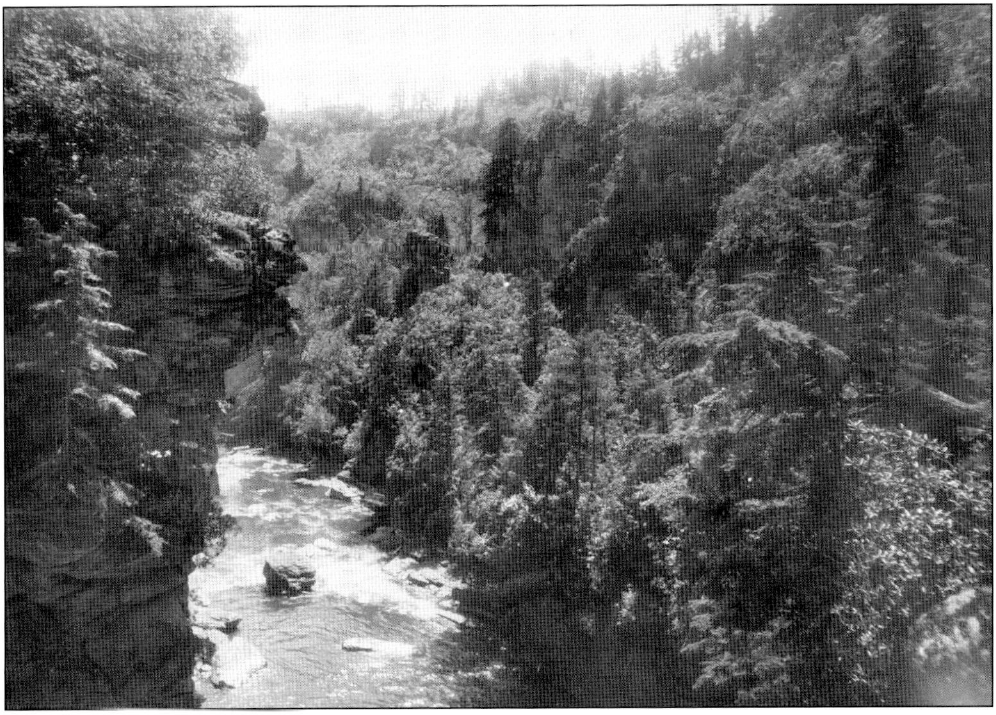

Linville River at the Bank. Frank W. Bicknell titled this photograph, "Over the brink of the falls, down toward Ervin's [*sic*] View, 31 May, 1906." (Courtesy of North Carolina State Archives.)

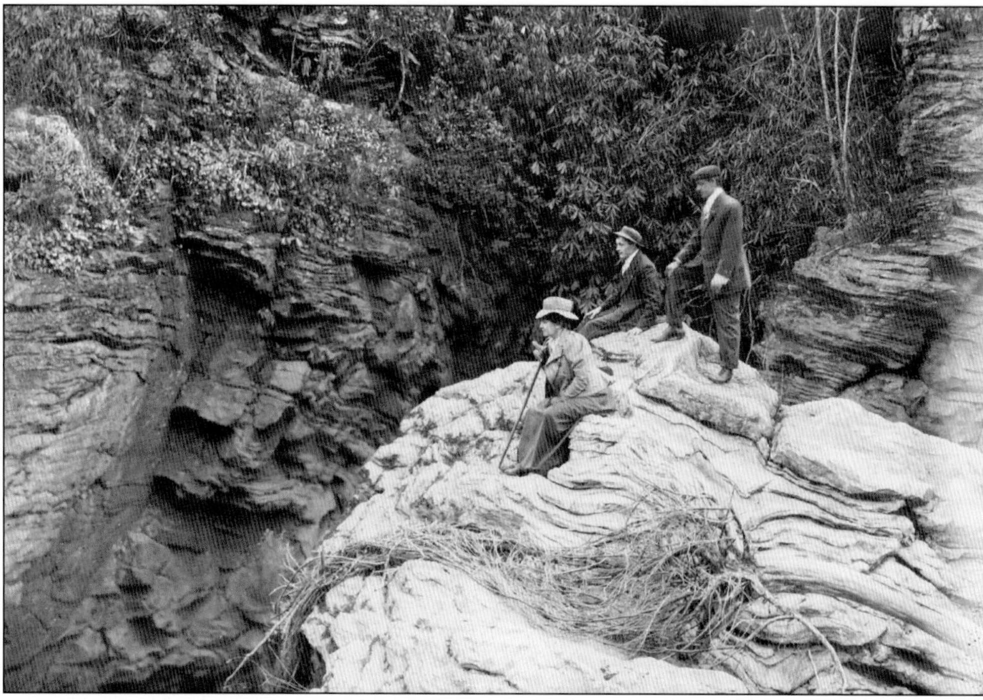

"Great Rock Brink of Lower Fall." Frank Bicknell captured his friends Ben Watrous and Dowle and his wife, Jessie, in October 1909 on the rock that Rufus Morgan had photographed 36 years earlier. Bicknell notes that this is the vantage point from which the previous photograph was taken. (Courtesy of North Carolina State Archives.)

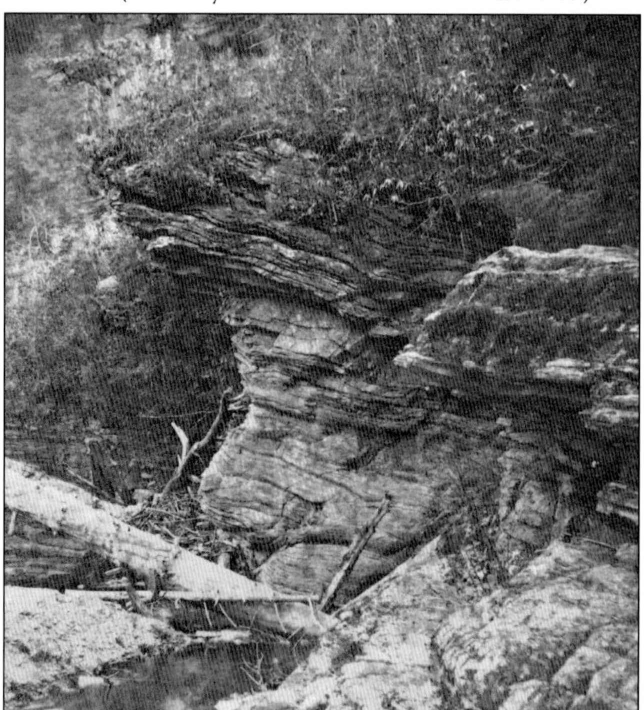

"The Banks of the River Just Above the Falls." The rhododendron-covered crag over the tree trunk is on the west side of the Linville Falls directly above the window. This is the same rock shown in Bicknell's photograph above. (Courtesy of the North Carolina Collection, Wilson Library, University of North Carolina at Chapel Hill.)

"THE LINVILLE FALLS." This view of Linville Falls seems to suggest a geological change in the structure of the waterfall occurring some time after Rufus Morgan took the photograph around 1873. The water courses straight down making no side-steps into a window-like opening. At the top is the "gap," as it's commonly called (top image on page 17 and bottom image on page 20). (Courtesy of the North Carolina Collection, Wilson Library, University of North Carolina at Chapel Hill.)

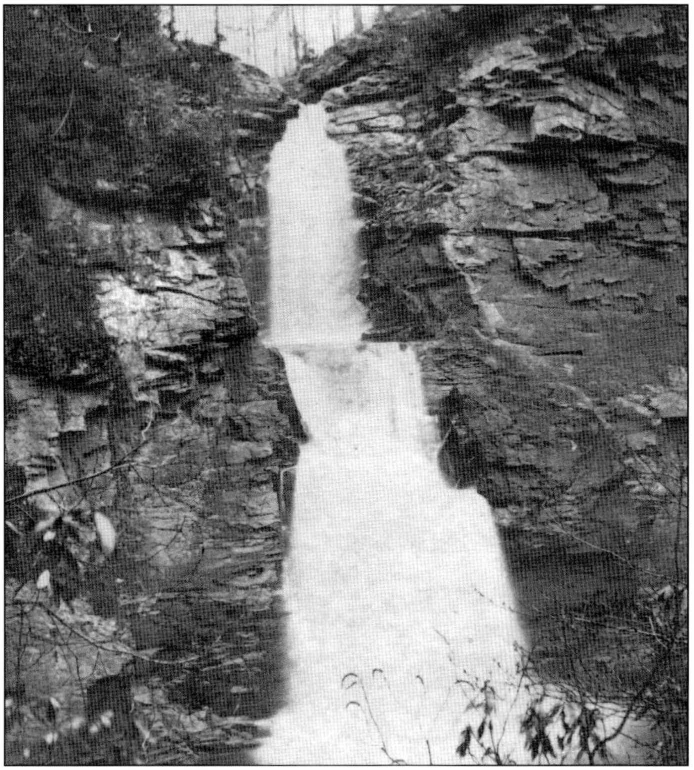

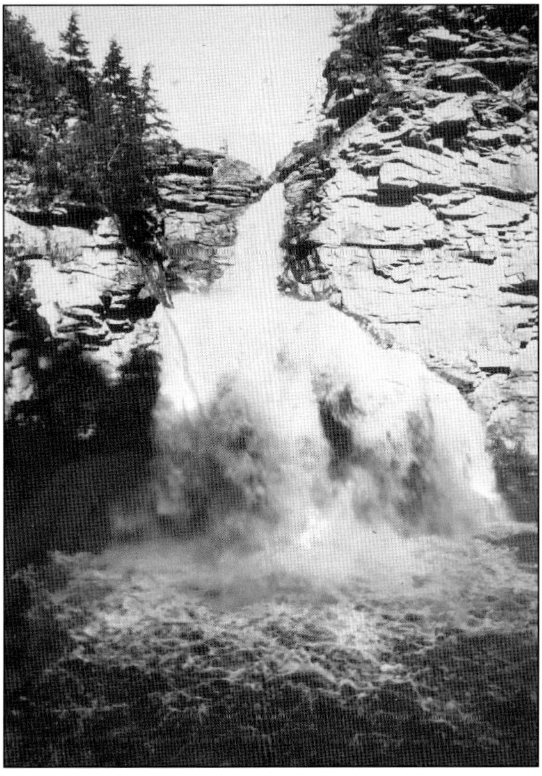

"FALLS AFTER HEAVY RAIN." In this February 16, 1909, photograph by Frank Bicknell, the swollen Linville River charges through the gap at the top and falls in a direct line, similar to Rufus Morgan's view above. (Courtesy of the North Carolina State Archives.)

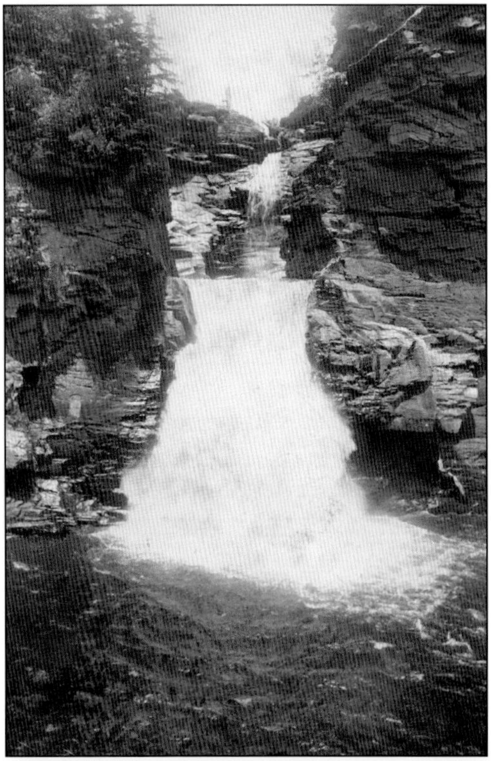

"The Falls at Low Water." The waterfall again pours through the gap to descend in a straight line without zigzagging through the window. Given that this was a day of low water in the river, there must have been an obstruction to the current that was severe enough to dam up the window. (Courtesy of the North Carolina State Archives.)

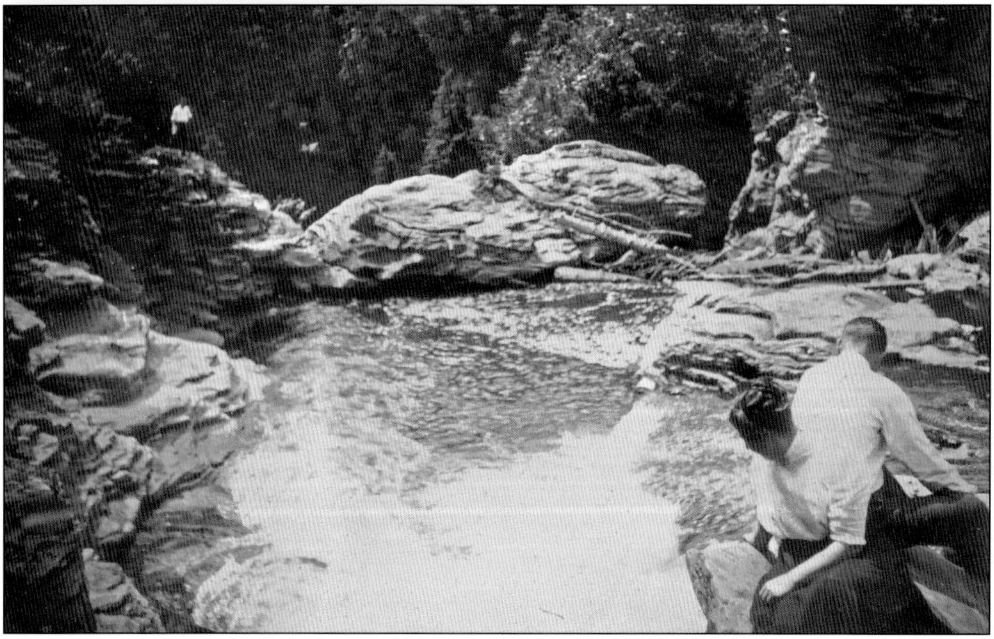

"Three Hossfelds above the Lower Falls." Bicknell's photograph, made on August 1, 1910, reveals major debris building up above the window and a river level approaching the gap through which the falls descend in a straight line. The Hossfelds are Fritz Jr., in the distance, and William, and Eleanor, seated together, on the same day as the bottom photograph on page 14 was taken. (Courtesy of the North Carolina State Archives.)

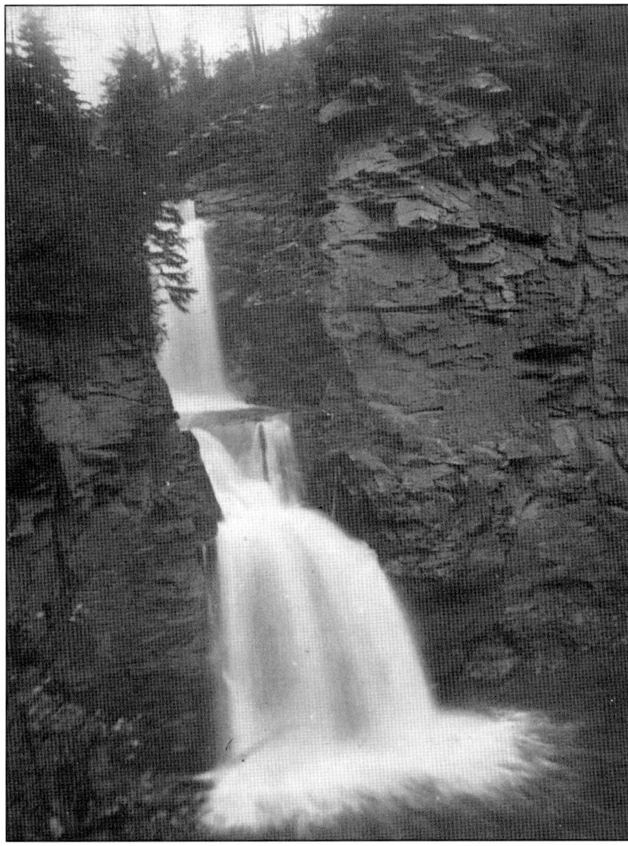

Linville Falls in 1914. Johnson City, Tennessee, architect D. R. Beeson made a three-day trip to Linville Gorge in July 1914 with three companions. Towards dusk on July 5th, Beeson clambered down a crevice on the west side of the Linville Falls and made this picture from the edge of the Plunge Basin pool. Yet again, the water falls in a straight line. (Courtesy of East Tennessee State University.)

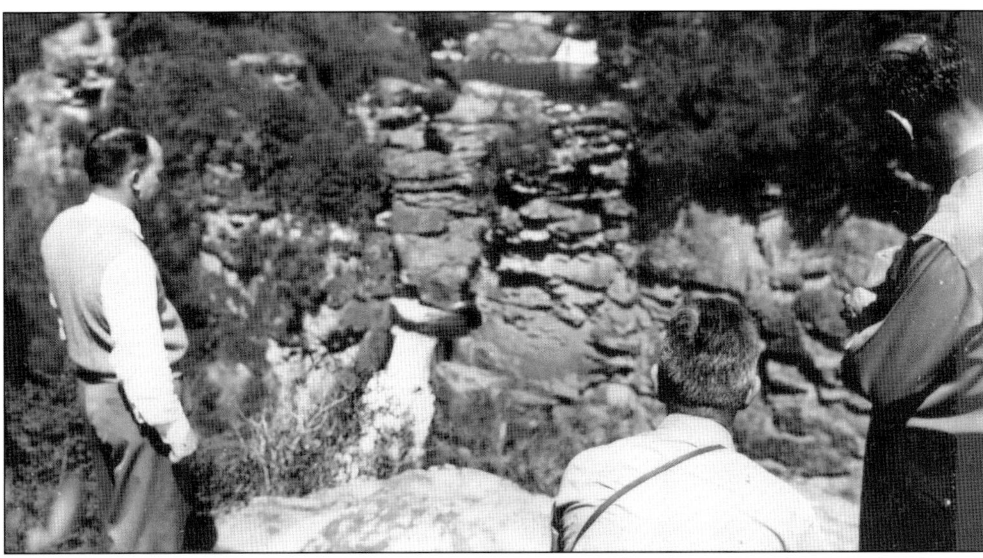

Government Officials at Chimney View. This National Park Service photograph taken on May 13, 1947, records a visit to the Linville Falls by government officials while the area was still owned by the Hossfelds. From left to right are Elbert Cox (southeast regional director of the National Park Service), John Siefer (U.S. Forest Service), and Conrad Wirth (director of the National Park Service 1951–1964). (Courtesy of the Blue Ridge Parkway Archives.)

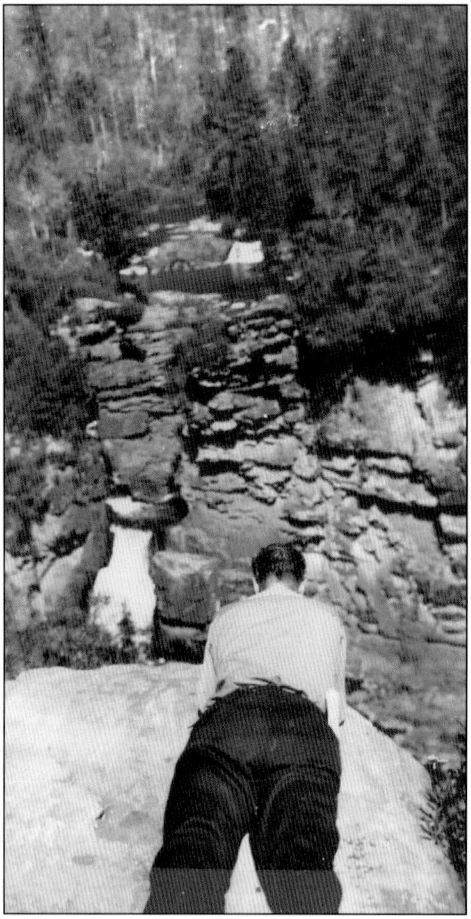

Conrad Wirth Inspects Gorge from Chimney View. Another official National Park Service photograph made on May 13, 1947, records Conrad Wirth exercising safety precautions to peer at the river 150 feet below. Before becoming director of the National Park Service in 1951, Wirth was chief of Branch of Lands, an office charged with investigating proposed new parks, extensions to existing areas, and the drafting work. Chimney View (two balconies actually) lies halfway between the Upper Falls View and Erwin's View. (Courtesy of the Blue Ridge Parkway Archives.)

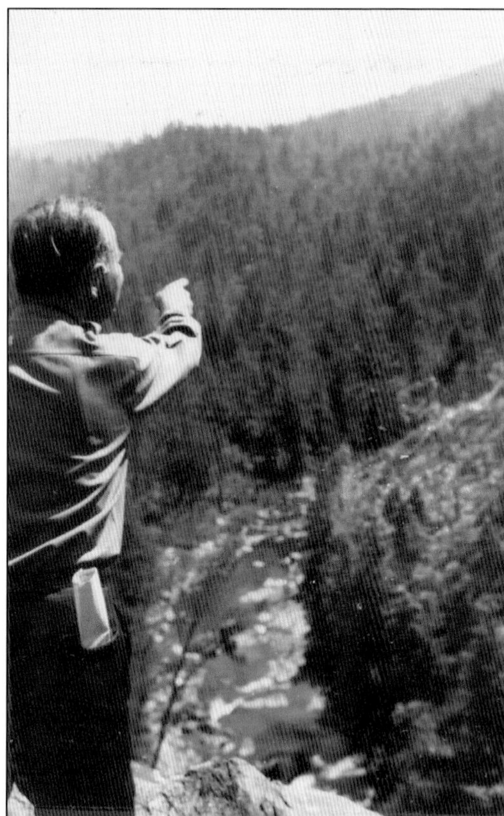

Conrad Wirth Inspecting Gorge from Erwin's View. A National Park Service photographer photographed chief of Branch of Lands Conrad Wirth at Erwin's View on May 13, 1947. Wirth is pointing downriver, perhaps at the boundary of Hossfeld and public lands. (Courtesy of the Blue Ridge Parkway Archives.)

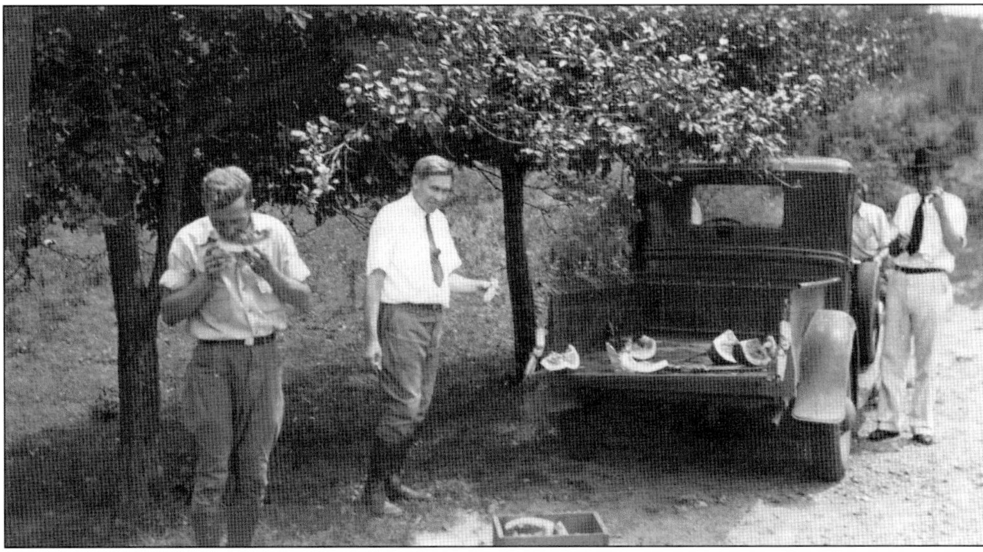

"Mr. Gibbs and Party." A National Park Service supervisory landscape architect captured what is probably a National Park Service landscape crew enjoying watermelon on a hot summer day, July 31, 1935. Once in parkway ownership, the landscape of the Linville Falls area changed considerably, with the addition of a picnic area, a campground, and a spur road crossing the Linville River twice (at the Riverbend area) on its way to a visitor center. (Courtesy of the Blue Ridge Parkway Archives.)

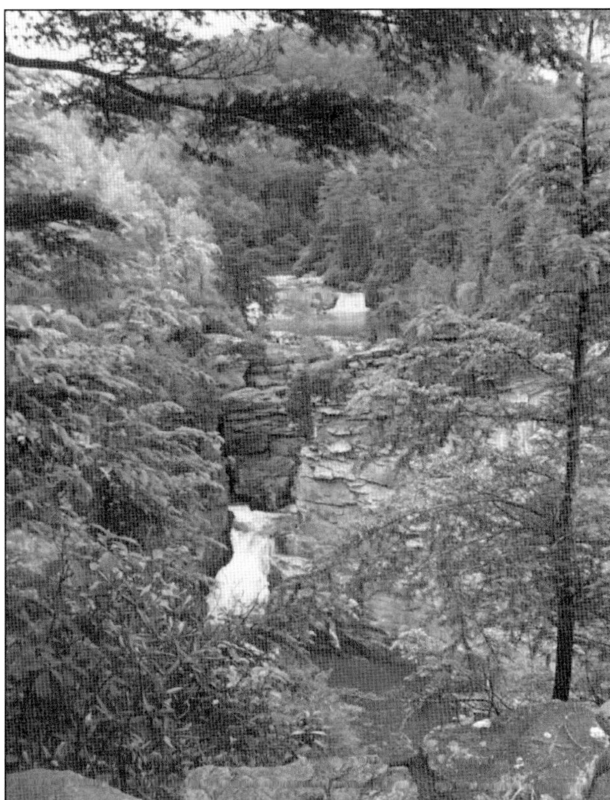

Linville Falls from Chimney View. This popular Linville Falls view was captured by National Park Service photographer C. E. Westveer on July 31, 1973, from the Chimney View balcony. Mountain laurel clings to the cliff face just past the rock wall, and the waterfall descends in its familiar zigzag through the window, while, above and behind, the cataract lies the Upper Falls. (Courtesy of the Blue Ridge Parkway Archives.)

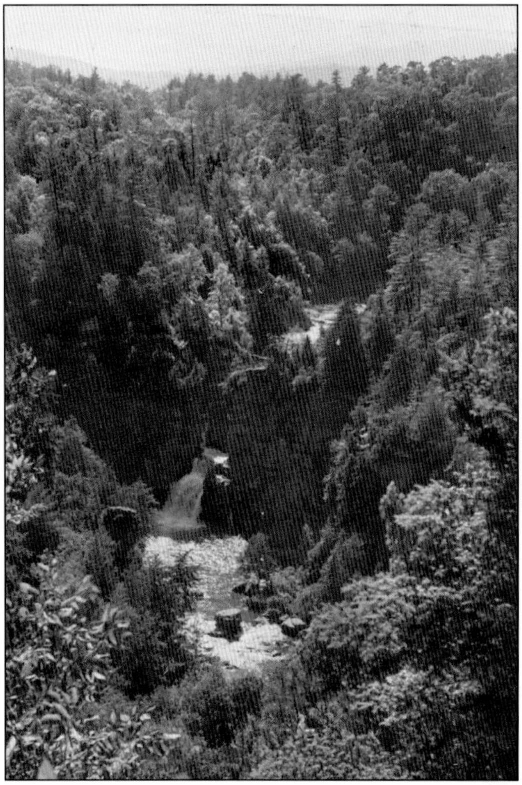

Linville Falls from Erwin's View. Barely visible as a narrow white-water stream above the last major drop of the waterfall, the river is passing through the window. Also visible in this National Park Service photograph by C. E. Westveer on June 12, 1974, is the cube-shaped boulder in mid-river below the Linville Falls. The "chimney rock" formation, as it's commonly called, can be seen to the left. (Courtesy of the Blue Ridge Parkway Archives.)

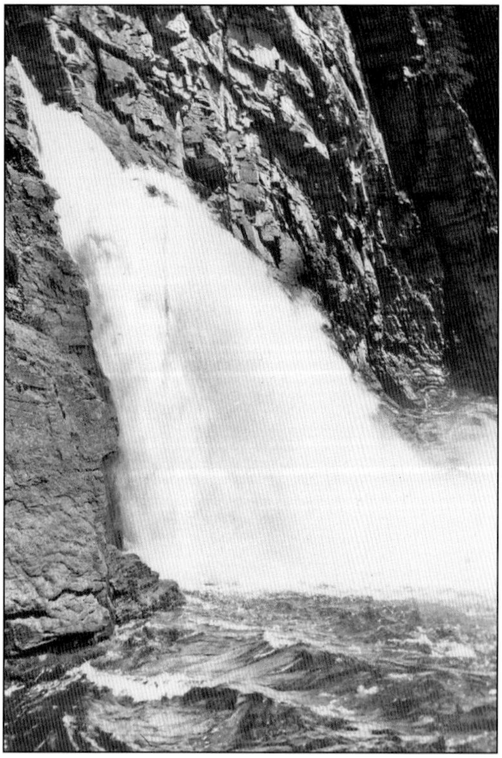

Linville Falls at High Water. Clinchfield Railroad chief engineer William Cary Hattan (1875–1929) ventured down below the Linville Falls around 1907 to take this view of turbulent white water dashing into the plunge basin. Early postcard companies were fond of this view as well. (Courtesy of East Tennessee State University.)

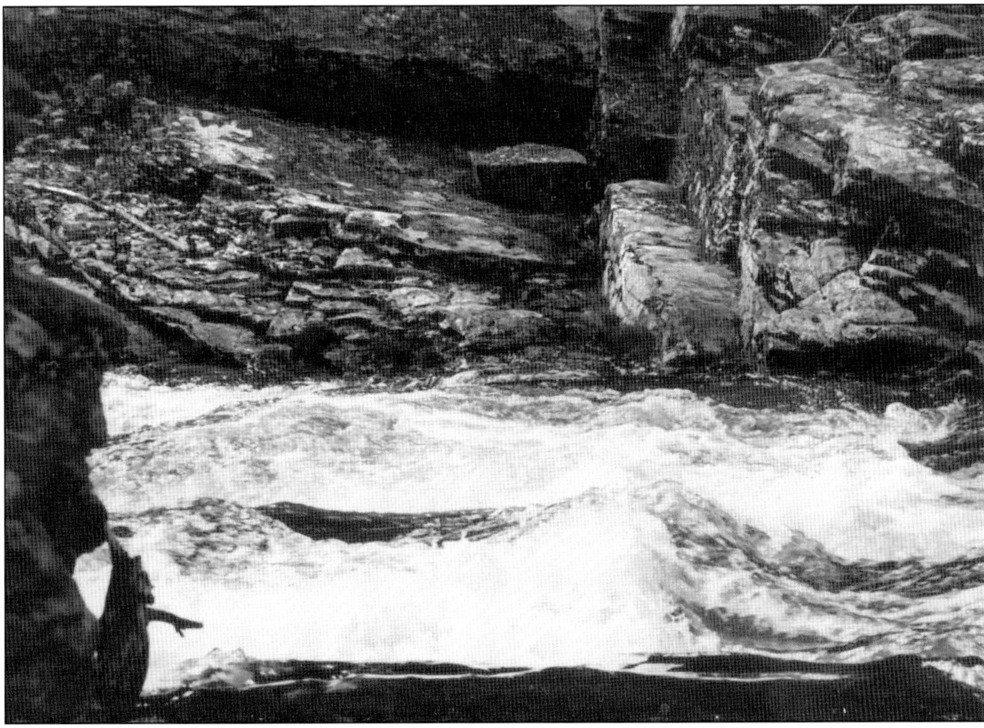

Waves on Linville River. C. E. Westveer took this undated photograph, probably sometime in the early 1970s, of choppy water on the Linville River. More than likely, the shot depicts the river above the Linville Falls. (Courtesy of the Blue Ridge Parkway Archives.)

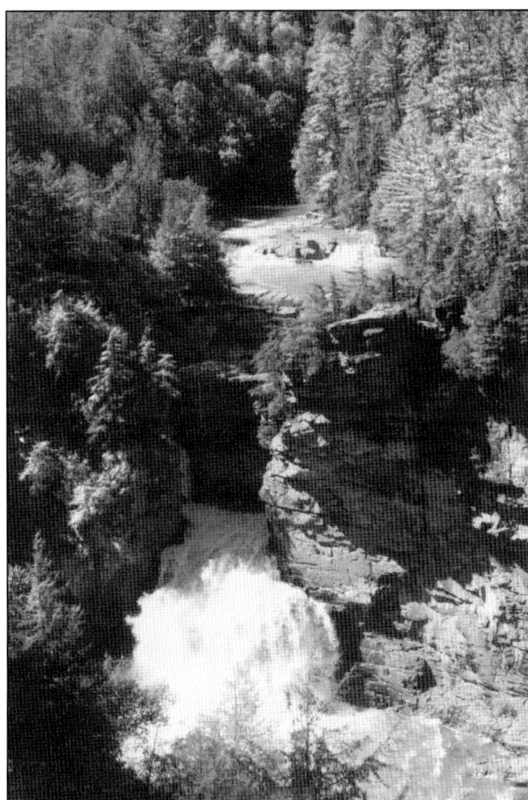

Hurricane Frances Floodwaters. In this 2005 picture taken from Chimney View, the floodwaters have started to recede. The flooding destroyed the Linville Falls Visitor Center, wrecked the footbridge behind the center, and tore away part of the rock wall at the Upper Falls balcony. Notice that the central rock in Upper Falls is visible here. (Courtesy of the Friends of Linville Gorge.)

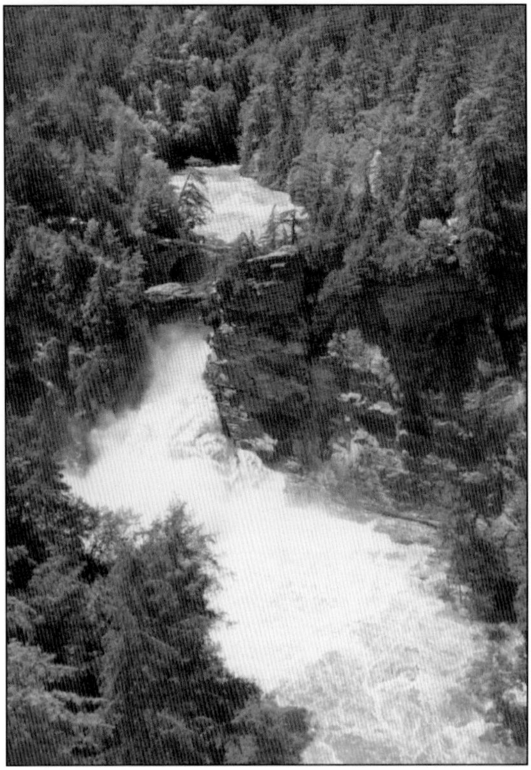

Hurricane Ivan Floodwaters. The swollen angry torrent has totally submerged Upper Falls in this view made after Hurricane Ivan swept through the Blue Ridge in September 2004. Flooding from storms in 1916 remains the worst ever to hit the Linville Falls area. (Courtesy of the Friends of Linville Gorge.)

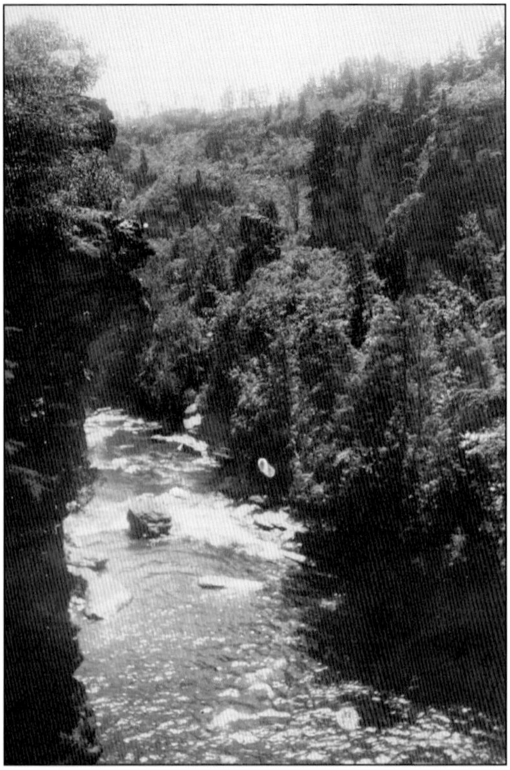

"Looking Down Gorge from Rock Above." Frank Bicknell took this photograph on May 31, 1909, including in his view the giant cube-shaped boulder below the Linville Falls and the ridge where the National Park Service would later construct three overlooks. (Courtesy of the North Carolina State Archives.)

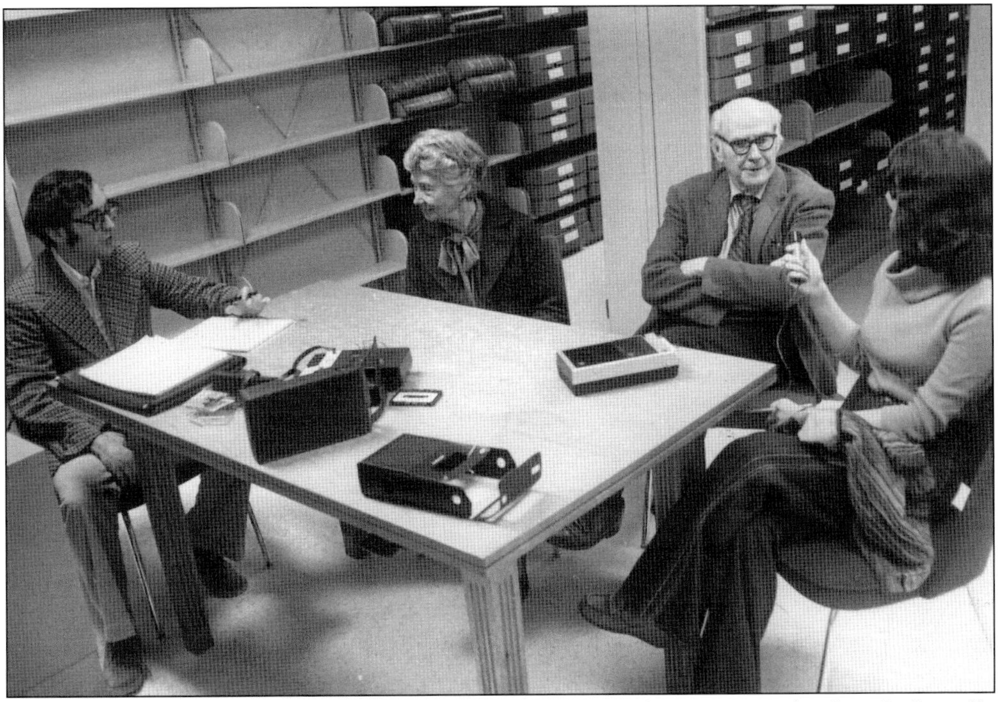

MARION A. WRIGHT (1894–1983). It is due to the efforts of Marion Wright that the Linville Falls area today belongs to the American people. A lawyer, author, and member of the board of directors of the American Civil Liberties Union, Wright moved to the village of Linville Falls in 1948. He petitioned Parkway superintendent Sam Weems and philanthropist John D. Rockefeller Jr. to add the Linville Falls to the National Park System. The three men are honored by a plaque at the Linville Falls Visitor Center. Dr. Arnold Shankman (left) records memoirs of Alice Spearman Wright and Marion A. Wright with help from student Pam Zagaroli at Winthrop University in Rock Hill, South Carolina, around 1980. (Courtesy of the Winthrop University Archives.).

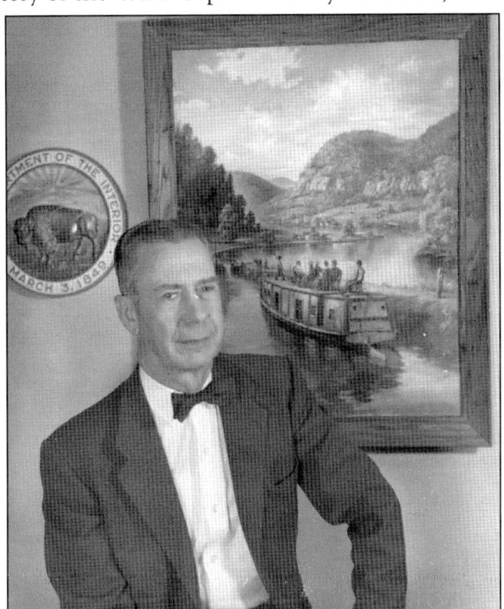

SAM WEEMS. First superintendent of the Blue Ridge Parkway, Sam Weems was notified by Marion Wright and National Park Service director Horace Albright of Rockefeller's interest in the Linville Falls area. Weems invited Rockefeller and his son, David, to a riverside picnic close to the waterfall. Rockefeller's son David was excited about the falls and wildflowers, which he described to his father, who was unable to walk the distance. A month after the visit, Rockefeller offered to negotiate a purchase at a reduced price, which was finally agreed upon by the Hossfeld heirs. (Courtesy of the Blue Ridge Parkway Archives.)

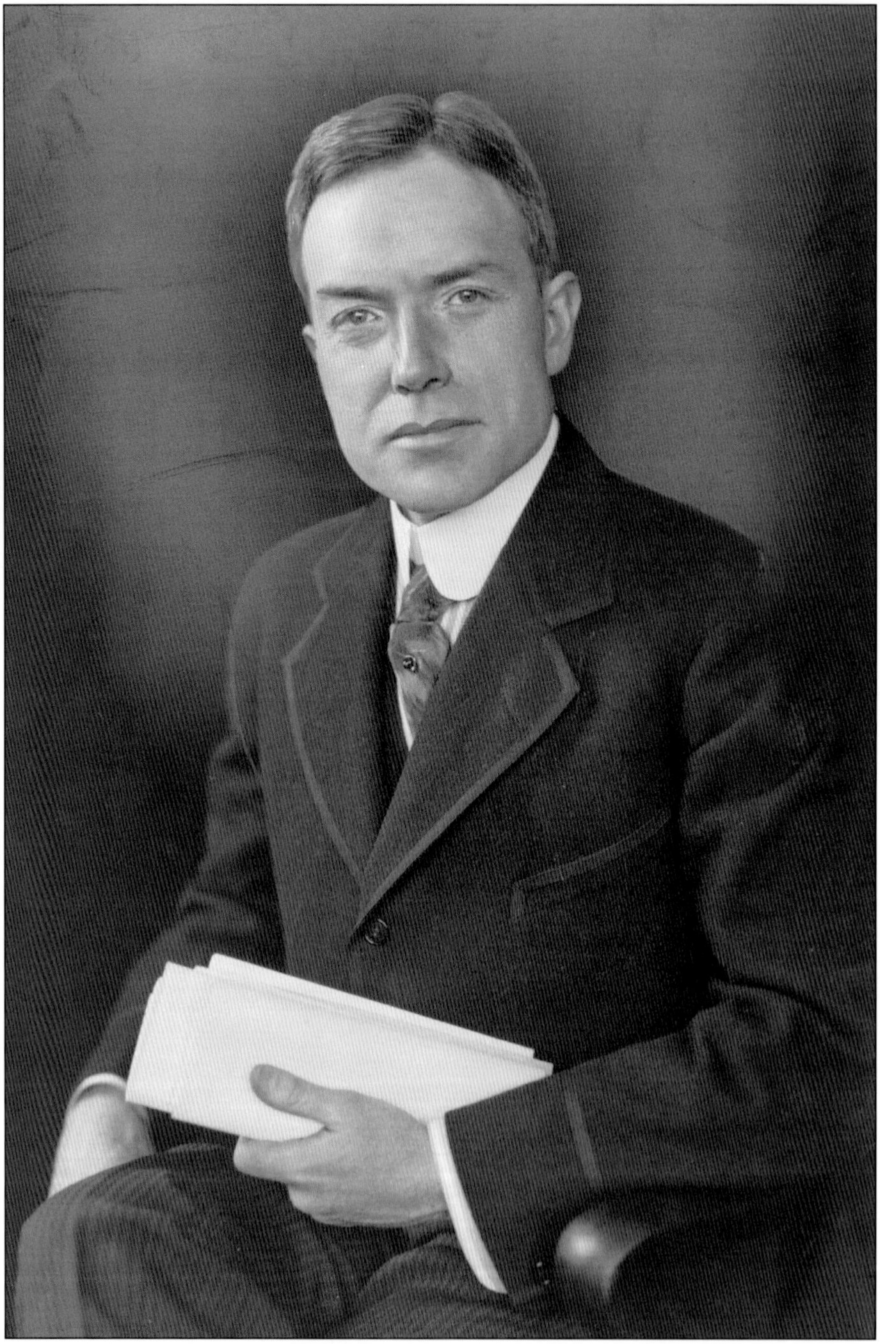

John D. Rockefeller Jr. (1871–1960). Through his Rockefeller Foundation, John D. Rockefeller had already contributed five million dollars for the purchase of the Great Smoky Mountains National Park when he came to Linville Falls in the early 1950s to meet with Wright and Weems. Wright and Weems held a lavish picnic on the river that was within hearing distance of a busy sawmill to convey to their guest a sense of urgency to the land deal. Convinced of the threat from logging to this scenic area, he purchased the 1,200-acre tract, paying $92,000 in 1951. (Courtesy of the Library of Congress.)

Two

LINVILLE RIVER
"ESSEEOH OR 'RIVER OF CLIFFS' "

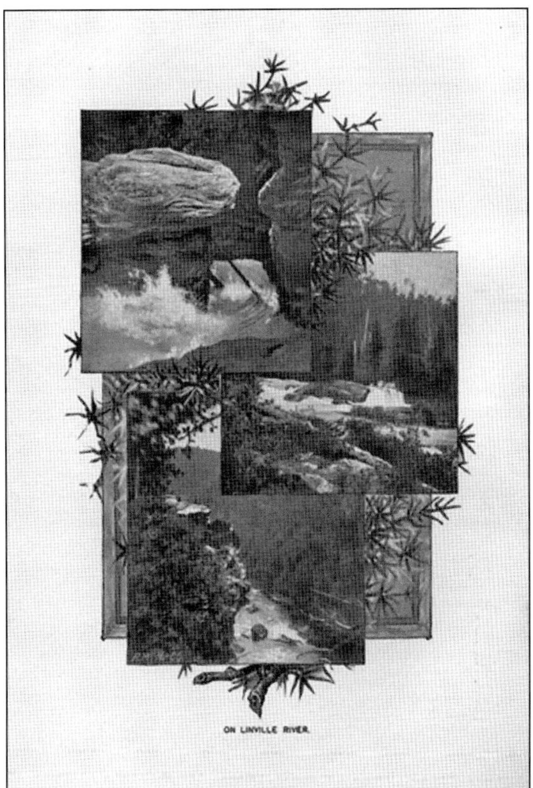

"ON LINVILLE RIVER." This three-panel design appeared in the book *North Carolina and Its Resources*, published by the State Board of Agriculture in 1896. Against a decorative spray of branches appear (from top to bottom) the window, the Upper Falls, and a view down into the river, the next stage in the pictorial history of the wilderness. (Courtesy of Documenting the American South, Wilson Library, University of North Carolina at Chapel Hill.)

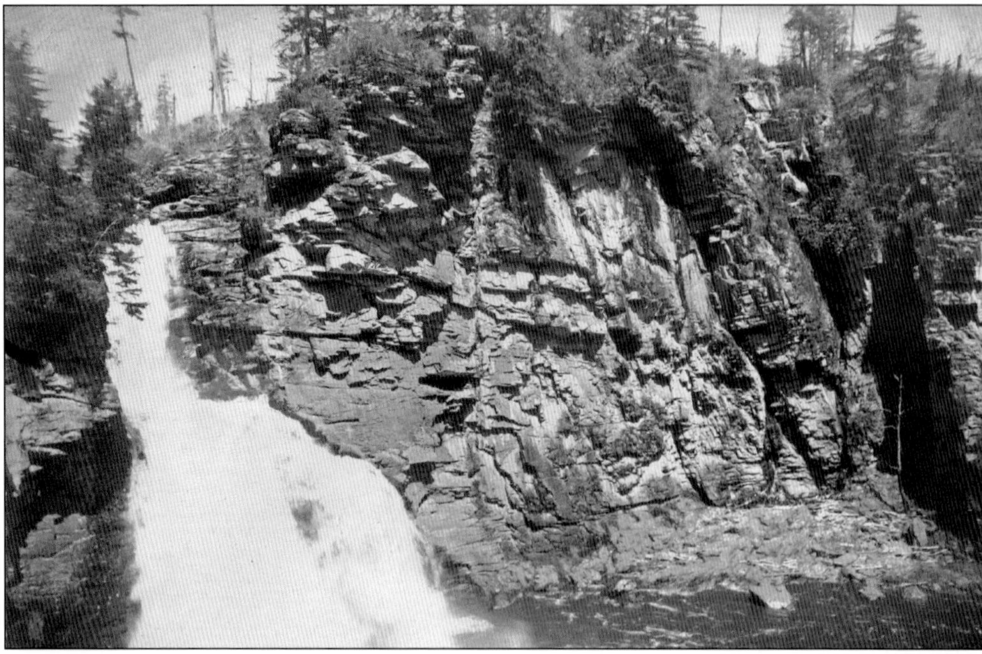

"The Great Ledge at the Lower Falls." On April 6, 1911, Frank Bicknell took this view of the river in full spate with the Linville Falls descending in a straight line. To the right of the dark fissure in the cliffs, the National Park Service has built a walled overlook, the Plunge Basin View. (Courtesy of the North Carolina State Archives.)

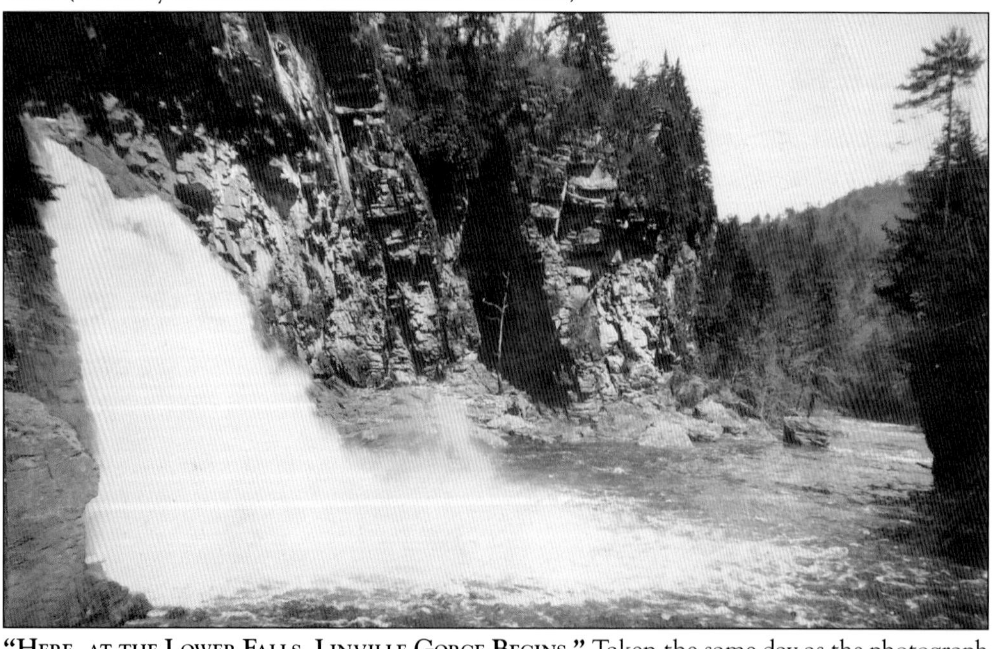

"Here, at the Lower Falls, Linville Gorge Begins." Taken the same day as the photograph above, this view by Bicknell conveys the sweep of the river from the plunge basin southward through the steep cliffs of the Linville Gorge. Given the impassability of the rock walls, there is no trail of any great distance along the river on this side. (Courtesy of the North Carolina State Archives.)

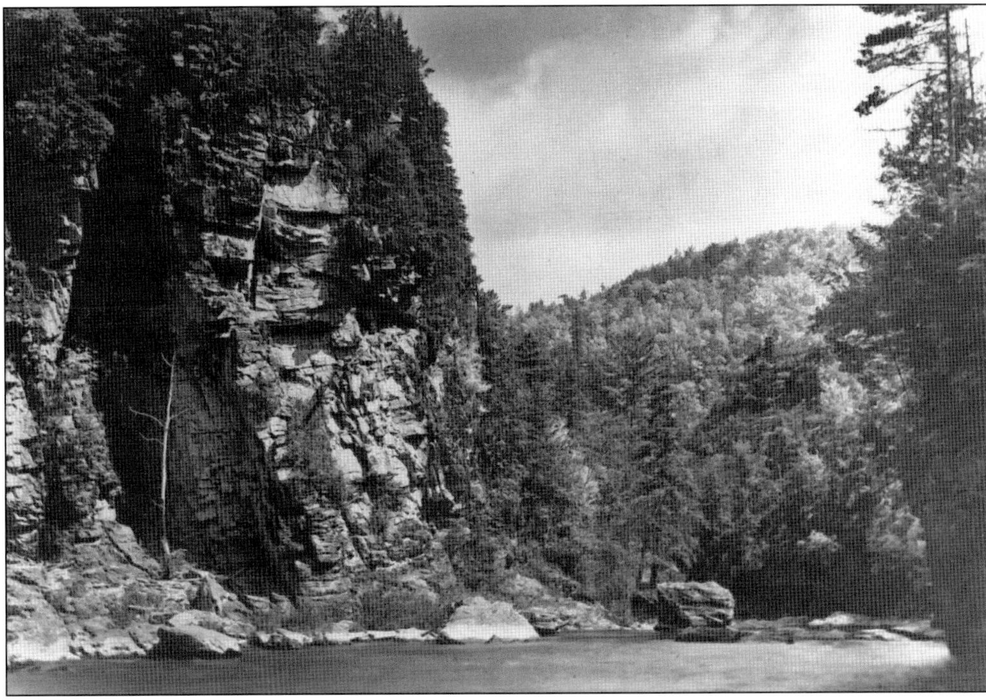

SOUTHWARD VIEW FROM PLUNGE BASIN. Just beyond the big boulder midstream, the Linville River cuts sharply to the left and begins a torturous meander for a couple of miles downstream. The Linville Gorge Trail, paralleling the river for 14 miles, rises and dips on the right (west) bank. A series of trails from the gorge's rim lead down to it. (Courtesy of East Tennessee State University.)

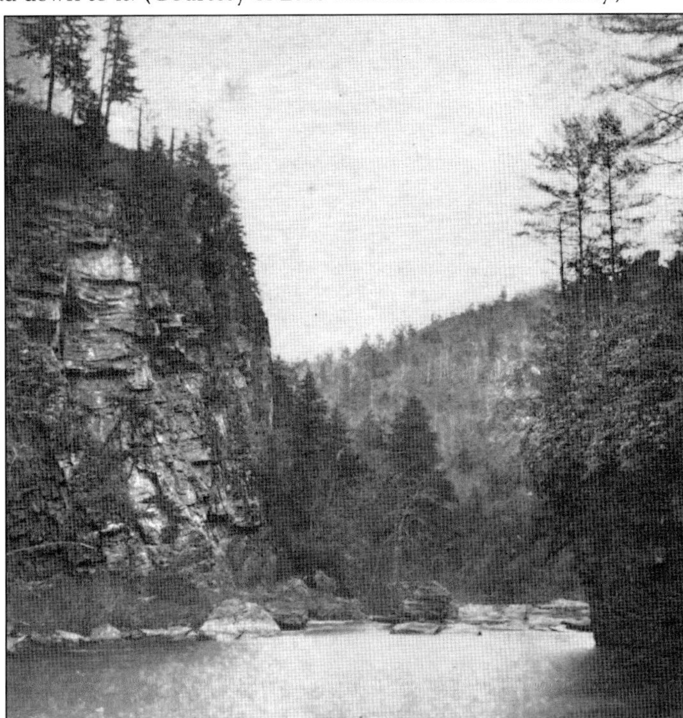

DOWNSTREAM FROM PLUNGE BASIN. Rufus Morgan photographed what was much the same scene as Bicknell above only here he has also recorded a large chimney rock just beneath Erwin's View to the right. (Courtesy of the North Carolina Collection, Wilson Library, University of North Carolina at Chapel Hill.)

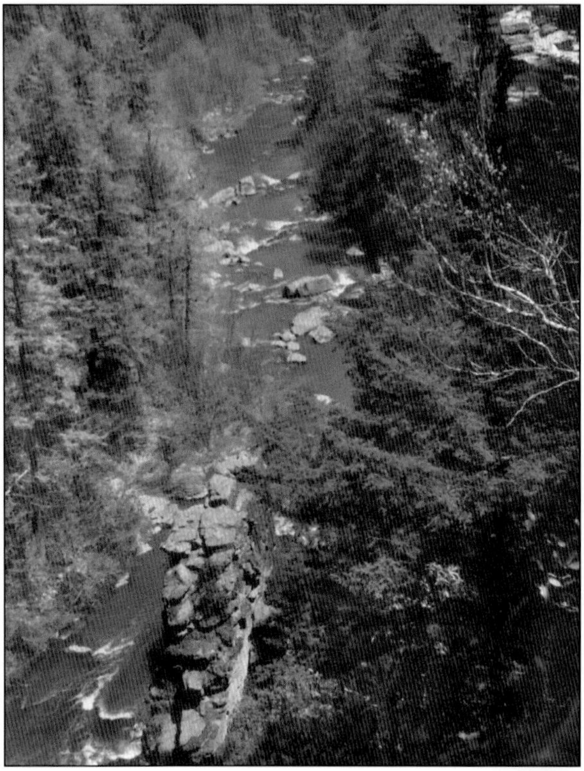

View of the Chimney. This dramatic freestanding rock spire or "chimney," underneath, stands directly below what is called the "Chimney View" just below the Linville Falls. Such chimney-shaped rock formations are even more plentiful on the east side of the Linville Gorge, south of Table Rock Mountain. This picture was taken by National Park Service photographer C. E. Westveer on June 12, 1974. (Courtesy of the Blue Ridge Parkway Archives.)

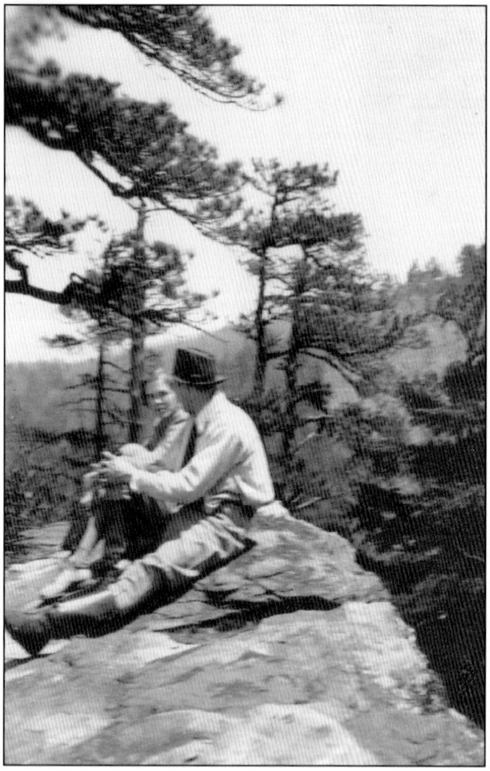

Couple at Linville Falls. Several of the National Park Service archival photographs of the Linville Falls record public visitors enjoying the views. This picture is anonymous and undated but was probably made in the early 1950s. Sightseers scramble around on the crags even today, contributing to the steady number of accidental falls. (Courtesy of the Blue Ridge Parkway Archives.)

"DR. CLARK AT LOWER FALLS." Frank Bicknell caught his friend Dr. Clark angling in the choppy waters of the plunge basin on a summer's day, June 26, 1909. (Courtesy of the North Carolina State Archives.)

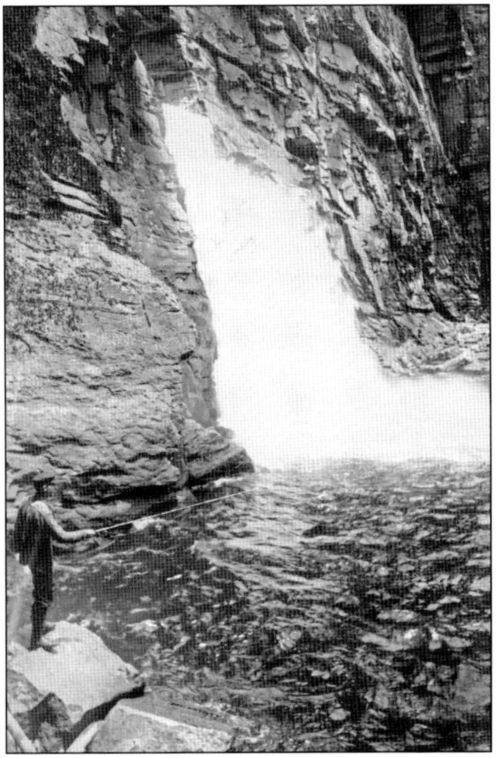

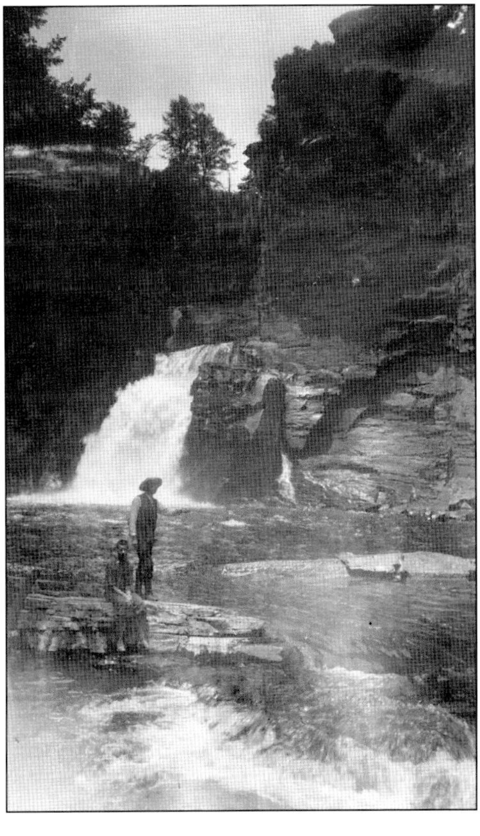

"DR. CLARK AND WILLIAM [HOSSFELD]." Bicknell has photographed his two friends against the dramatic backdrop of Linville Falls. Just to the right of the base of the Linville Falls is a small gushing stream of water, which is often visible when the river is high. (Courtesy of the North Carolina State Archives.)

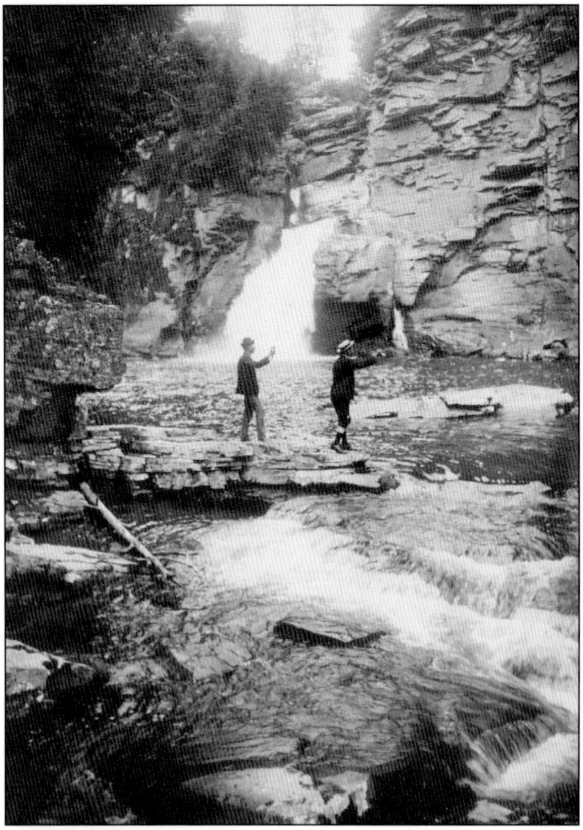

"**At the Outlet of the Big Pool.**" Here two other friends of Bicknell's, Ben Watrous and C. B. Carpenter, are angling in the plunge basin on July 18, 1909. (Courtesy of the North Carolina State Archives.)

"**Of a Rainy Day No Spot More Tempting to Fishermen.**" Jessie Bicknell photographs her husband, Frank, in his waders as he angles in the plunge basin on August 25, 1911. (Courtesy of the North Carolina State Archives.)

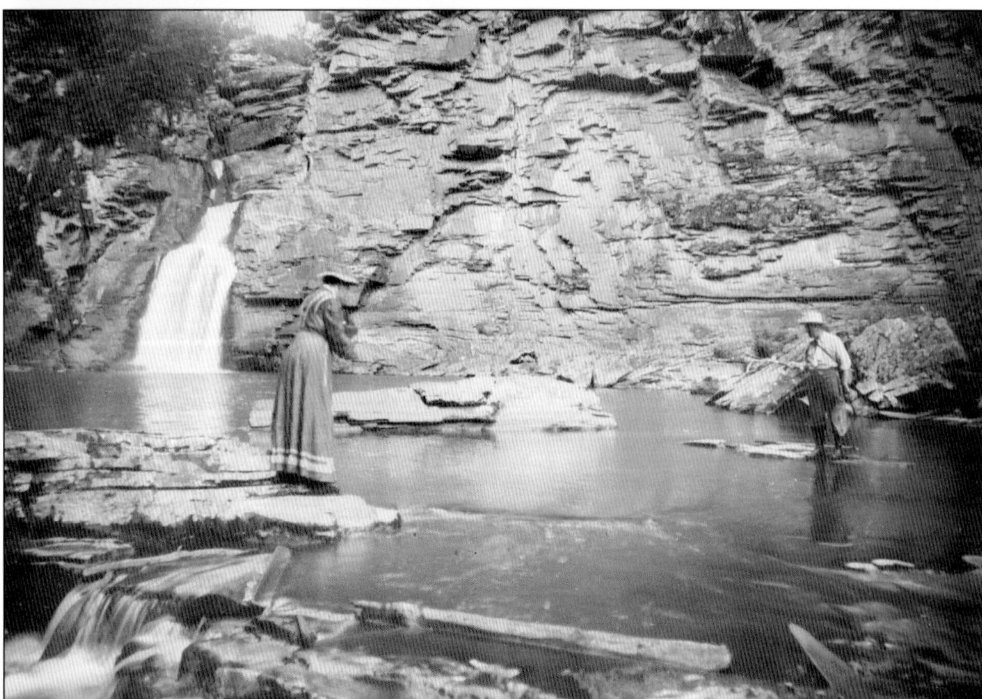

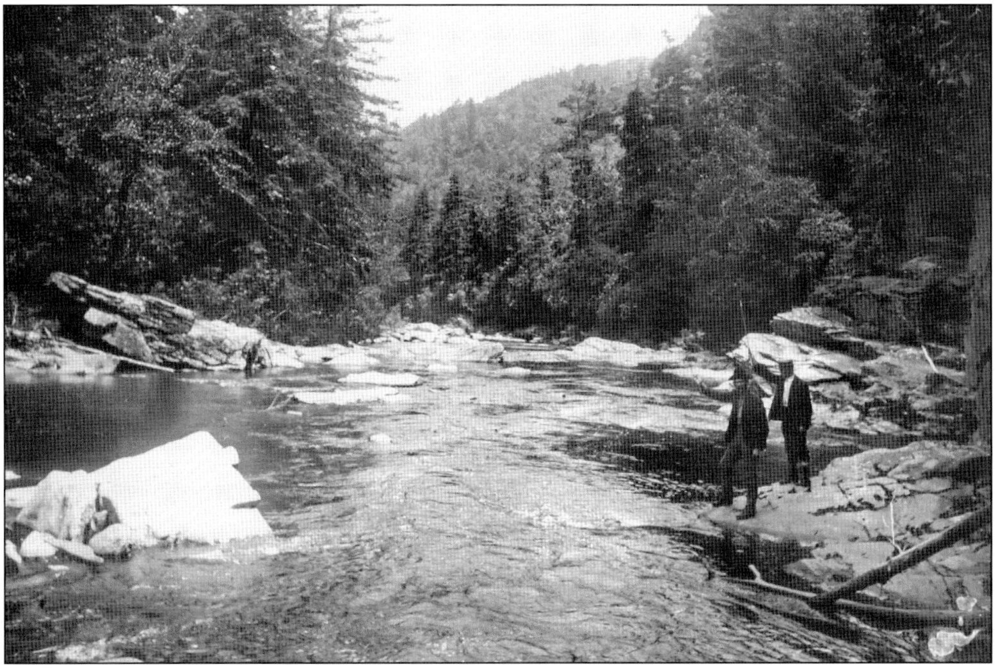

"WATROUS AND CARPENTER BELOW LOWER FALLS." Frank Bicknell photographed his two outdoor companions on July 18, 1909. (Courtesy of the North Carolina State Archives.)

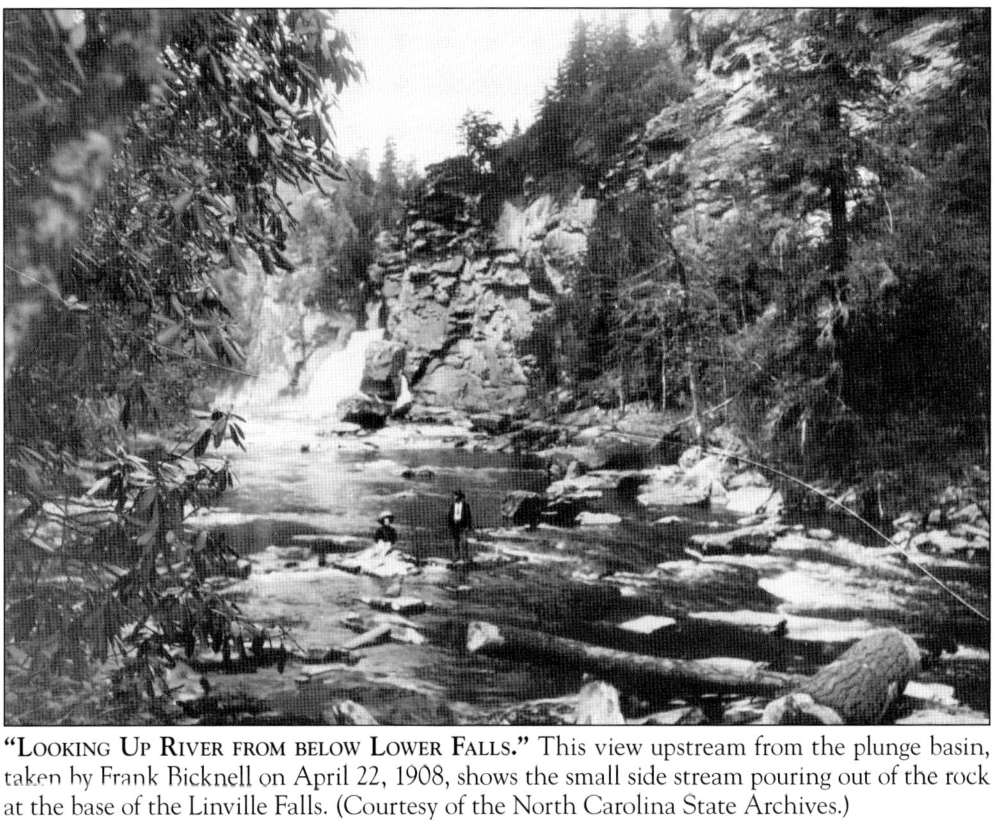

"LOOKING UP RIVER FROM BELOW LOWER FALLS." This view upstream from the plunge basin, taken by Frank Bicknell on April 22, 1908, shows the small side stream pouring out of the rock at the base of the Linville Falls. (Courtesy of the North Carolina State Archives.)

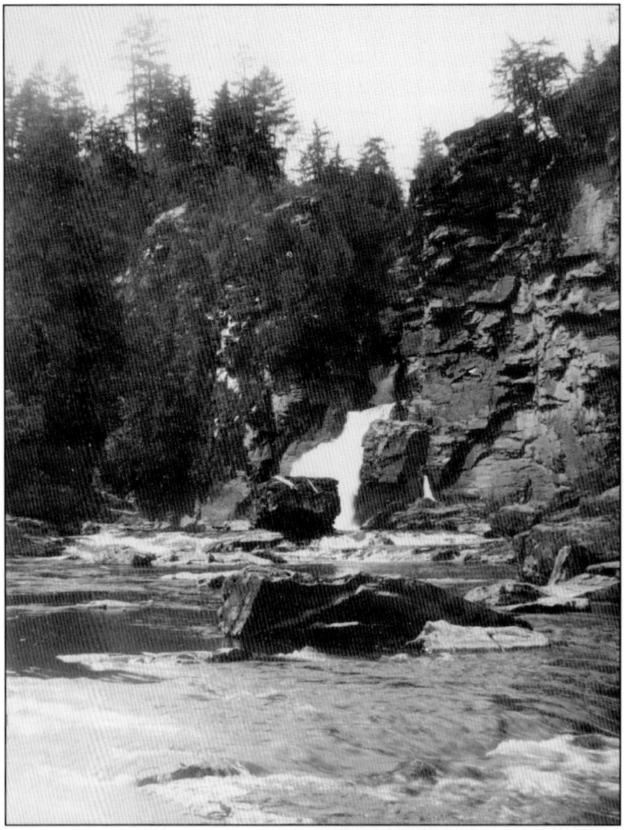

"IN THE RIVER BELOW THE FALLS, OUR FIRST SITE [SIC] OF IT, GUIDED BY SHEPHERD M. DUGGER." The Bicknells had an excellent guide in Banner Elk, North Carolina, resident Shepherd M. Dugger, surveyor, teacher, and self-styled "Bard of Ottaray" (his name for North Carolina). In 1892, Dugger published a novel, *Balsam Groves of the Grandfather Mountain*, which includes a romantic wedding service at the base of Linville Falls. The National Park Service has named a small creek and nature trail for Dugger; it is at the entrance of the visitor center parking lot. (Courtesy of the North Carolina State Archives.)

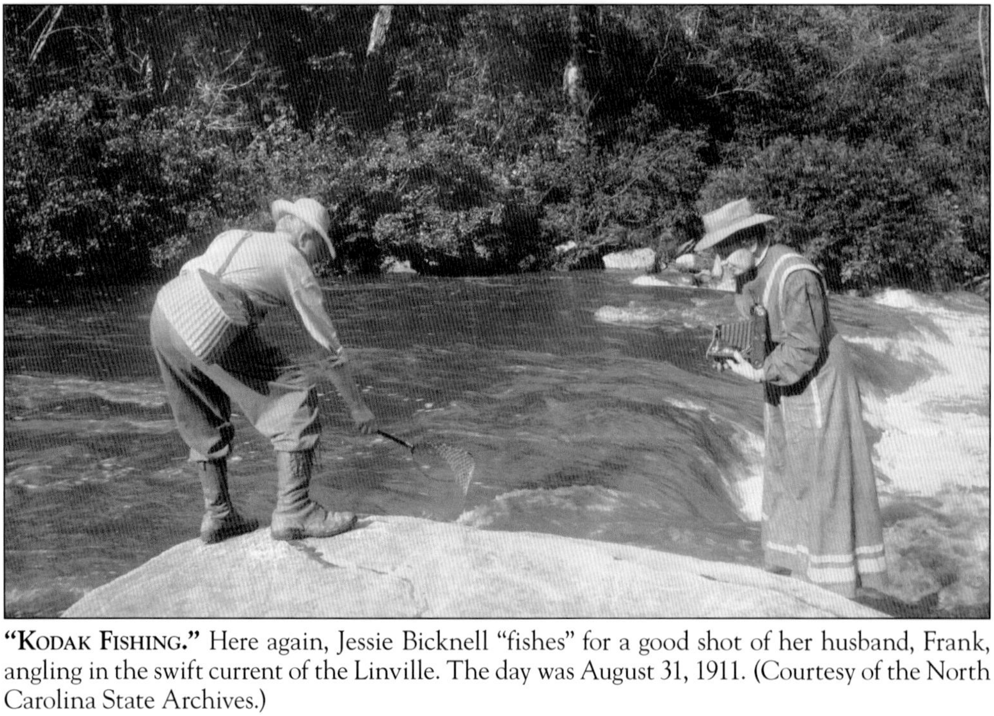

"KODAK FISHING." Here again, Jessie Bicknell "fishes" for a good shot of her husband, Frank, angling in the swift current of the Linville. The day was August 31, 1911. (Courtesy of the North Carolina State Archives.)

"Looking Up over Bynum's Bluff Falls." Bynum's Bluff, a ridgeline on the west side of the Linville Gorge with a trail down to the river, was named for lawyer John Bynum. The pools where the trail meets the riverside are still favorite spots for trout fishermen. (Courtesy of the North Carolina State Archives.)

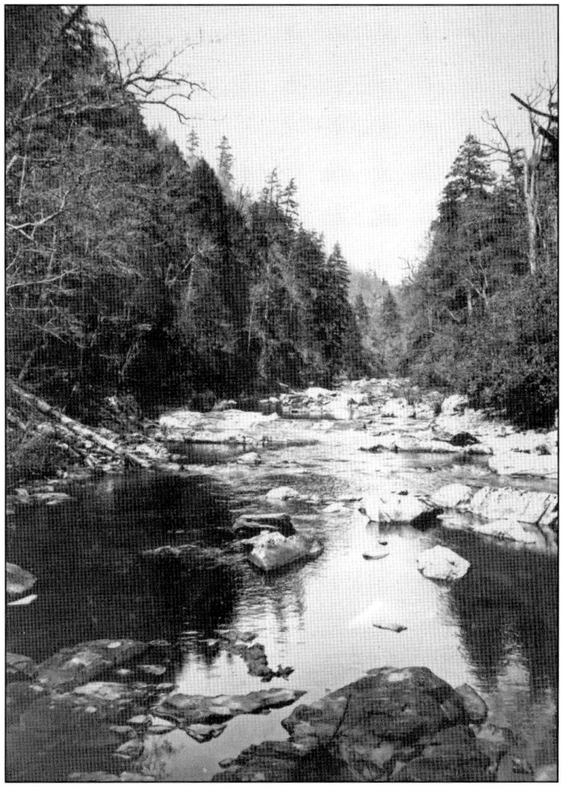

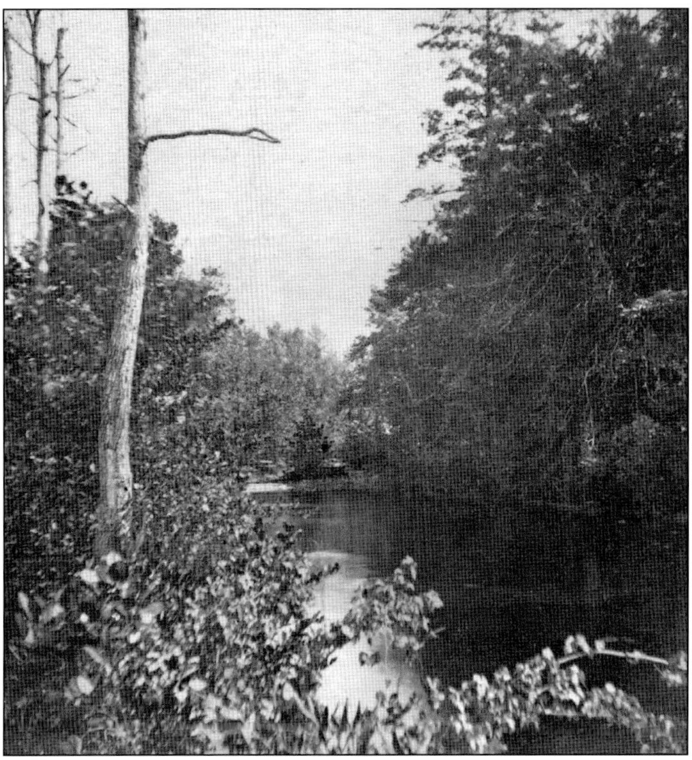

Linville River in a Quiet Mood. For considerable stretches and at periods of low water, the Linville River flows placidly with barely a ripple. Rufus Morgan caught the stream in such a mood around 1873. (Courtesy of the North Carolina Collection, Wilson Library, University of North Carolina at Chapel Hill.)

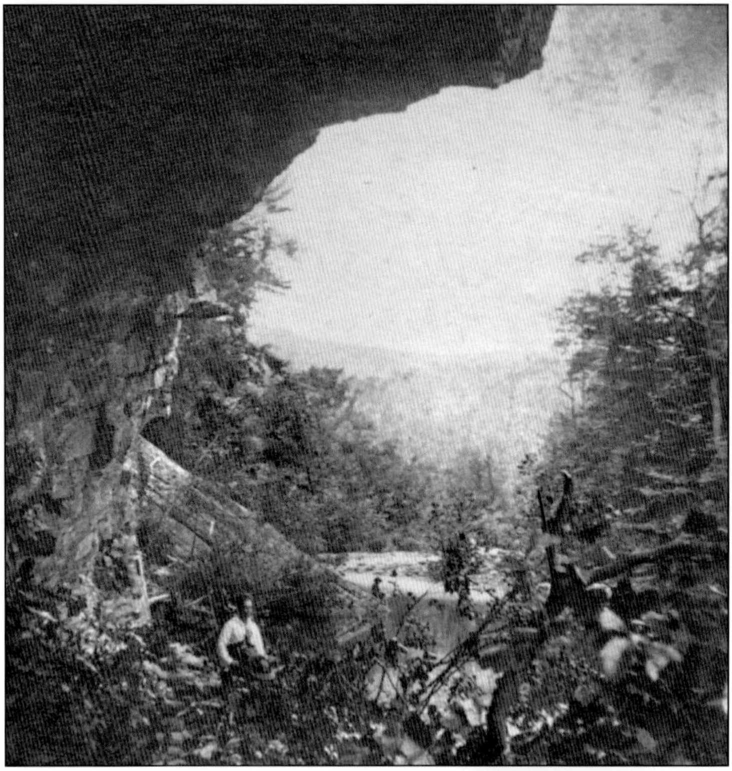

Overhang on the River. Such overhanging rock cliffs are a common sight along the river. Telltale smoke on the surface of the rock indicates their popularity as campsites. They are also shelters from rainstorms. (Courtesy of the North Carolina Collection, Wilson Library, University of North Carolina at Chapel Hill.)

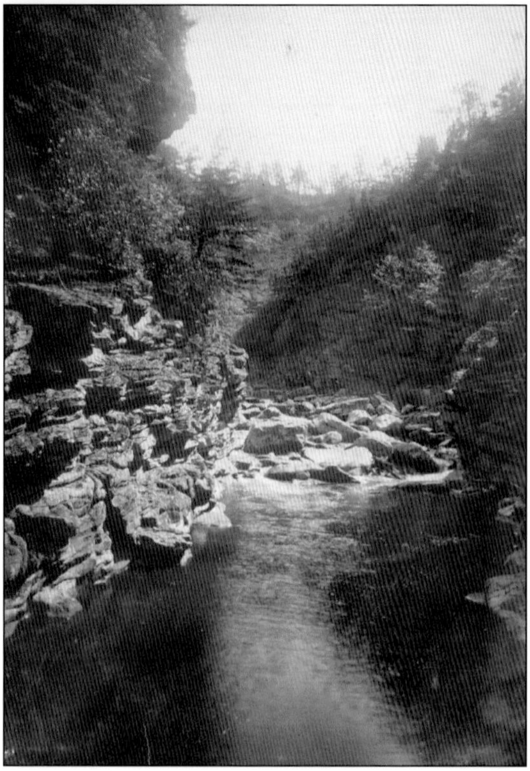

"From the Cliff, Middle of Pool, Looking Up." Bicknell recorded the cliff side near the Babel Tower Trail on October 6, 1911. (Courtesy of the North Carolina State Archives.)

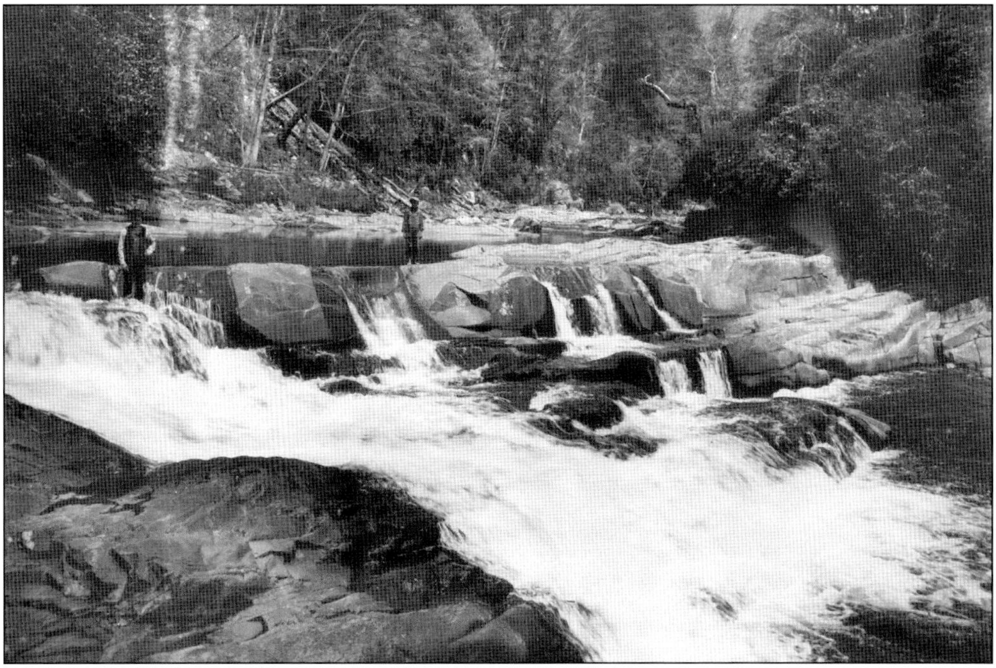

"BYNUM'S BLUFF FALLS." Behind Bicknell's two unnamed friends, one can see evidence of a washout on the slope. Hurricane and tropical rainstorms periodically cause rock slides, forcing the rerouting of trails. This view was taken on Sunday, May 1, 1910. (Courtesy of the North Carolina State Archives.)

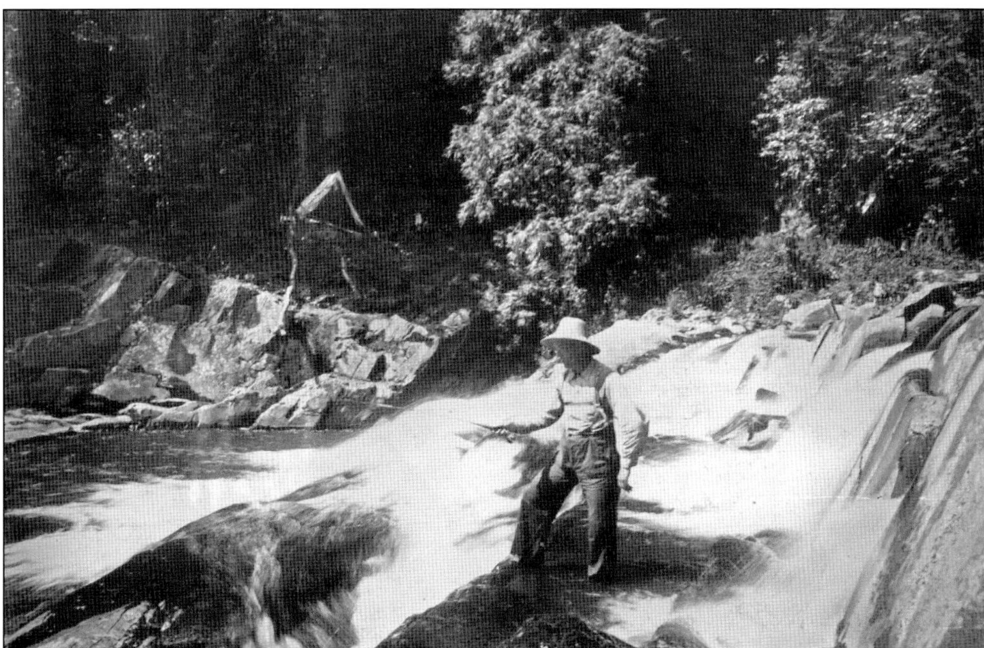

"TROUT FOR SUPPER, CAMP PETERSON." Bicknell jocularly named this campsite after his companion on the trip, G. H. Peterson. The location is Bynum's Bluff Falls on May 27, 1911. (Courtesy of the North Carolina State Archives.)

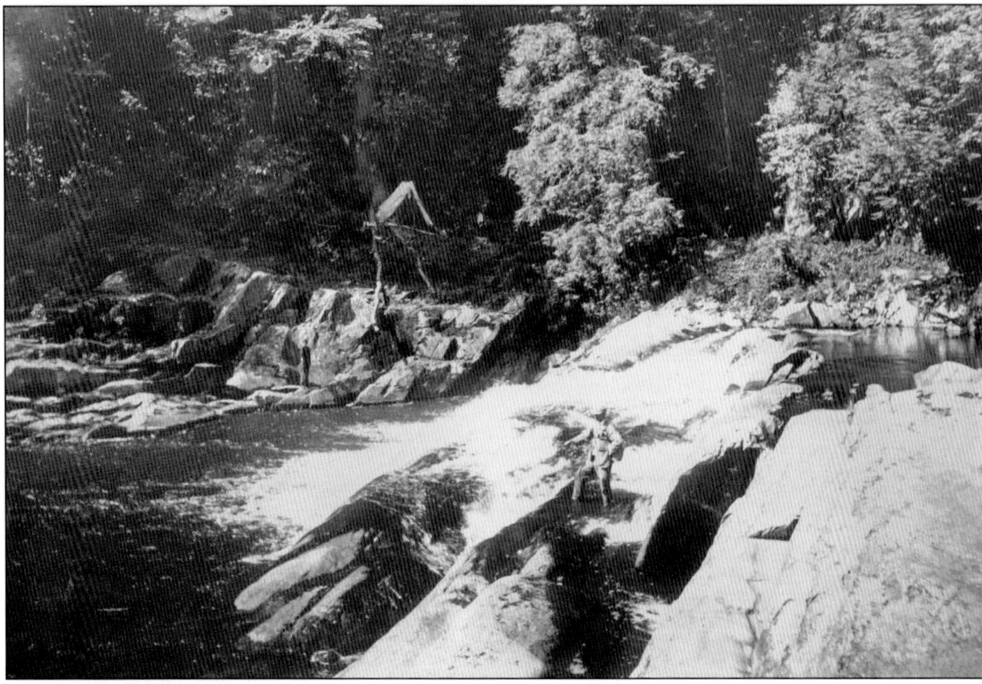

"G.H.P. [Peterson] Fishing in Bynum's Bluff Pool." Here is another photograph dating from May 27, 1911, and showing a friend of Bicknell's engaged in providing dinner for the campers. (Courtesy of the North Carolina State Archives.)

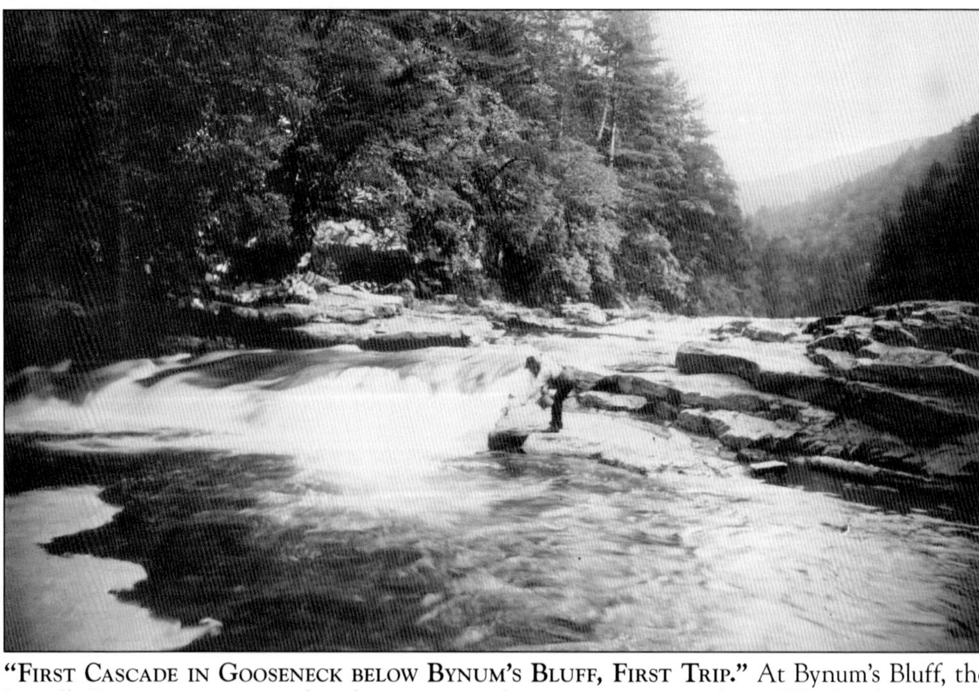

"First Cascade in Gooseneck below Bynum's Bluff, First Trip." At Bynum's Bluff, the Linville River executes one of its sharpest turns (see picture on top of page 58). On this visit on September 12, 1910, Bicknell was accompanied by his friends Vance Turner, Crockett, and C. B. Carpenter. (Courtesy of the North Carolina State Archives.)

"Another Splendid Trout Hole, Ruggedly Set." The river is captured here making one of its serpentine twists around a massive rock. At this point, the Linville Gorge Trail passes high above the cliffs, with no passage beside the stream being possible for much of its 14 miles. (Courtesy of the North Carolina State Archives.)

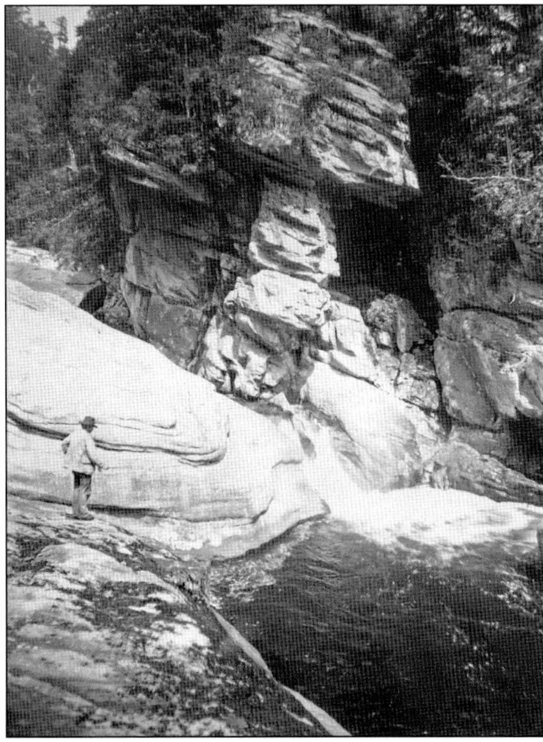

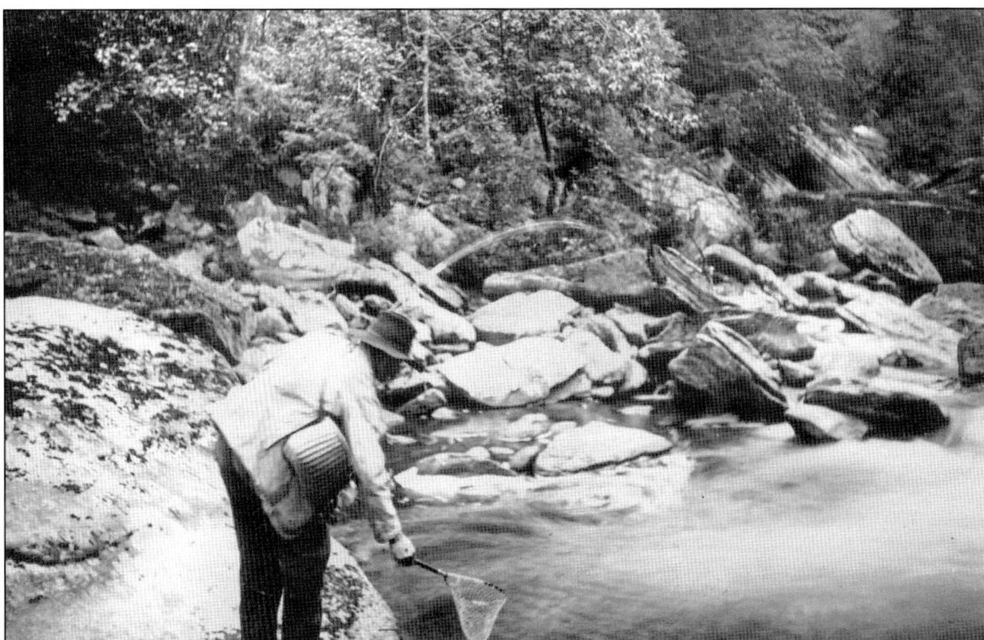

"Lifting One Out at Carpenter Trail Camp." Frank Bicknell made this shot of a successful catch on September 13, 1910. Carpenter Trail, perhaps descending the west side of the Linville Gorge near Laurel Knob, might have been scouted and cut by Bicknell and his friends. No such trail or trail name is recorded on the U.S. Geologic Survey topographical map of the Linville Gorge. (Courtesy of the North Carolina State Archives.)

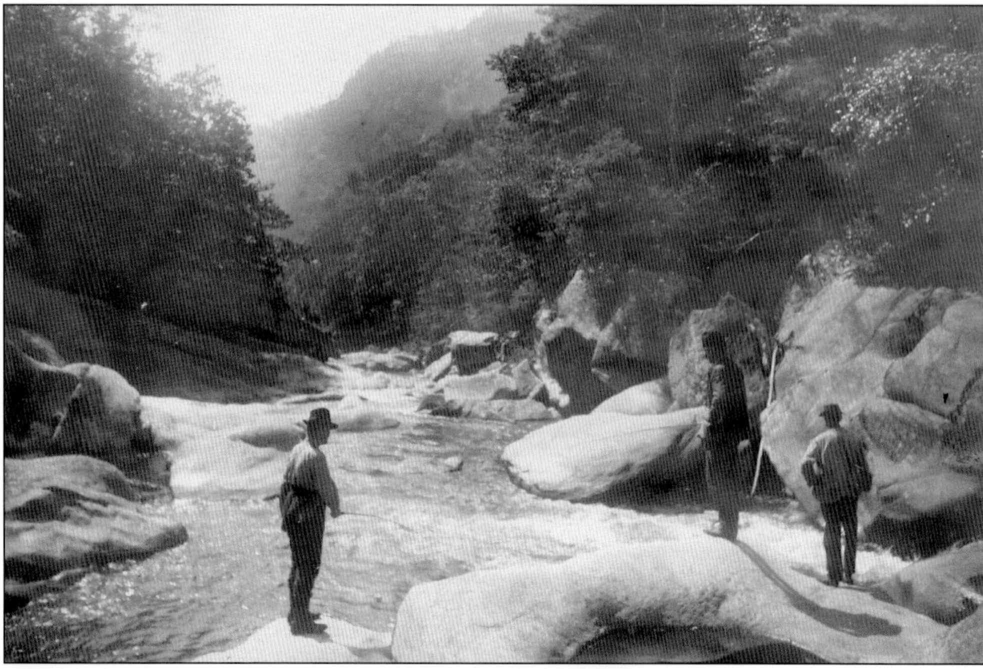

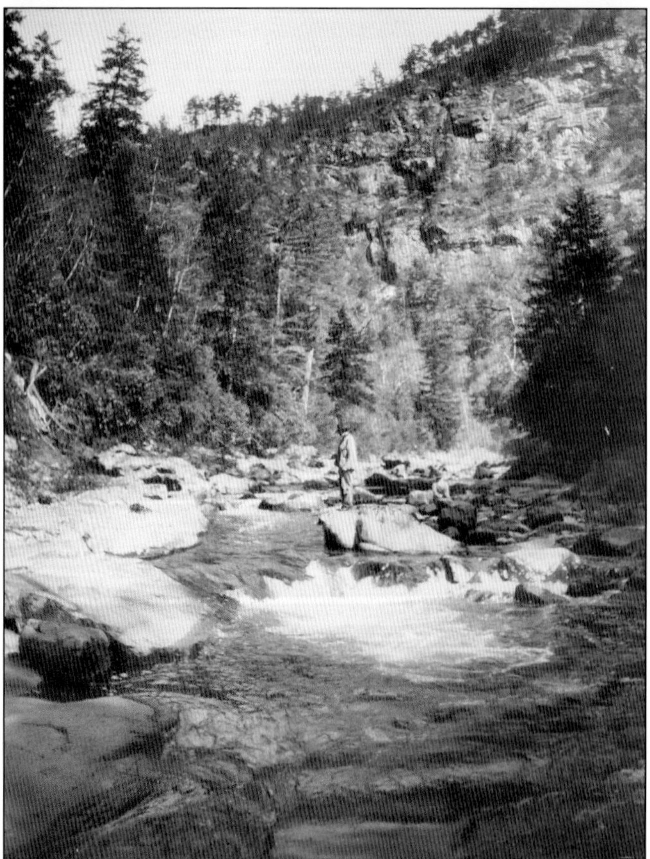

"At the Lucky Stone Ledge below Babel Towers." This photograph was taken the same day as the previous one. It might place Carpenter Trail in the vicinity of Babel Tower Trail. Notice the worn-and-sculpted river stone. (Courtesy of the North Carolina State Archives.)

"Rapids below Bull Face." Bull Face is a sheer cliff on the Linville Gorge's eastern side that overlooks the gooseneck bend in the river at the Bynum's Bluff Trail terminus. Bicknell was at its base on October 26, 1910. (Courtesy of the North Carolina State Archives.)

"A Famous Fishing Pool Containing Eels." Bicknell is careful not to give away the location of this eel pool, which he visited on September 23, 1910. (Courtesy of the North Carolina State Archives.)

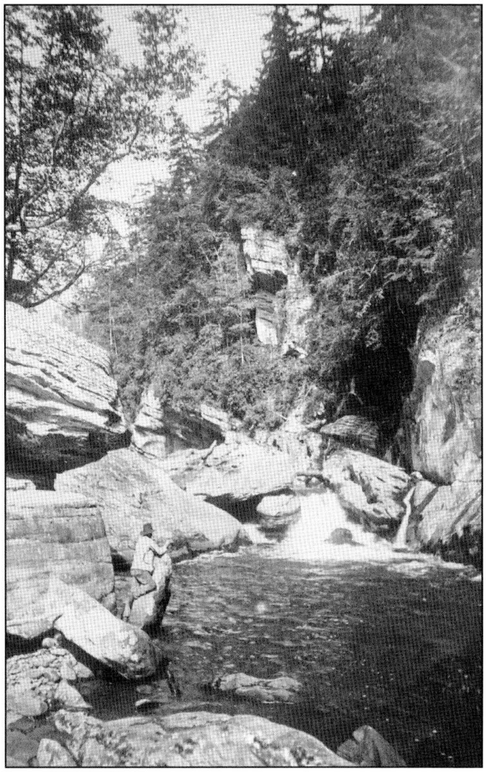

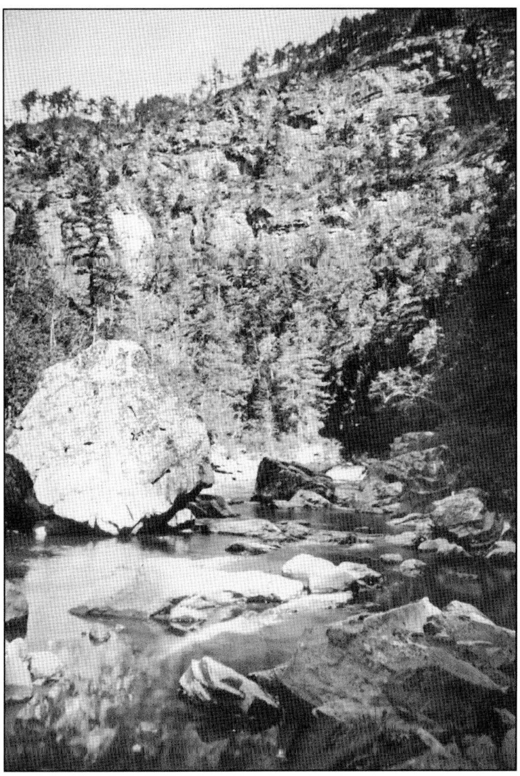

"Looking Up at Bull Face Cliff." The great round boulder near Bynum's Bluff Trail on the river gives some idea of the colossal size attained by such rocks, many of which have split off from the cliffs above to careen down to the water. (Courtesy of the North Carolina State Archives.)

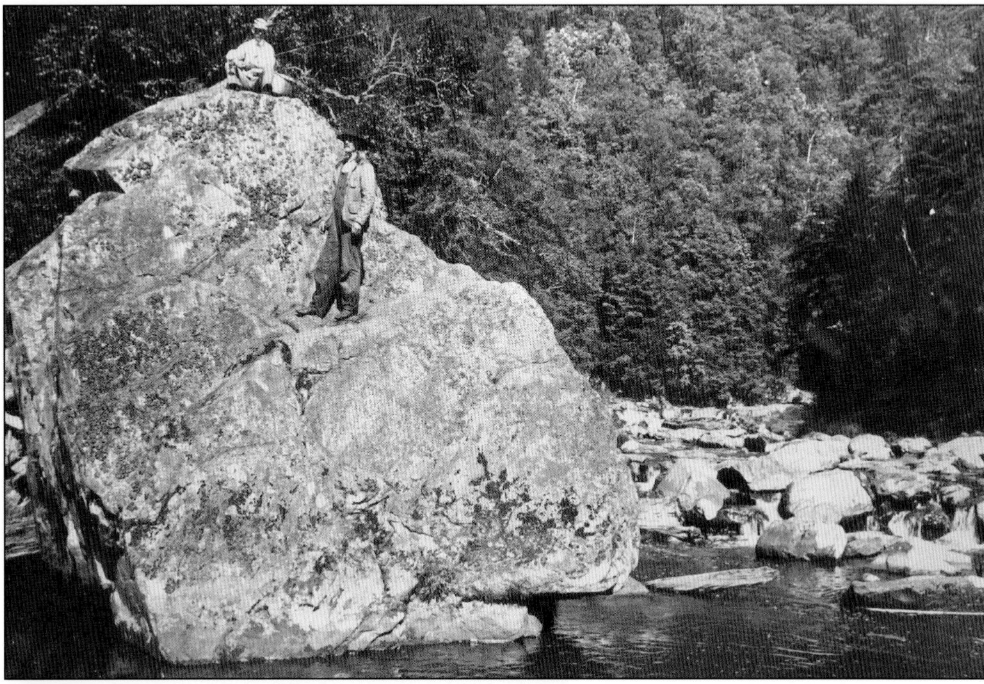

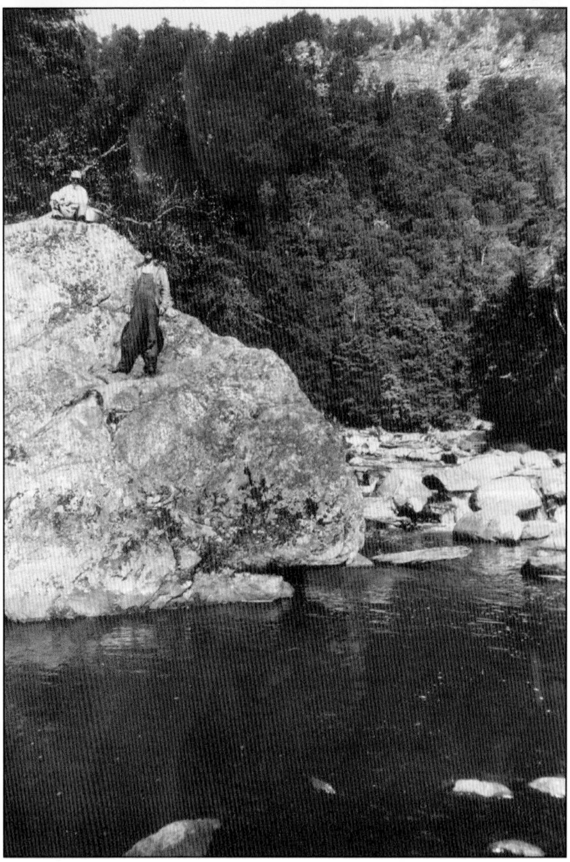

"Huge Rock Foot of Bynum's Bluff Pool." This is another monolith in the river with two of Frank Bicknell's fishing friends, G. H. Peterson (left) and Turner Vance (right), giving scale to the rock on May 27, 1911. A common sight all over the Linville Gorge, notice the lichen flecking the stone surface (May 27, 1911). (Courtesy of the North Carolina State Archives.)

"The Great Rock and Bluff Behind." This is much the same view as the photograph above and made by Bicknell on the same day. On the ridgeline, the exposed rock of the bluff is visible. Today this is a popular camping area. (Courtesy of the North Carolina State Archives.)

"A Bit of Roughness, Babel Tower Gorge." Babel Tower Trail reaches the Linville River at a point some two miles below the Bynum's Bluff Trail. Bicknell's caption means the small canyon formed by the projection of the Babel Tower ridge. (Courtesy of the North Carolina State Archives.)

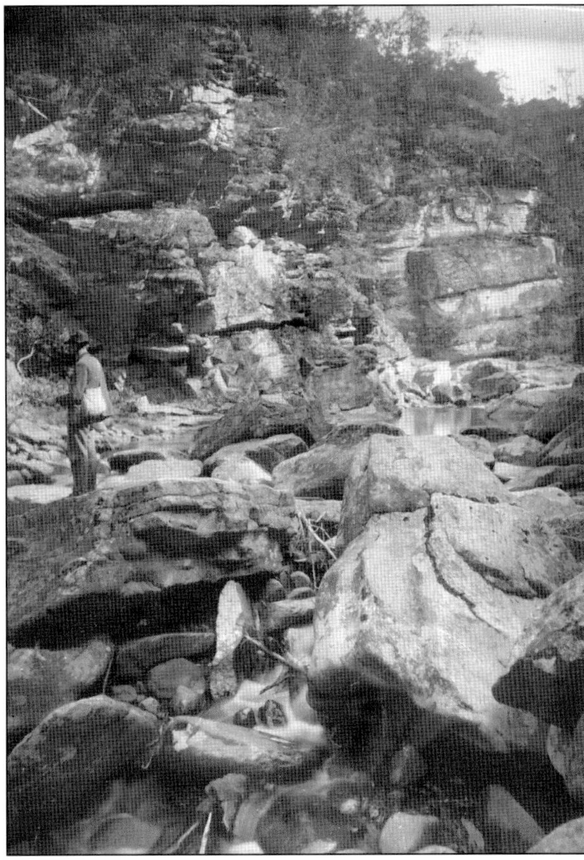

"J. is Now Ready to Start from Camp to go through Babel Tower Gorge." A friend might have snapped Bicknell's picture as he turned his back to face downstream on June 1, 1912. The figure seated on a rock to the right is probably Jessie Bicknell. (Courtesy of the North Carolina State Archives.)

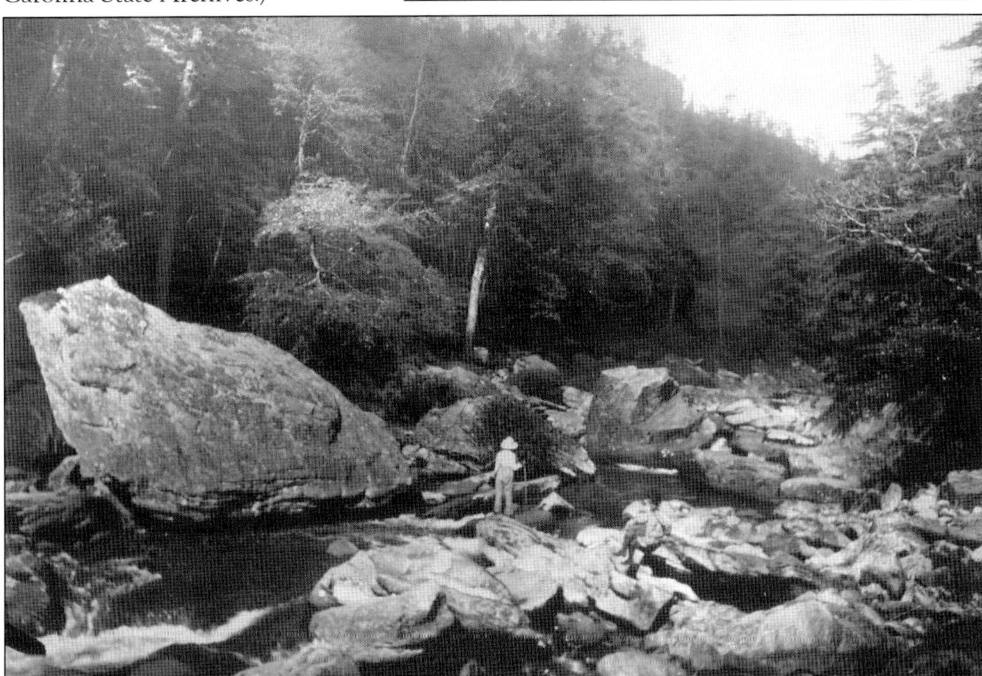

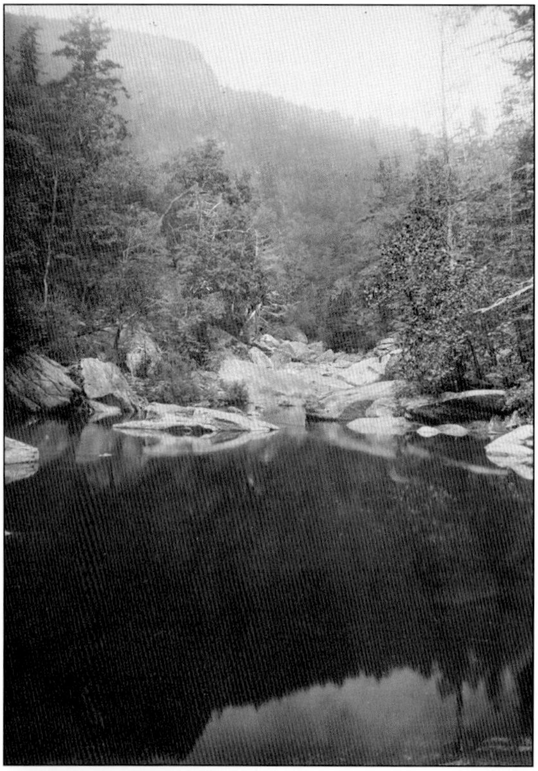

"WISEMAN'S VIEW FROM BELOW, FROM A ROCK IN MID-RIVER." Wiseman's View is the rock buttress projecting into the west side of the Linville Gorge from Linville Mountain. It faces directly between Hawksbill Mountain on the left and Table Rock Mountain on the right on Jonas Ridge to the east. On September 23, 1910, Bicknell and friends are near the Spence Ridge Trail leading up to a gap between the two peaks. (Courtesy of the North Carolina State Archives.)

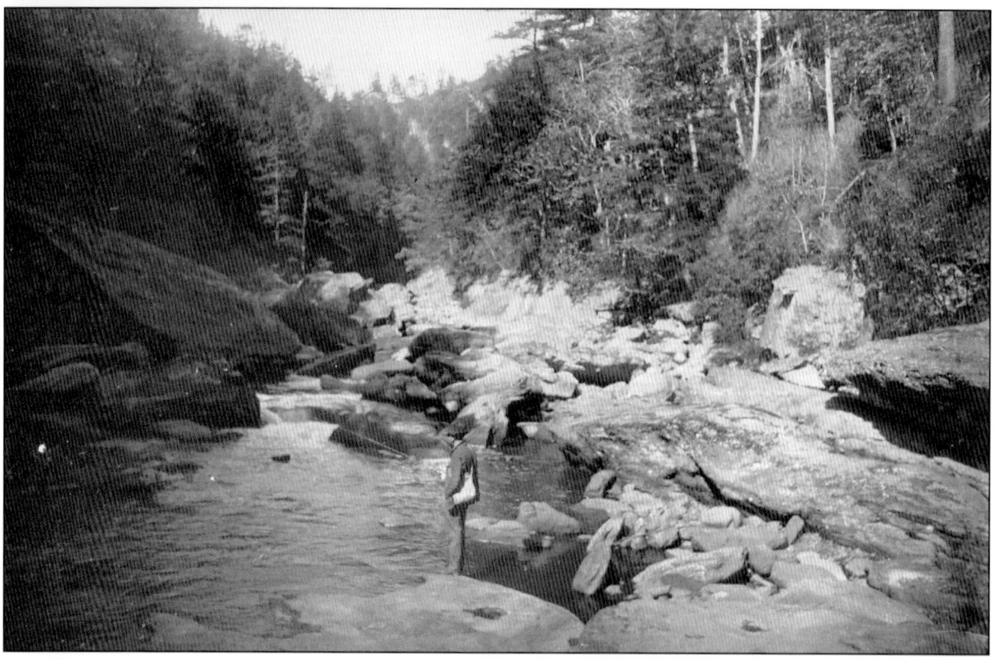

"UP RIVER FROM ROUGH RIDGE CAMP AFTER COLD NIGHT." Trail and landscape names throughout the Linville Gorge have changed over the years. The location of the camp where the party spent a chilly night could be anywhere along miles of the Linville River. The campers headed up the river on October 6, 1911. (Courtesy of the North Carolina State Archives.)

JESSIE BICKNELL FISHING AFTER NIGHT CAMP WITH CARPENTER AND JOHN DEANE." On May 4, 1912, the group broke camp and headed off to climb Table Rock Mountain. They had spent the night near the base of Conley Cove Trail. This trail, south of Wiseman's View, terminates on the west side of the river directly below Table Rock Mountain. (Courtesy of the North Carolina State Archives.)

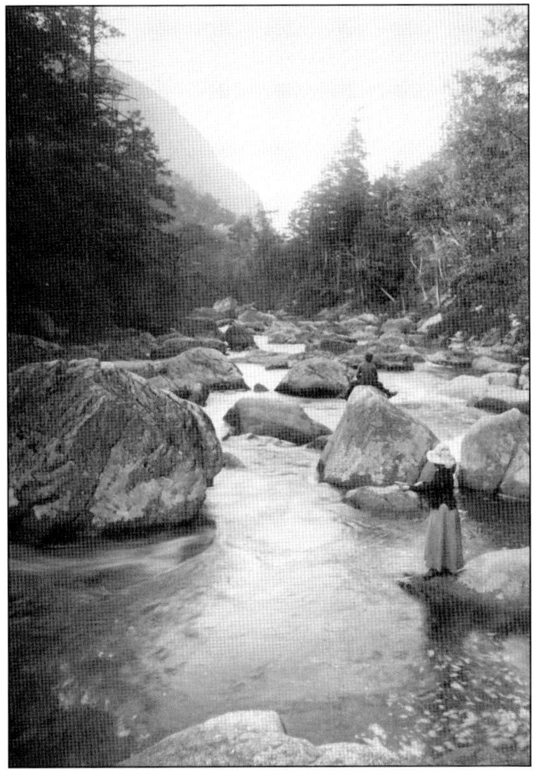

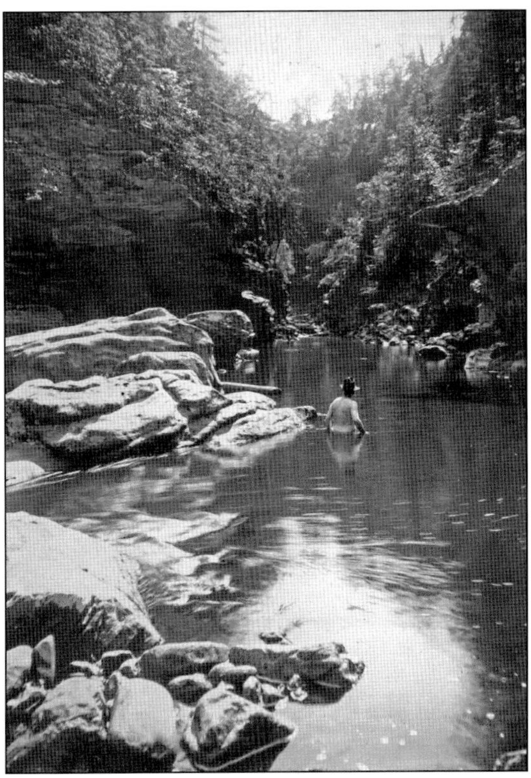

"LOWER END OF BABEL [TOWER] GORGE, READY TO SWIM." With his hat on his head, this unidentified man clad in his long johns is more likely seeking a suitable route to traverse the steep riverside than to swim. There is no continuous trail on the east side of Linville River; boulder scrambling and wading await those who travel that side of the stream. The photograph was taken on October 16, 1911. (Courtesy of the North Carolina State Archives.)

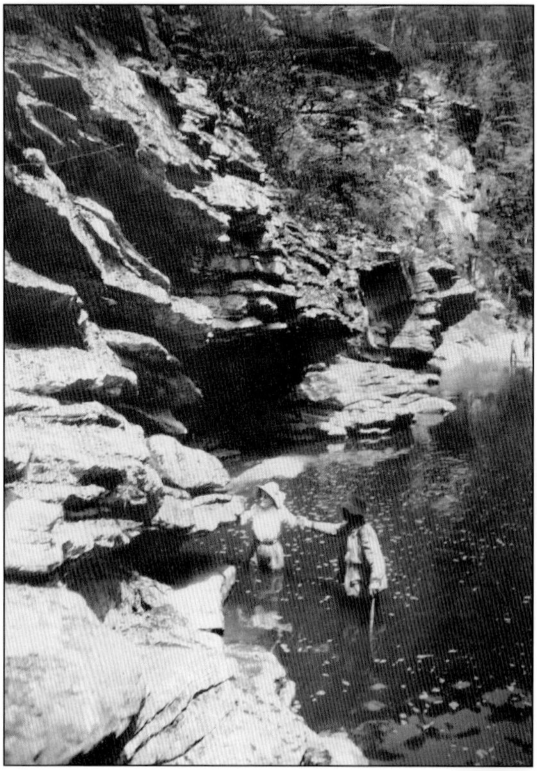

"NOTHING FOR IT BUT TO WADE AROUND." This picture of Jessie Bicknell being assisted around river rocks by an unidentified man in an undated shot clearly shows the difficulty of maneuvering along the *Eeseeoh*, or "river of many cliffs." (Courtesy of the North Carolina State Archives.)

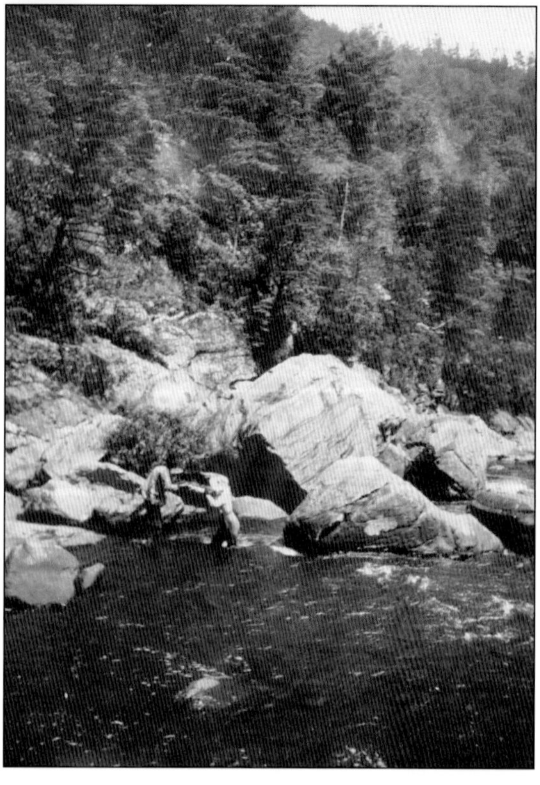

"GETTING ACROSS A RAPID." Jessie Bicknell is assisted again in negotiating the rocks and currents of the Linville River in this photograph taken on June 1, 1912. Depending on the water level, the river can be waded easily in places or crossed only at personal risk. (Courtesy of the North Carolina State Archives.)

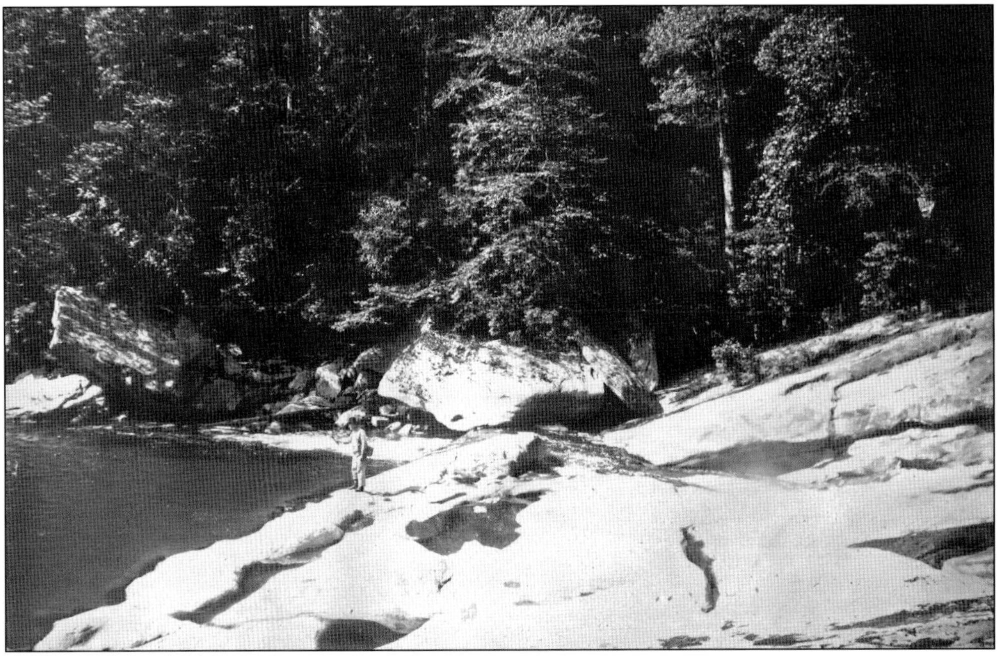

"Part of the Big Holly Falls and Pool." This immense slab of rock resembles one located in the northern end of the Linville Gorge between Cabin and Bynum Bluff Trails. The name "Big Holly" does not appear in any recent maps or trail guides. Frank Bicknell recorded the scene on September 24, 1910. (Courtesy of the North Carolina State Archives.)

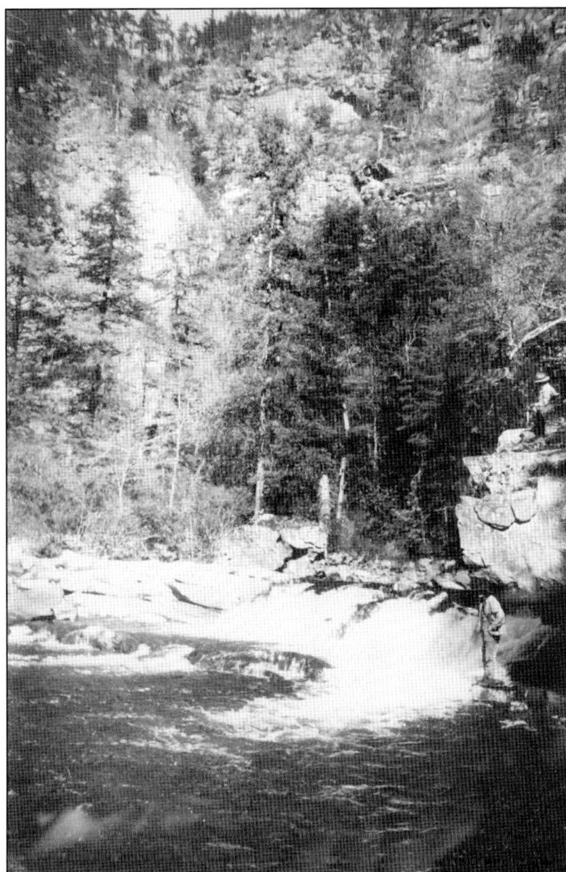

"Bull Face Falls, Turner Vance Fishing." Turner Vance, fish and game warden and close friend of the Bicknells, fishes in the cascade at the bottom of Bynum's Bluff Trail below Bull Face Cliffs. The date is October 26, 1910. (Courtesy of the North Carolina State Archives.)

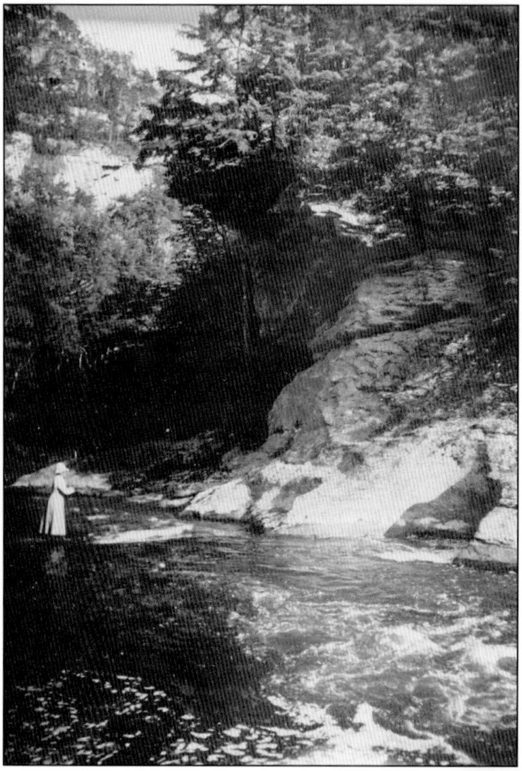

"The Sounding Board in front of Camp, Half Mile below Babel Tower Gorge." This 1912 photograph made by Frank Bicknell depicts his wife, Jessie, creating echo effects as she stands in the river and shouts at a cavity in the cliff facing her. (Courtesy of the North Carolina State Archives.)

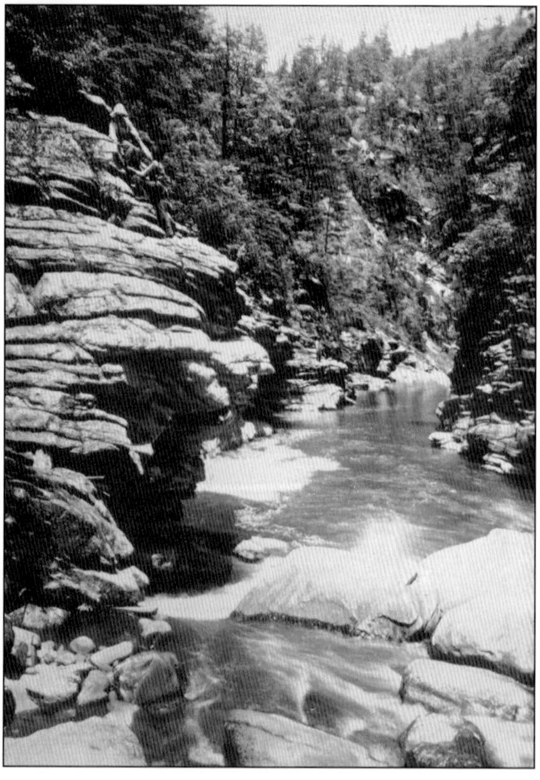

"The Jumping-Off Place, 40 Feet down an Overhanging Cliff, Babel Tower Gorge." It is highly unlikely that any of the party jumped from this rock; rather, it appears to be another obstacle in their route down the east side of the river. In this photograph dated June 1, 1912, Jessie Bicknell is assisted by friend Carpenter. (Courtesy of the North Carolina State Archives.)

"JUST BELOW BABEL TOWER FALLS." This photograph conveys to perfection the dwarfing of human visitors by the landscape of the Linville Gorge. A friend made this picture of the diminutive Frank and Jessie and their companion, C. B. Carpenter, on June 1, 1912. (Courtesy of the North Carolina State Archives.)

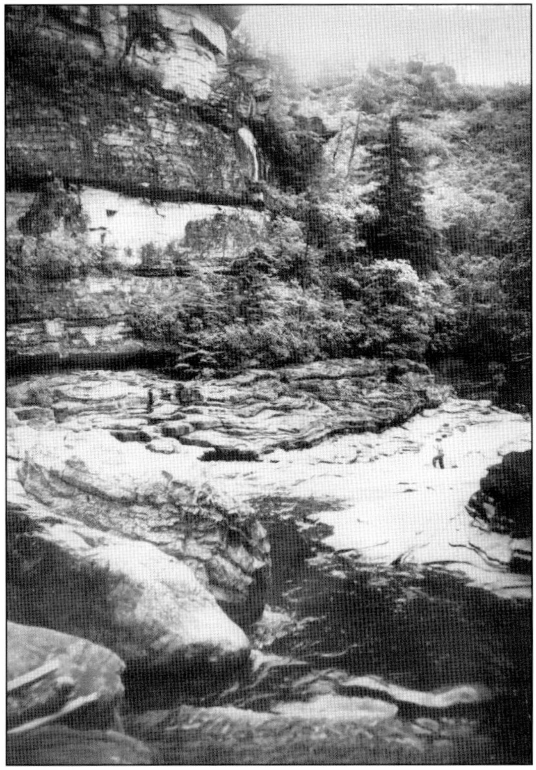

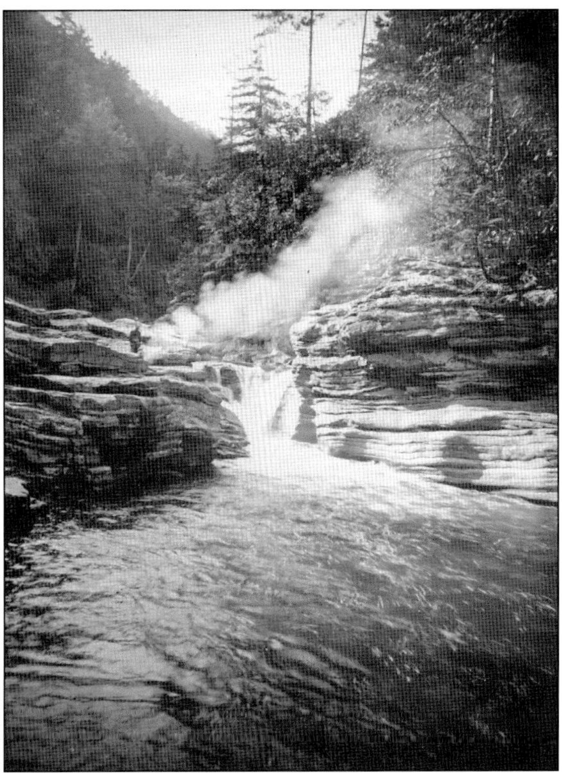

"BABEL TOWER FALLS, WHERE THE WILDEST OF THE GORGE BEGINS." It is difficult to say why Bicknell considered the gorge below the Babel Tower to be any "wilder" than other areas. The river here offers an exceptionally delightful swimming hole. This photograph was taken on the October 6, 1911, outing Bicknell made with friends. (Courtesy of the North Carolina State Archives.)

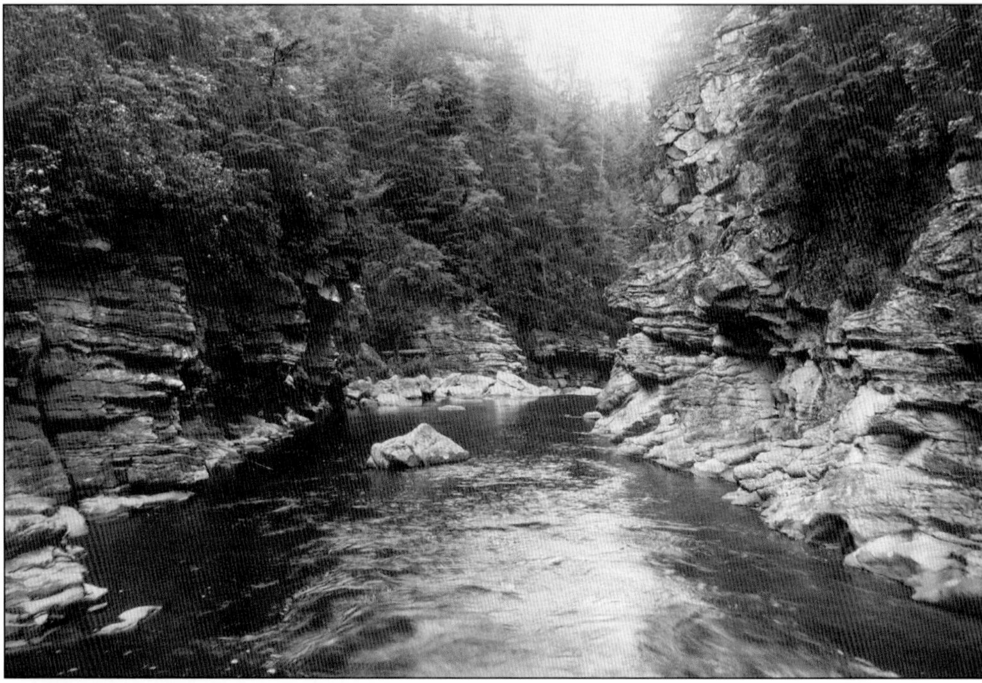

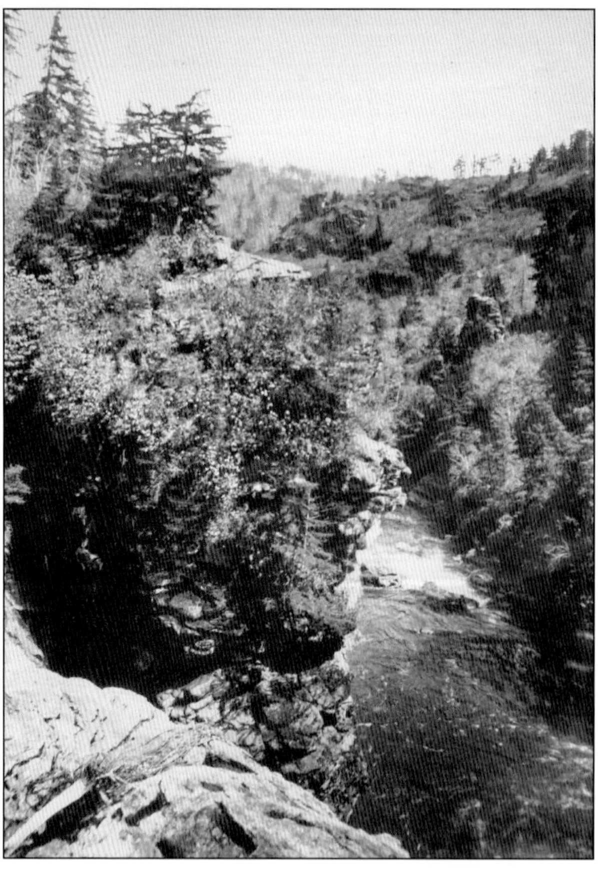

"Looking Down in Babel Tower Gorge. Deep Water and Precipitous Cliffs Call for Climbing." Skirting the rock walls by climbing to the wooded slopes above them is the only sensible passage downstream at this point in Bicknell's journey on June 1, 1912. (Courtesy of the North Carolina State Archives.)

"Down Gorge from Observation Rock on Trail." This is another of Bicknell's photographs whose location could be practically anywhere in the Linville Gorge. The view was taken on April 6, 1911. (Courtesy of the North Carolina State Archives.)

"GLIMPSE OF THE CANON FROM PINE GAP." Pine Gap is an area of Linville Mountain less than a mile below the Linville Falls that offers easy access to the river on a relatively short trail. This trail is the northernmost in the U.S. Forest Service trail system on the Linville Gorge's west side. (Courtesy of the North Carolina State Archives.)

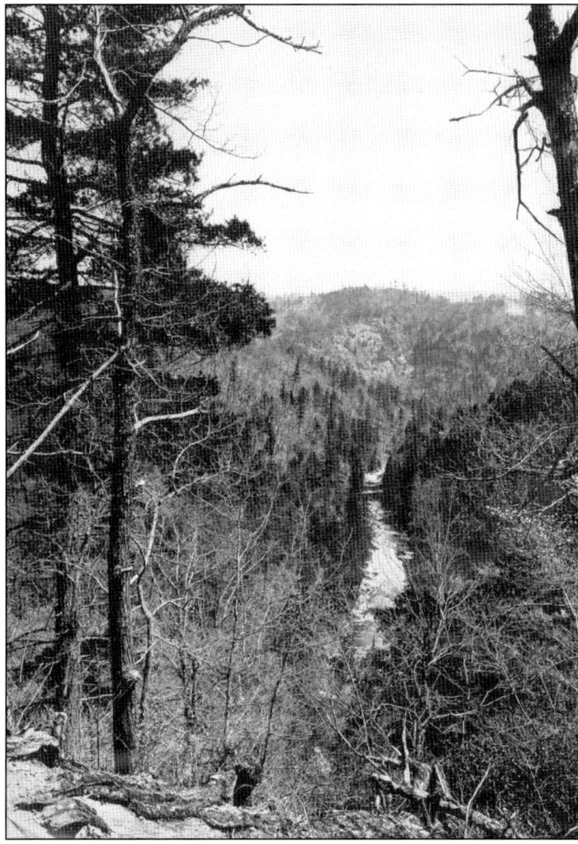

"LAKE JAMES FROM SHORTOFF." This contemporary photograph by Brad Sanzenbacher of Greensboro, North Carolina, shows Lake James, completed by Duke Power Company in 1923. The Catawba and Linville Rivers and Paddy's Creek flow into the lake, which is overlooked by the southernmost mountain on Gorge's east side, Shortoff Mountain. (Courtesy of Brad Sanzenbacher.)

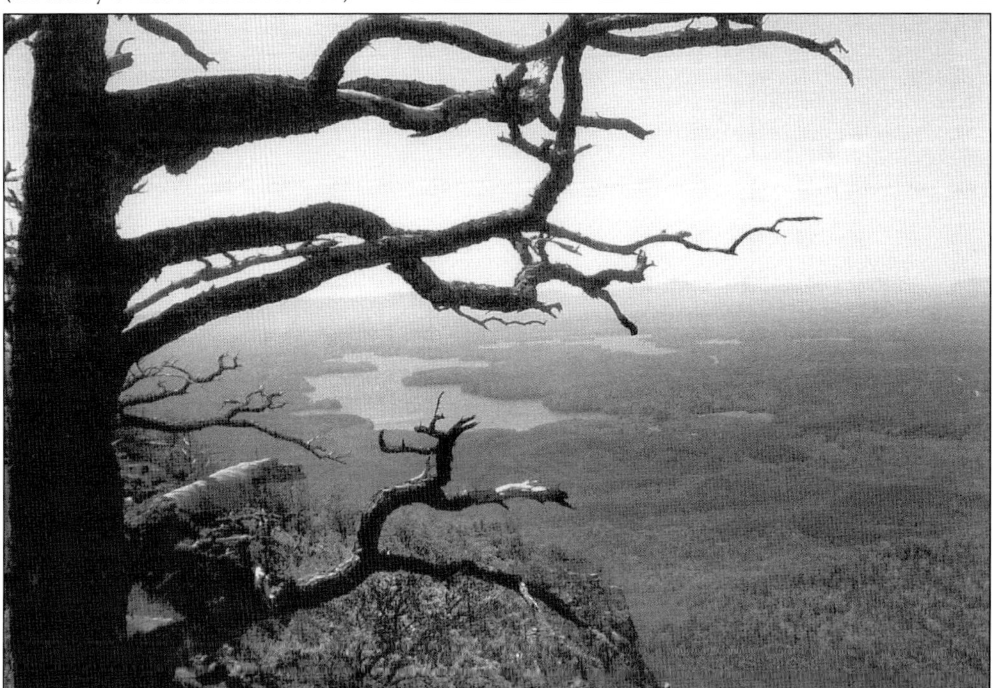

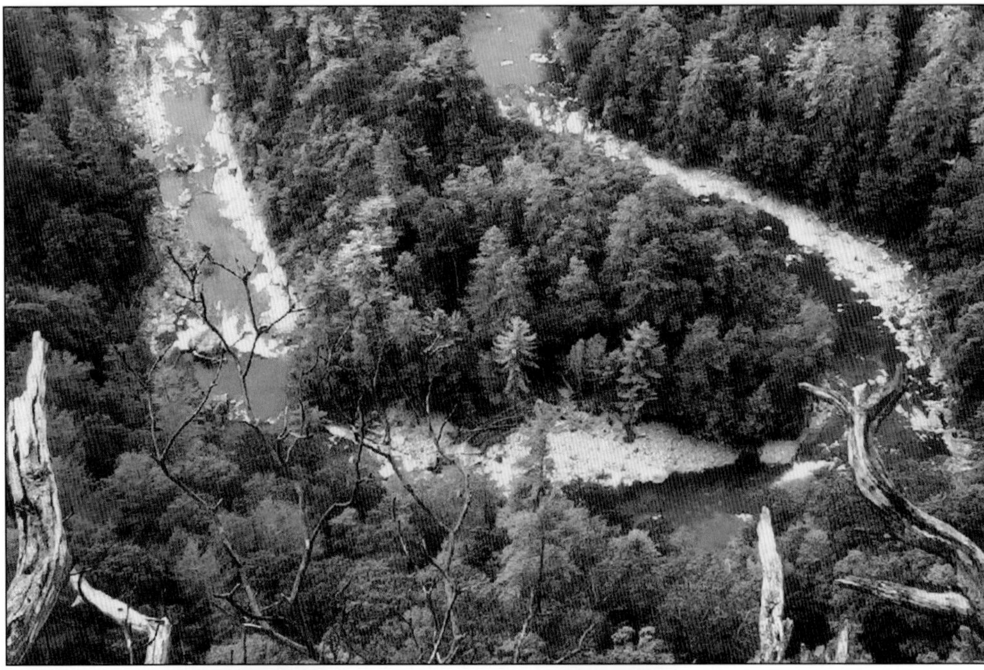

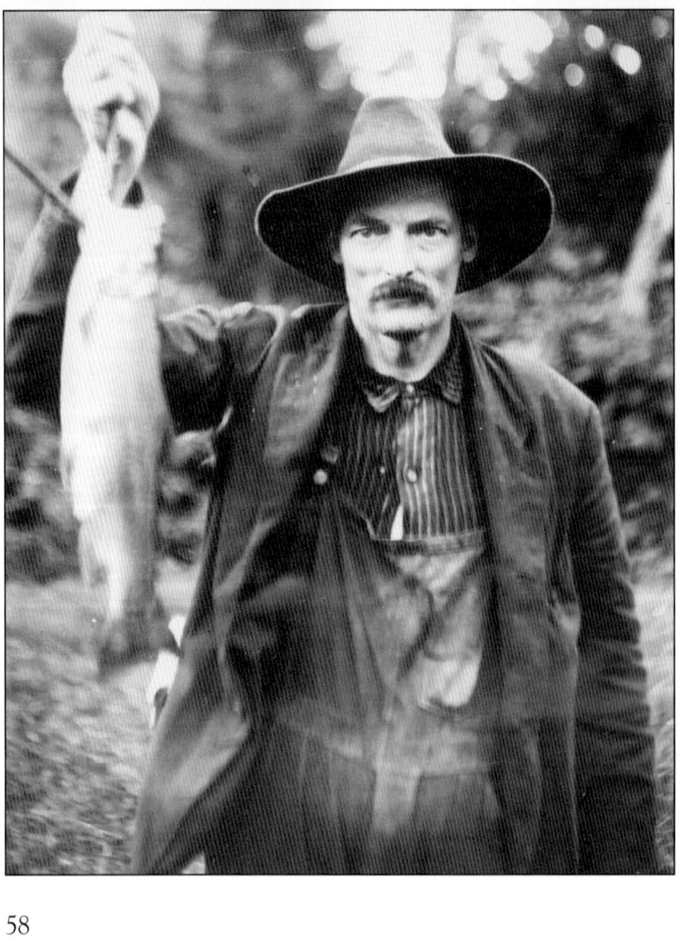

BEND IN RIVER FROM BULL FACE CLIFF TOP. The gooseneck-like curve of the Linville River at the bottom of Bynum's Bluff Trail was one of the favorite fishing spots for the Bicknells and their friends. Compare with Bicknell's photograph on the bottom of page 47. (Courtesy of the Friends of Linville Gorge.)

"TURNER VANCE AND PETERSON'S 18-INCH TROUT." Fish and game warden Turner Vance holds up one of the game fish for which the Linville Gorge is renowned among white-water fishermen. Frank Bicknell recorded Peterson's catch on July 28, 1910. (Courtesy of the North Carolina State Archives.)

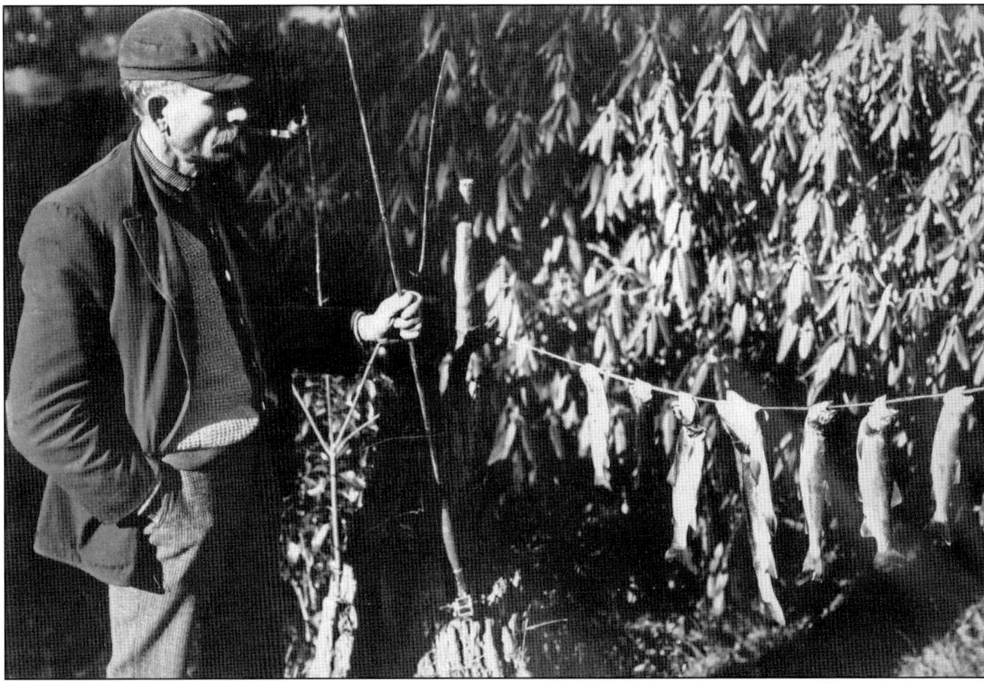

"C. B. Carpenter and Rainbow Trout." Here is another photographic record of a good trout catch in the limpid waters of the Linville—this one made by Frank Bicknell on November 30, 1909. (Courtesy of the North Carolina State Archives.)

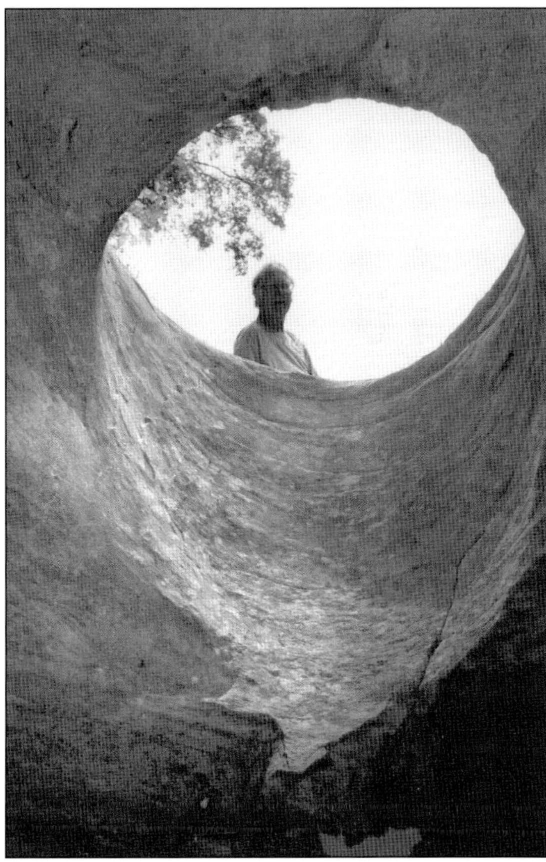

Bob Underwood in Hole Rock. Caving expert Cato Holler took this picture of Bob Underwood looking down into a deep hole worn by river water into a rock north of the Devil's Hole Trail. Underwood first visited Linville Gorge in 1962; in October 1964, he explored the North Carolina Wall area. In 1969, he created the Rock Jock Trail on the gorge's western side and has explored continuously in the area since then. He posts information daily on the wilderness for his Linville Gorge Yahoo group. (Courtesy of Brad Sanzenbacher.)

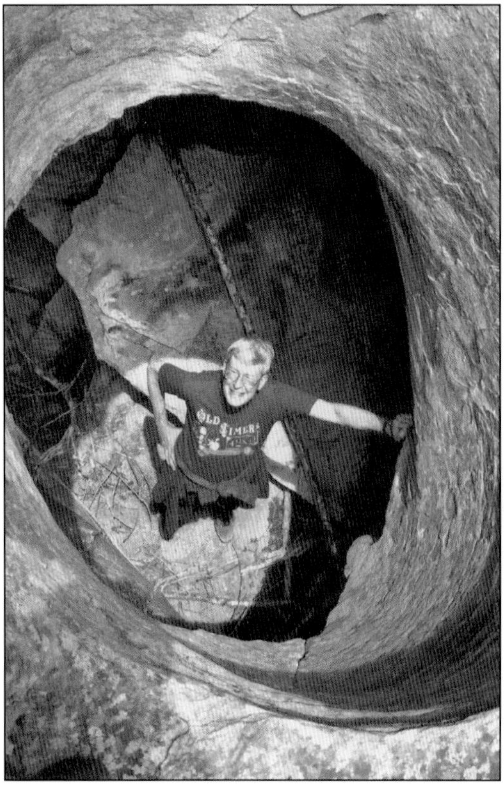

Cato Holler in Hole Rock. Brad Sanzenbacher captured Cato Holler, director of the North Carolina Cave Survey, in a pothole-like stone eroded by the Linville River. Holler has explored and described all caves in the Linville Gorge and is an authority on nearby Linville Caverns. He is the founding member and chairman-emeritus of Flittermouse Grotto of the National Speleological Society and fellow of the Explorers Club. (Courtesy of Brad Sanzenbacher.)

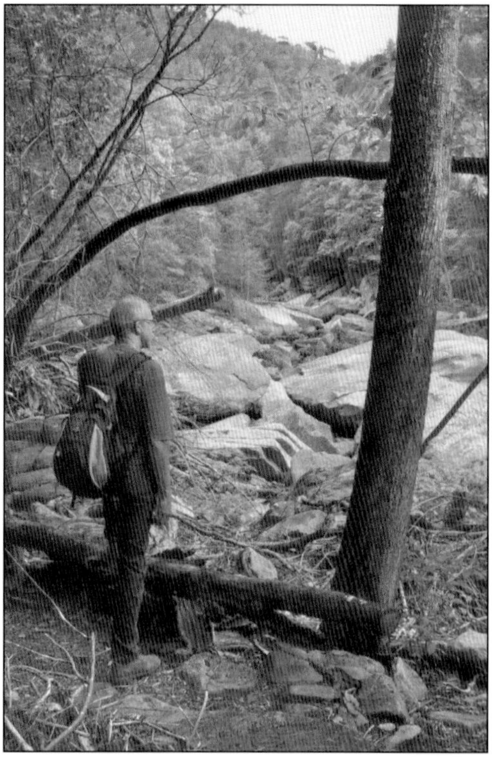

"Allen Hyde on Linville River between Dellinger Cabin and Daffodil Flats." Allen Hyde, author of *the Linville Gorge Hiker's Guide* and resident of the Gingercake Acres Community on Jonas Ridge at the gorge's north end, surveys the river at the bottom of the wilderness area. He was photographed by Jonathan Cox on July 20, 2007. Daffodil Flats is a riverside area that glows with daffodils each spring. Floodwaters often carry plants downstream, where they take hold and thrive. All that remains of Dellinger Cabin is a freestanding chimney. (Courtesy of Allen Hyde.)

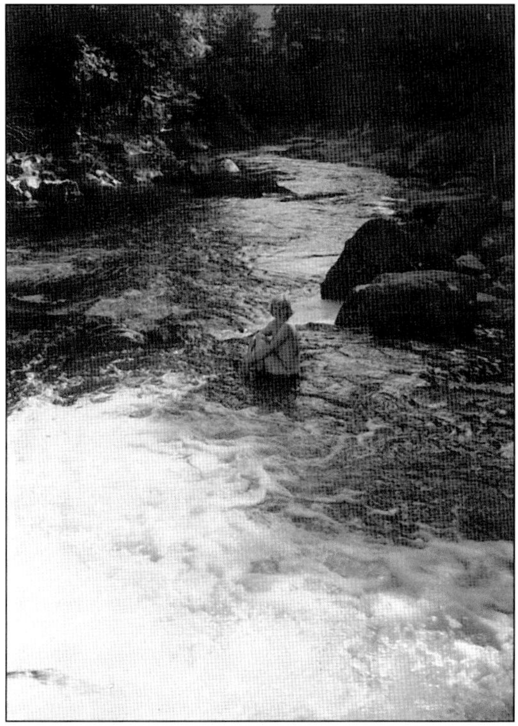

Bathing Beauty. In Victorian times no less than today, hot and weary hikers have loved to avail themselves of the refreshing currents of the Linville River. Churning white water invites adventurous souls to shed their inhibitions and jump in. (Courtesy of the Friends of Linville Gorge.)

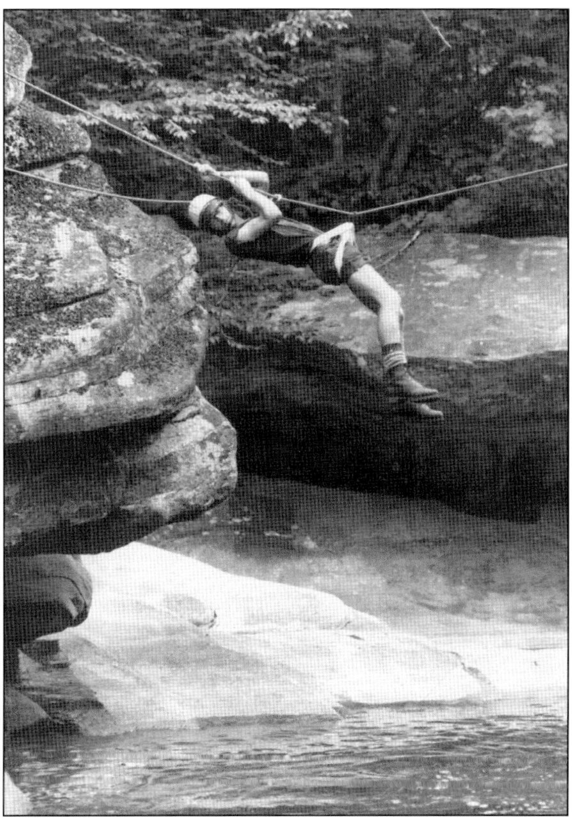

Tyrolean Traverse on Linville River. North Carolina Outward Bound School courses in mountaineering include the use of fixed ropes. This photograph made in the early 1970s shows a student traversing a fixed line by means of snap-links, or karabiners, connected to the student's harness and free to slide along the rope. (Courtesy of Mike Fischesser.)

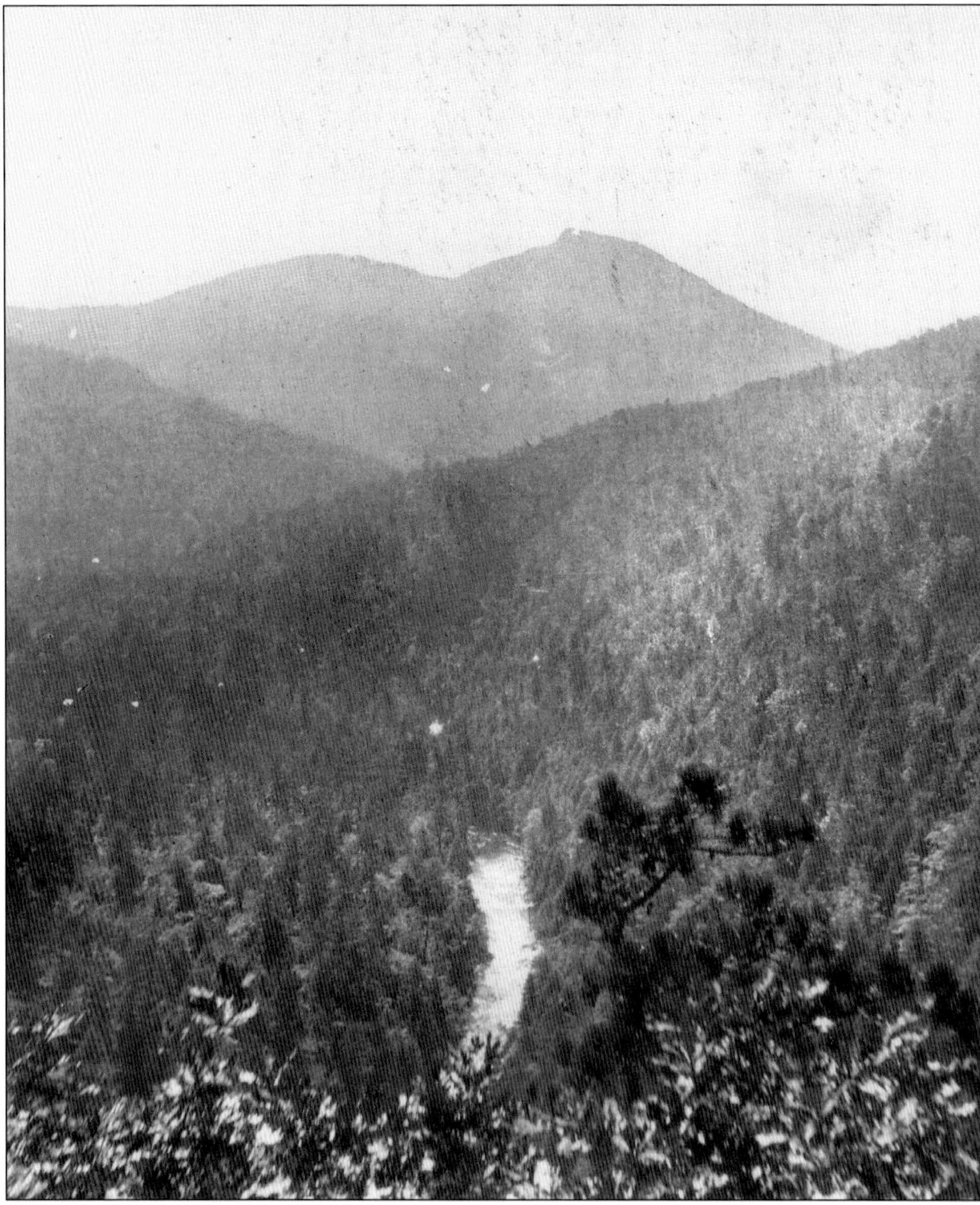

"Gorge of Linville Falls." This last shot of Linville River flowing south toward Hawksbill Mountain was taken by William Cary Hattan around 1907. The view prepares us for the next stage in our Linville Gorge journey, the cliffs and mountains of the area. (Courtesy of East Tennessee State University.)

Three

Peaks and Crags

"Cliffs of Fall, Frightful, Sheer."

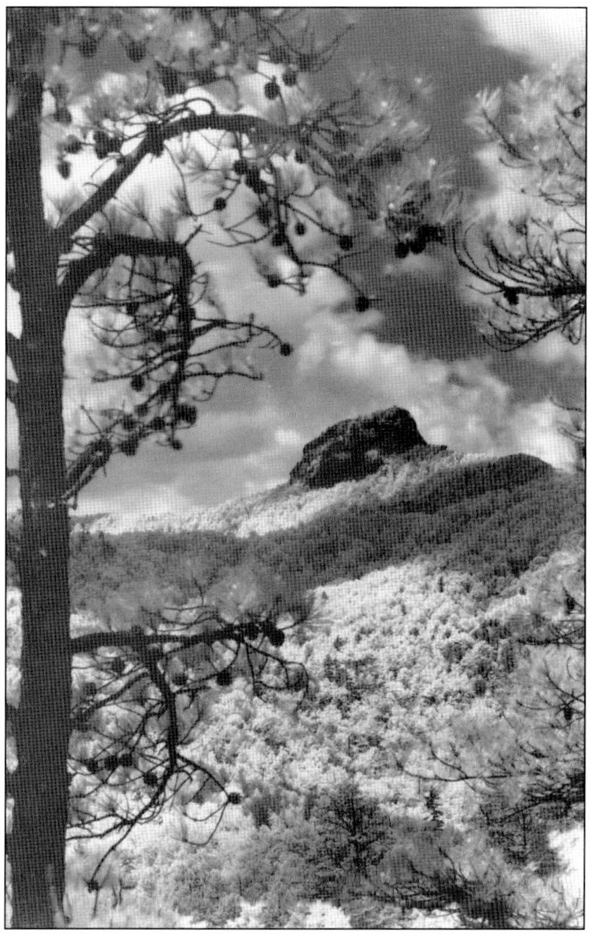

Table Rock, Table Mountain Pine. Gingercake Acres community developer and author J. Alex Mull took this photograph of Linville Gorge's most distinctive peak: Table Rock Mountain (3,918 feet). A mass of Chillhowie quartzite with cliffs ranging from 50 to 300 feet in height, the rock presents an impressively different appearance from alternate directions. Rock climbers love it, as have generations of sightseers, some of whom are recorded as far back as 1829. Table mountain pine prefers dry, rocky ridges; exposed to the winds of the Linville Gorge area, it takes on stunted, twisted shapes reminiscent of Japanese bonsai. (Courtesy of the Friends of Linville Gorge.)

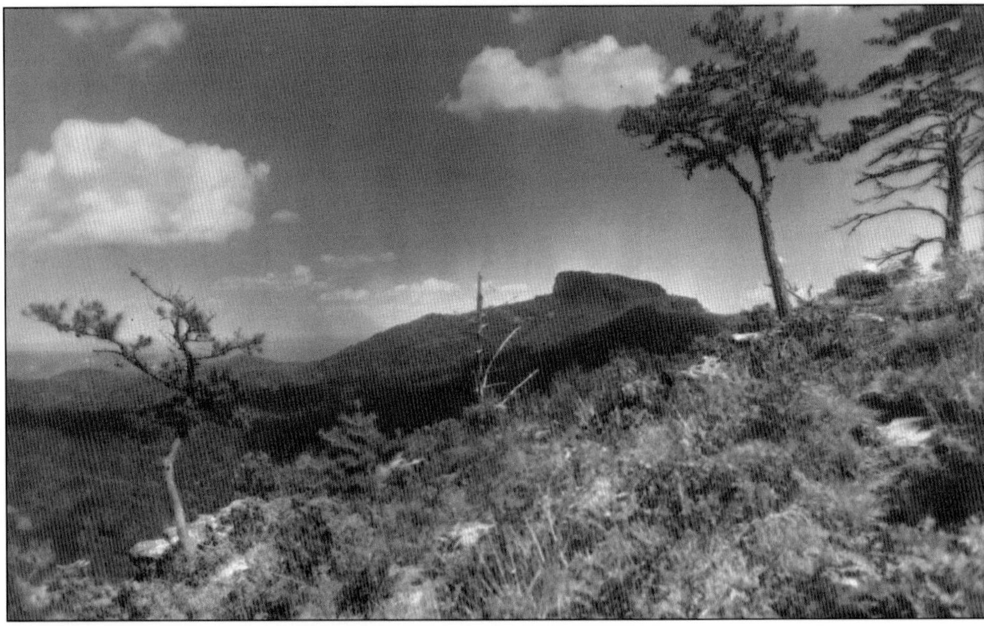

Table Rock Mountain and Clouds. Besides her famous studies of rural life in the Appalachians, Bayard Wootten was a masterful landscape photographer, often contrasting stark mountains with soft, nebulous skies. In the footsteps of her less well-known father, Rufus Morgan, she visited the west side of the gorge in the 1930s to take this atmospheric view of Table Rock. (Courtesy of the North Carolina Collection, Wilson Library. University of North Carolina at Chapel Hill.)

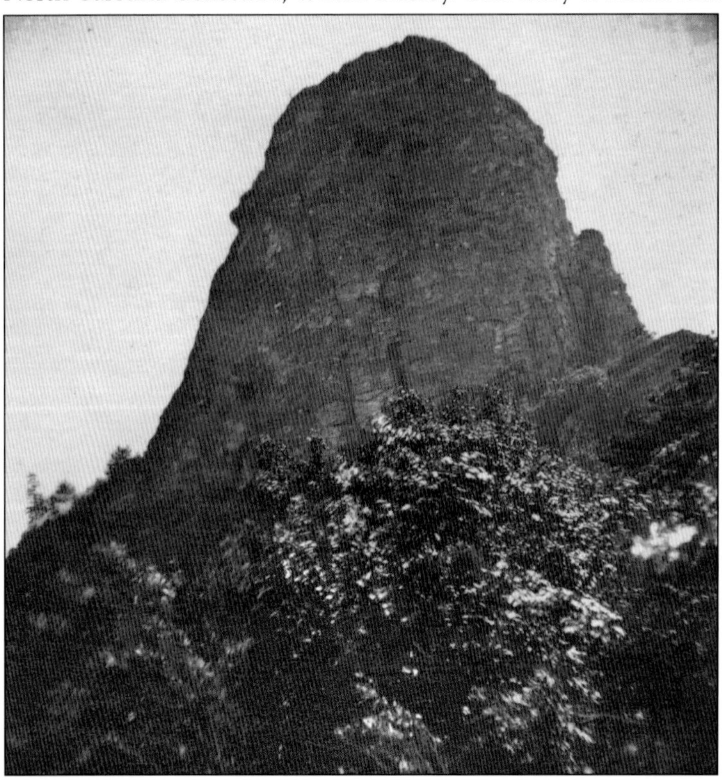

"Table Rock from the North." Not so well known is this conical view of the great rock taken from where the Mountains-to-Sea Trail now runs. The outcropping on the right marks the chasm called Devil's Cellar. (Courtesy of the North Carolina Collection, Wilson Library, University of North Carolina at Chapel Hill.)

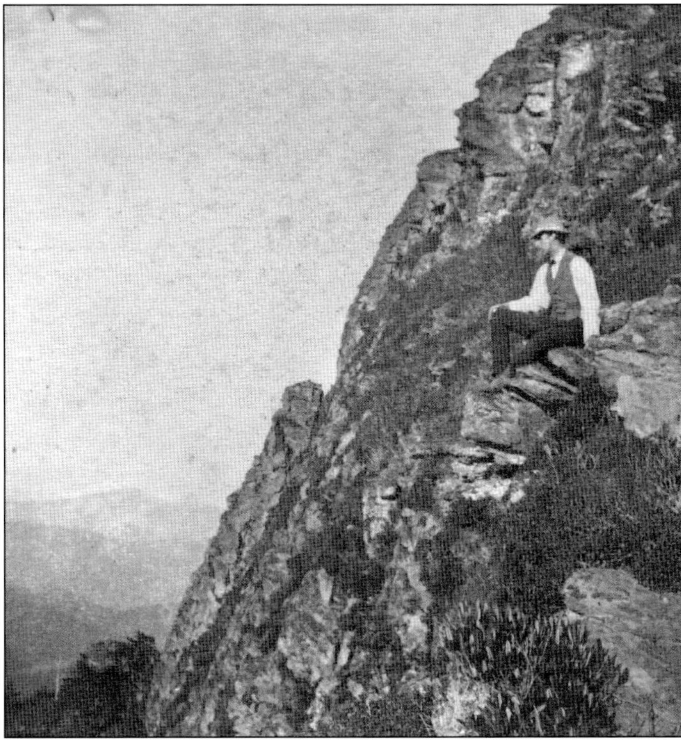

"North Face of Table Rock." The seated man is facing north towards Hawksbill, the sister peak of Table Rock Mountain on Jonas Ridge. (Courtesy of the North Carolina Collection, Wilson Library, University of North Carolina at Chapel Hill.)

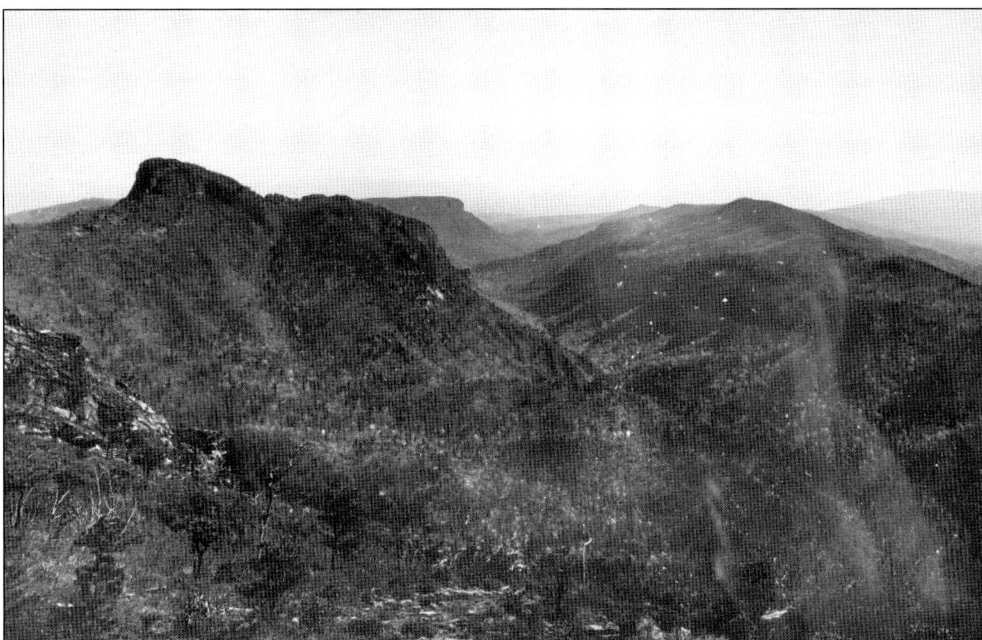

"Down Linville Canon from Summit of Hawksbill." Table Rock Mountain rears above Jonas Ridge on the left in this photograph taken by Frank Bicknell on April 24, 1909 (the same day this book's cover image was made). Beyond Table Rock Mountain, Shortoff Mountain marks the Linville Gorge's southern end. On the right, Linville Mountain forms the Linville Gorge's western side. (Courtesy of the North Carolina State Archives.)

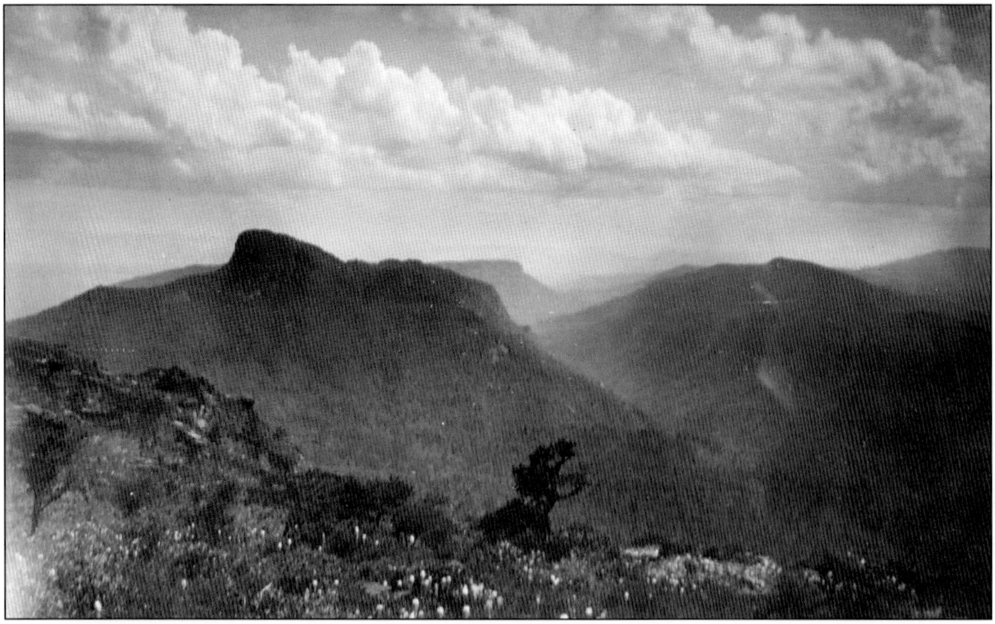

"From Top Hawksbill down Canon, Cloudy Day." The cloud cover over Linville Gorge is often striking. On June 17, 1912, Bicknell captured this brooding scene. (Courtesy of the North Carolina State Archives.)

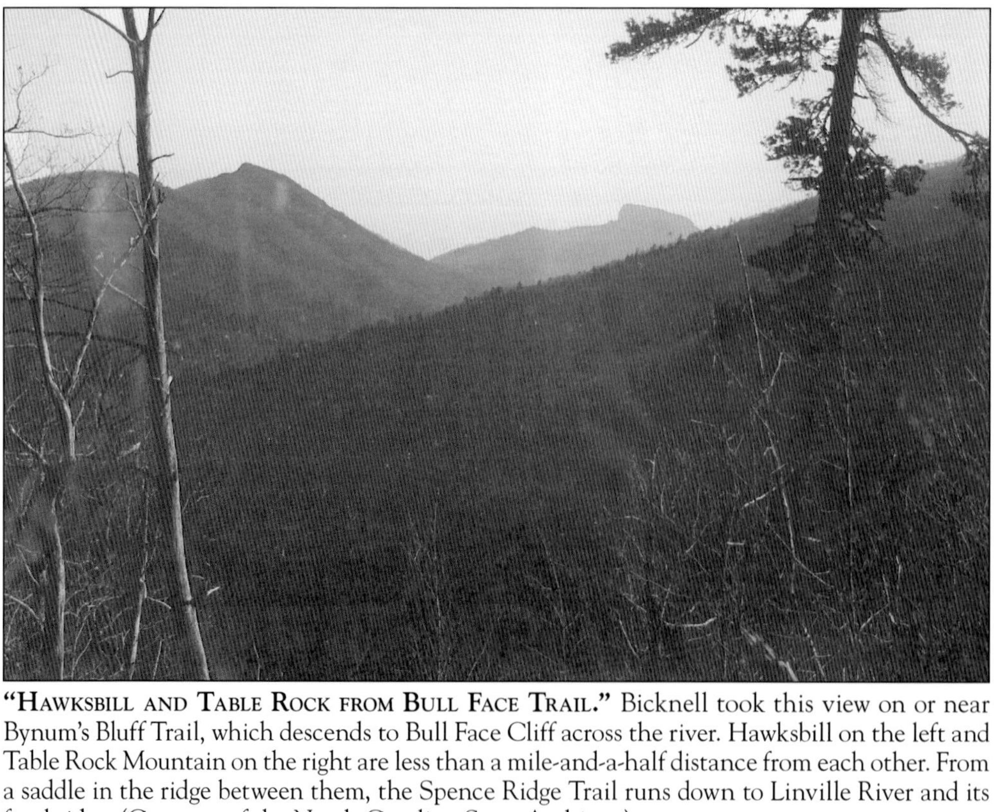

"Hawksbill and Table Rock from Bull Face Trail." Bicknell took this view on or near Bynum's Bluff Trail, which descends to Bull Face Cliff across the river. Hawksbill on the left and Table Rock Mountain on the right are less than a mile-and-a-half distance from each other. From a saddle in the ridge between them, the Spence Ridge Trail runs down to Linville River and its footbridge. (Courtesy of the North Carolina State Archives.)

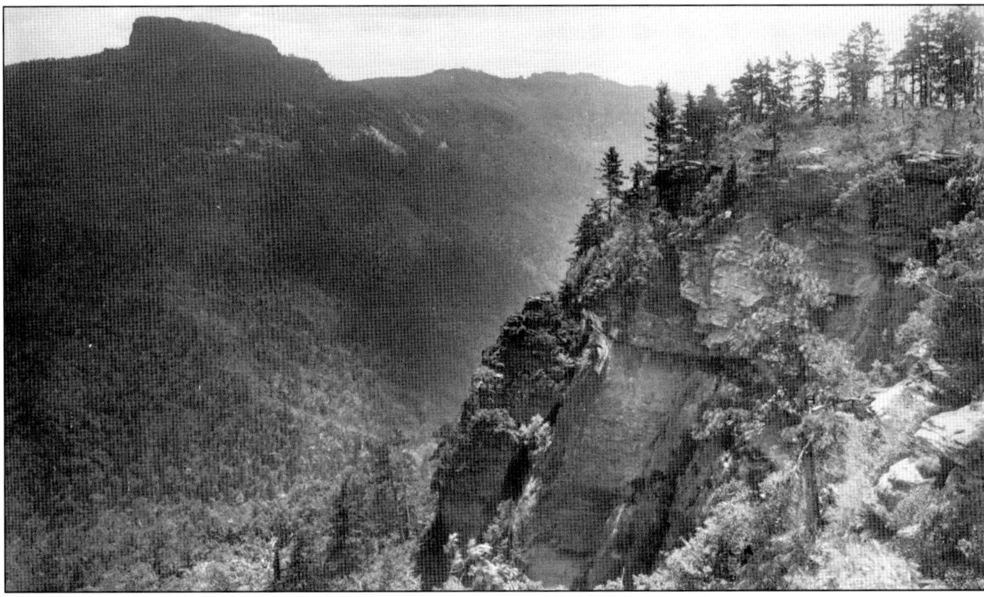

"Wiseman's View from UG's Cliff Just across Deep Hollow." Wiseman's View is the famed promontory from which the eerie Brown Mountain Lights are commonly seen. Bicknell's July 19, 1911, photograph shows the craggy ridgeline to the south (right) of Table Rock Mountain known as "the Chimneys." "U. G." was the nickname of A. M. Huger, a visitor from Charleston, South Carolina, who cleared many of the trails to today's spectacular views. (Courtesy of the North Carolina State Archives.)

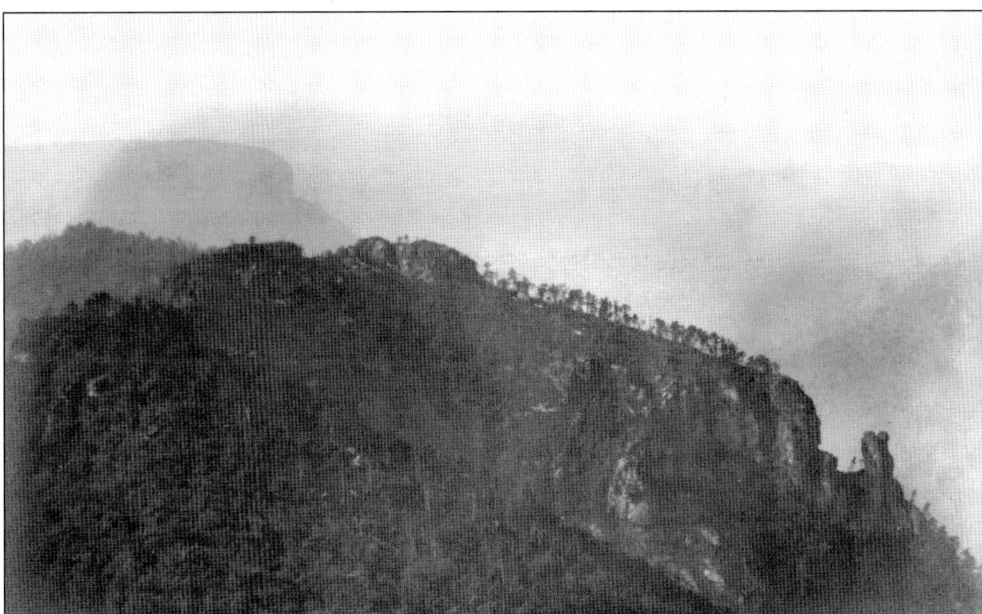

"From Tablerock." Donald R. Beeson subtitled this early morning vista as follows: "Linville Gorge to Right, Chimney Rock in foreground, Shortoff Mtn. in background." At the far right of the thinly wooded ridge stands the double-humped rock called "the Camel." The top picture on page 125 shows North Carolina Outward Bound students doing a rope traverse at the Camel. (Courtesy of East Tennessee State University.)

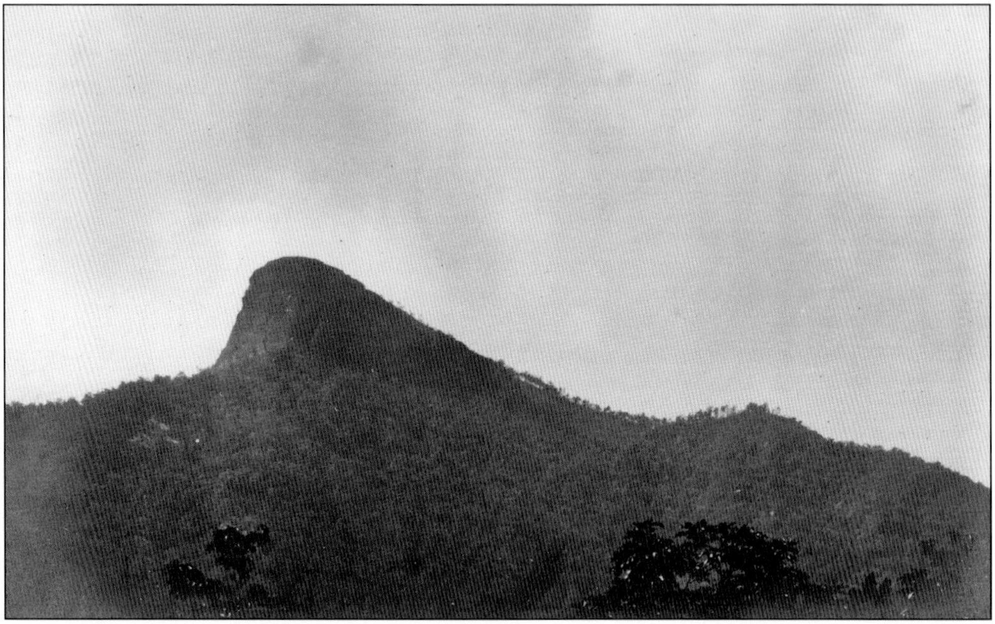

"Table Rock from the North." In another distinctive view of Table Rock Mountain, Beeson has caught the ridgeline running to the right of the mountain out to a bluff called Little Table Rock. (Courtesy of East Tennessee State University.)

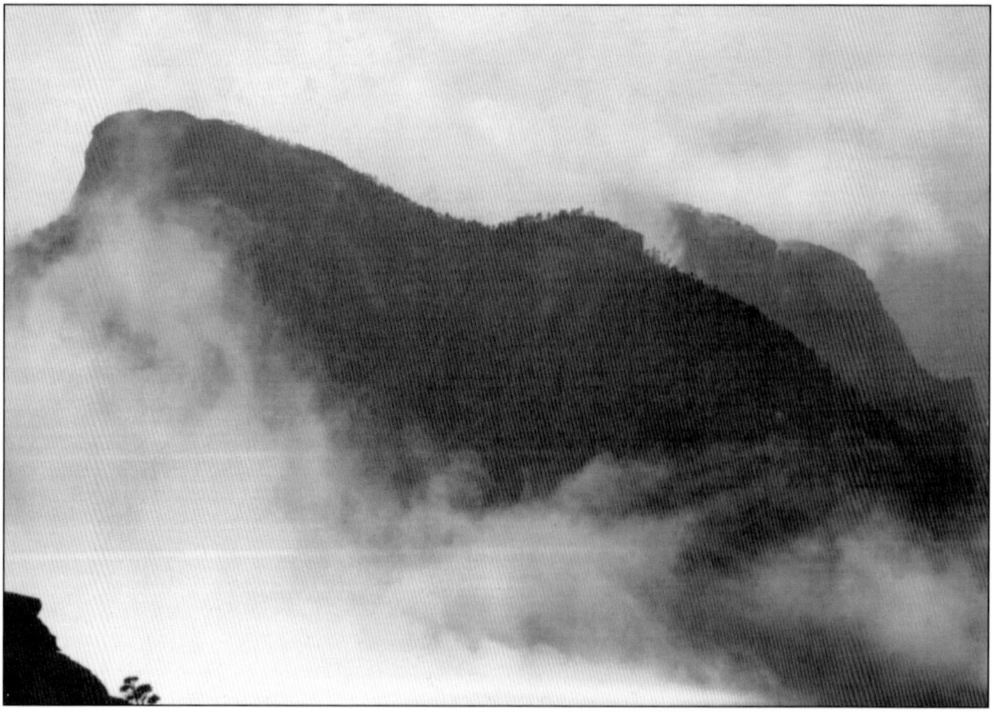

"Table Rock from the Hawksbill, Early Morning." Table Rock Mountain seems afloat in a sea of mist in this July 1914 photograph made by D. R. Beeson. To the right, the bluff called Little Table Rock is clearly visible, as is the distant group called the Chimneys. (Courtesy of East Tennessee State University.)

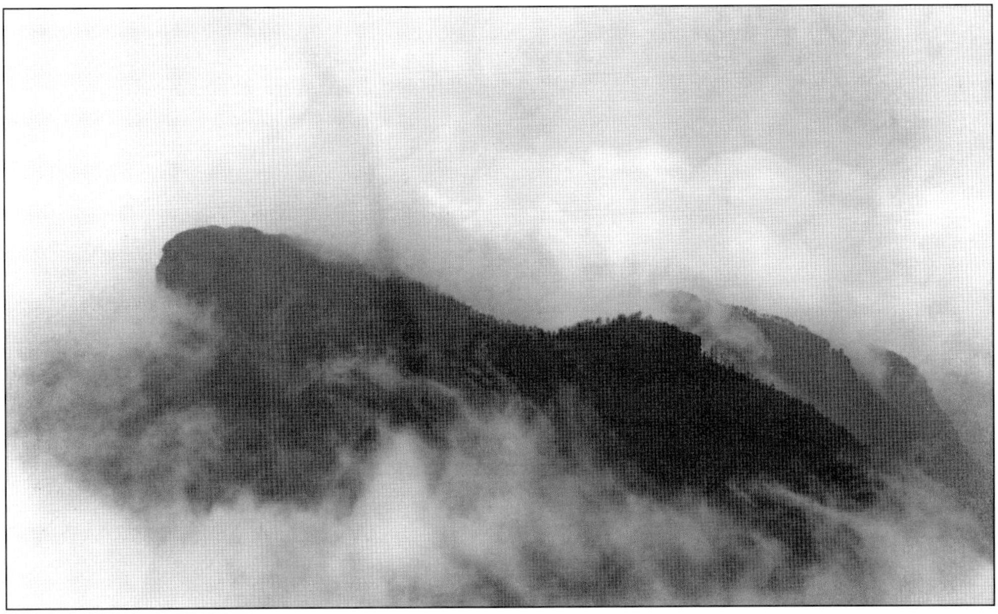

"Table Rock from the Hawksbill, Early Morning." Here is another atmospheric view of Table Rock Mountain in the mist. Beeson records that he made the picture around 7:00 a.m., July 5, 1914. (Courtesy of East Tennessee State University.)

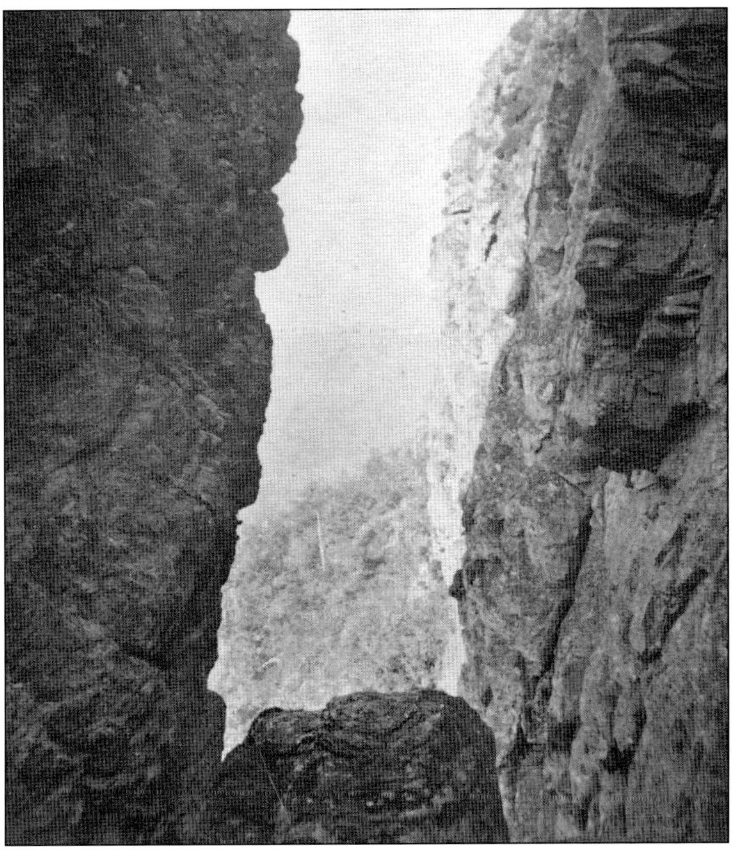

"The Cellar." This dramatic crevice on Table Rock Mountain's northwest side is a favorite place for rock climbers to rappel (slide down a fixed rope). Rufus Morgan took this picture around 1873. (Courtesy of the North Carolina Collection, Wilson Library, University of North Carolina at Chapel Hill.)

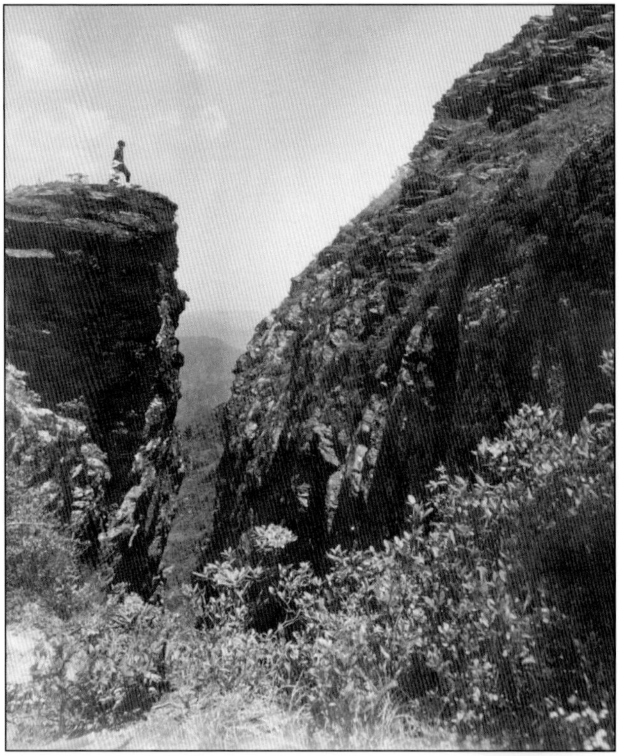

"The Devil's Cellar on Table Rock." Frank Bicknell included an unidentified friend in this picture of Devil's Cellar he made on May 23, 1912. (Courtesy of the North Carolina State Archives.)

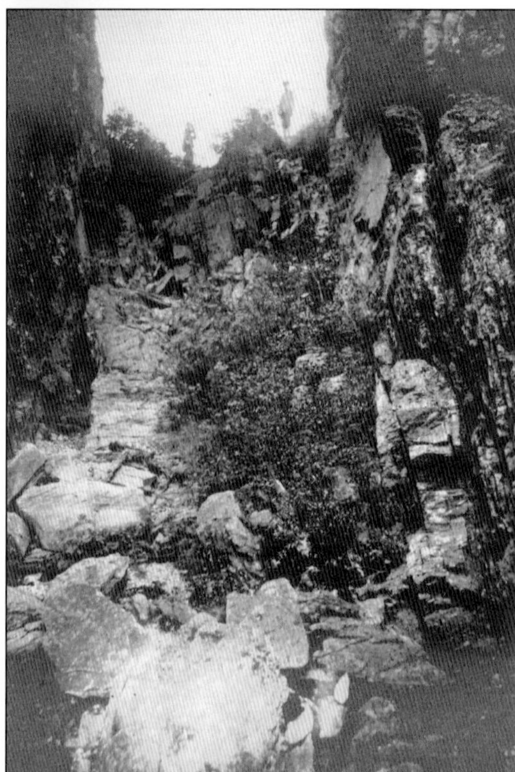

"Looking Up from Large Boulder in Devil's Kitchen." Visiting less than two years after Bicknell, D. R. Beeson took this picture (July 1914) of the cellar from the bottom up. In another instance of varying nomenclature in the Linville Gorge, Beeson has used an alternate name for the place. (Courtesy of East Tennessee State University.)

"LOOKING UP THRO DEVIL'S KITCHEN FROM EAST SIDE OF TABLE ROCK." Beeson has backed away from the crevice to give a clearer idea of the rock spire on its east (right) side. (Courtesy of East Tennessee State University.)

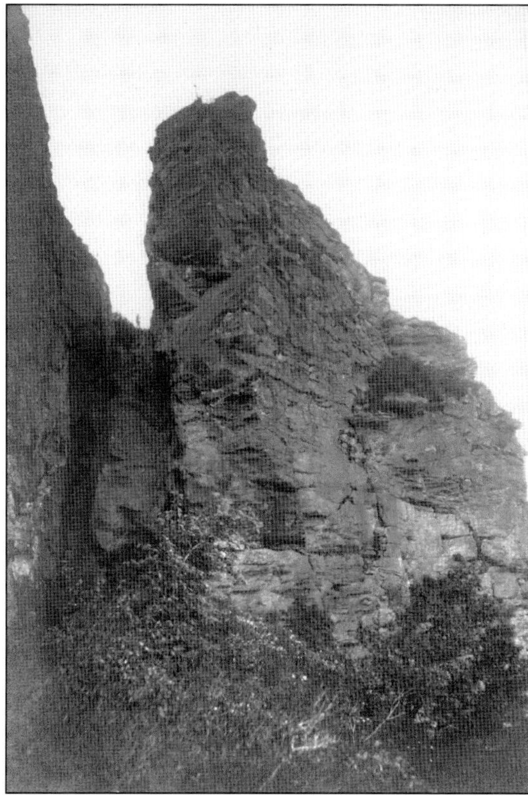

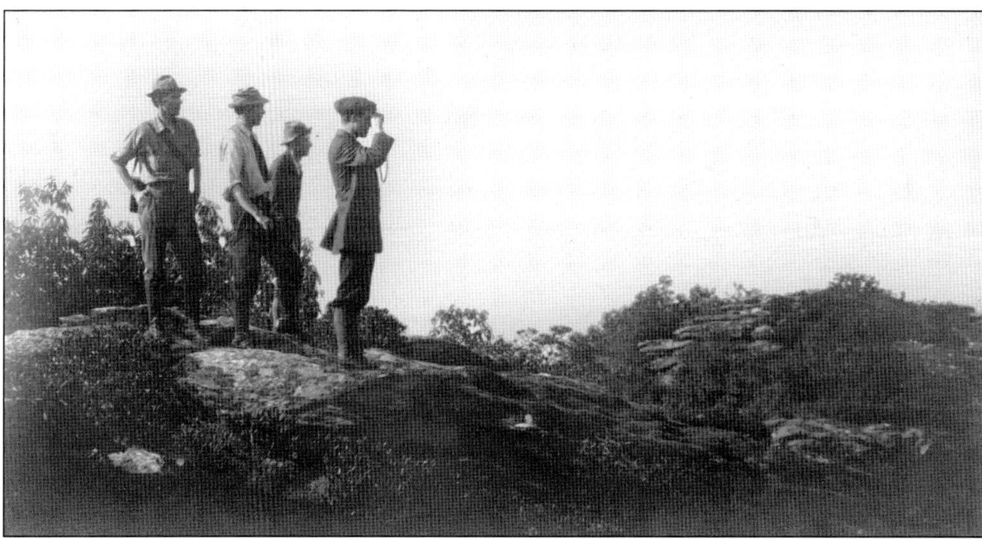

"THE PARTY ON TOP OF TABLE ROCK." D. R. Beeson has included himself in this photograph (second from left, gripping the fishing line he pulled to trip the camera shutter) atop Table Rock Mountain in July 1914. The party also includes Beeson's close friend C. Hodge Mathes, an English instructor at East Tennessee State Normal School (far left), Buford Mathes (second from right), and friend Schoen (far right). Beeson annotated his photographic records of his hiking trips to the Great Smoky Mountains, Mount Mitchell, and Grandfather Mountain. (Courtesy of East Tennessee State University.)

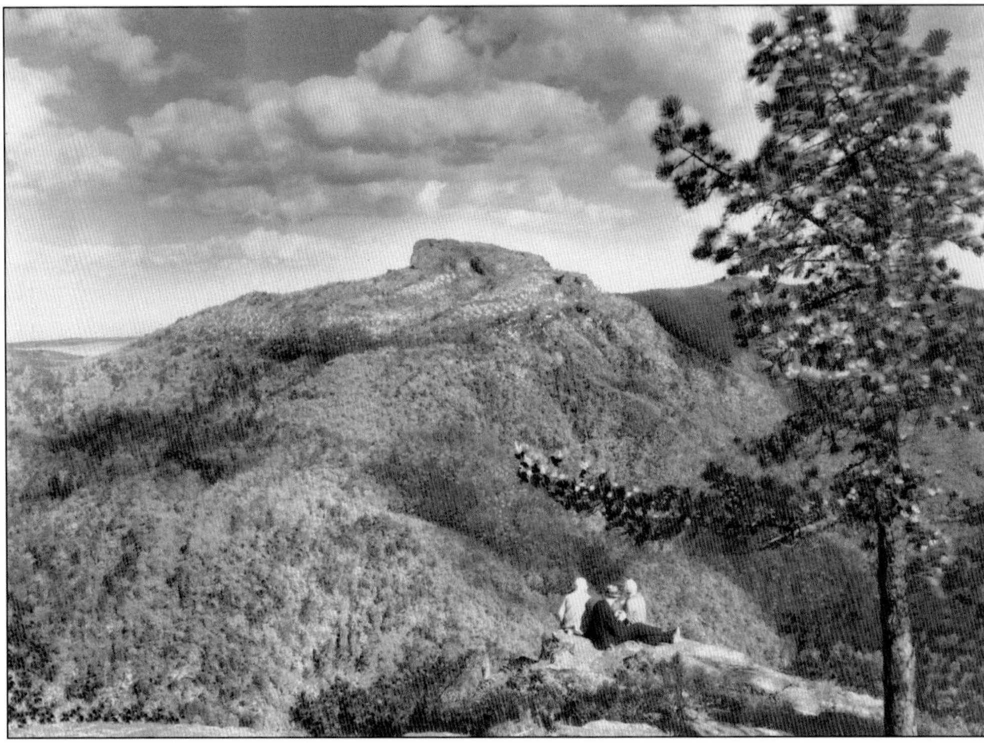

"View of Table Rock from Wiseman's View." George Masa was a Japanese-American photographer, an activist for the formation of a Great Smoky Mountains National Park, a pioneer in the routing and naming of the Appalachian Trail in the Smoky Mountains, and the founding member of the Carolina Mountain Club. He probably visited the Linville Gorge in the 1940s where he caught these day visitors admiring the view of Table Rock Mountain. (Courtesy of Pack Memorial Library.)

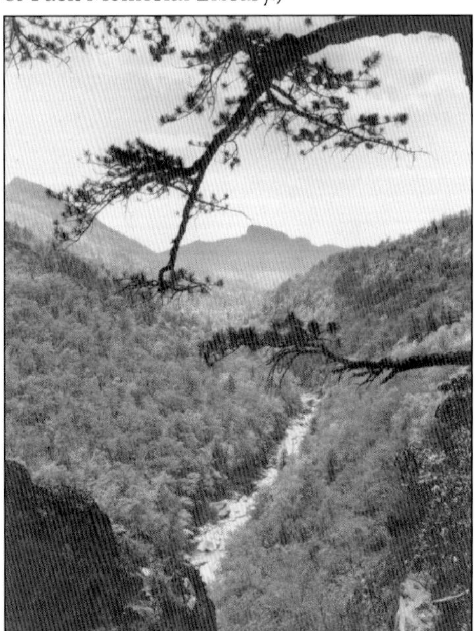

Table Rock with Hemlock Bough. Masa's friends in the Carolina Mountain Club recalled his penchant for pulling down tree branches to frame his pictures in a picturesque, so-called oriental manner. This view of Linville Gorge includes the river far below, Hawksbill on the left, and Table Rock Mountain on the right. (Courtesy of Pack Memorial Library.)

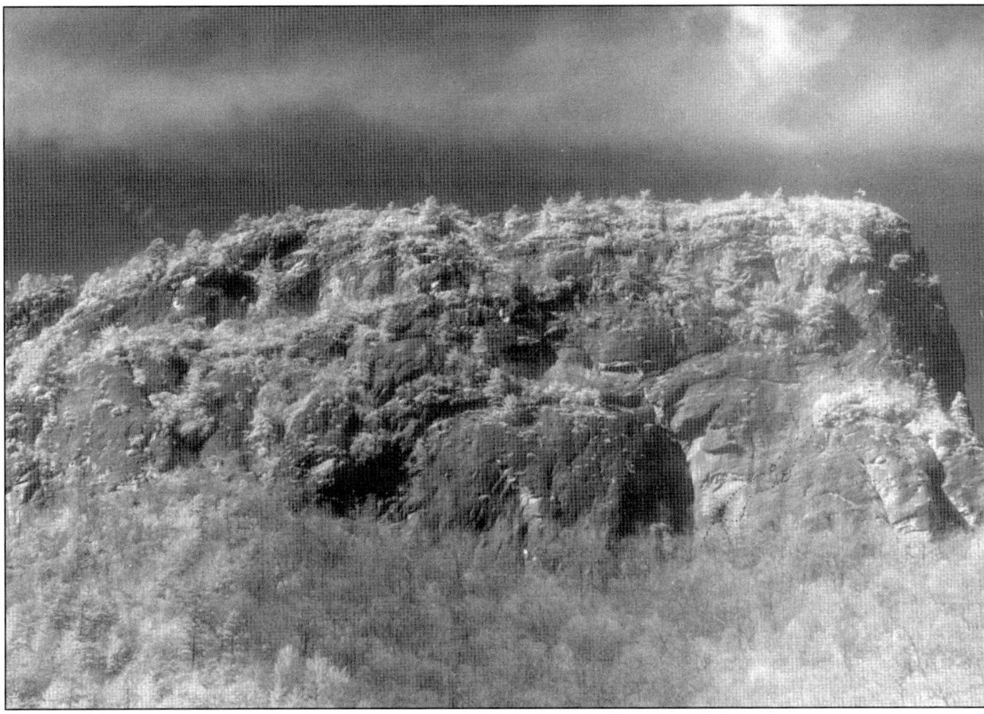

STORM CLOUDS OVER TABLE ROCK. Storm clouds mass ominously over Table Rock Mountain in this view from the south. (Courtesy of Mike Fischesser.)

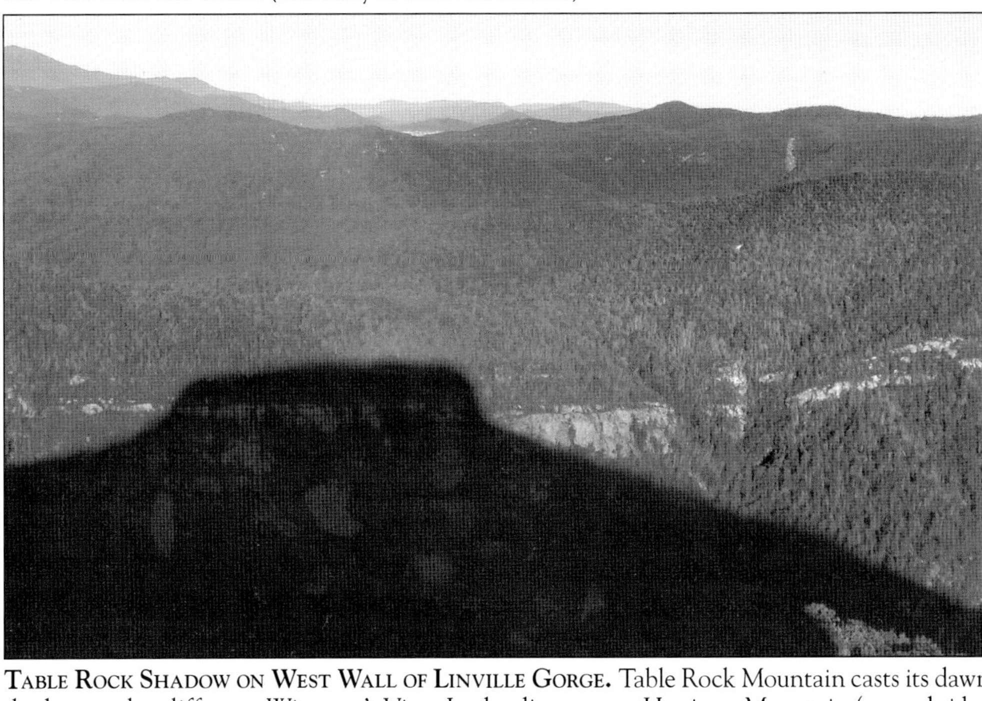

TABLE ROCK SHADOW ON WEST WALL OF LINVILLE GORGE. Table Rock Mountain casts its dawn shadow on the cliffs near Wiseman's View. In the distance on Hunicutt Mountain (second ridge back on the right), one can see the devastating mudslide on the Blue Ridge Parkway caused by Hurricane Katrina in 2005. (Courtesy of Mike Fischesser.)

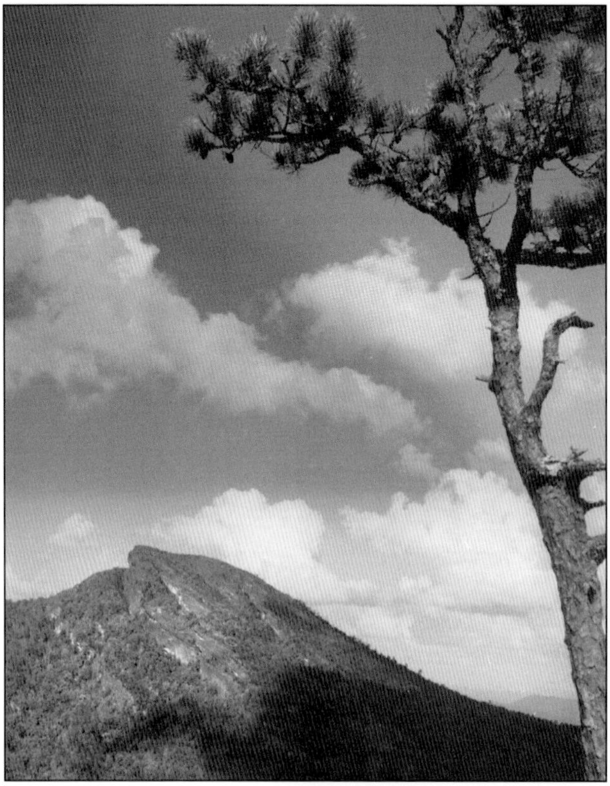

"HAWKSBILL WITH TABLE MOUNTAIN PINE." J. Alex Mull took this companion picture to the image on page 63 and again placed a Table Mountain pine in his foreground. The bill of the hawk is at the summit, and below are a series of sheer rock walls, one above the other, that are popular with rock climbers. The U.S. Forest Service trail to the top (4,090 feet) ascends the back (east) side. (Courtesy of the Friends of Linville Gorge.)

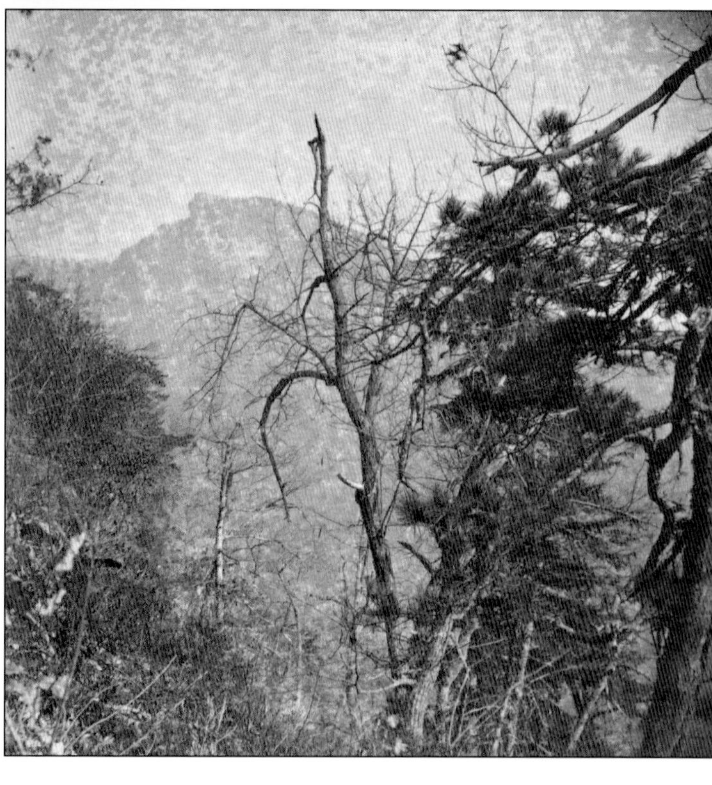

"HAWK'S BILL MOUNTAIN." Rufus Morgan's stereoscope view of Hawksbill was taken from a point below the Linville Gorge's western rim, perhaps from Sandy Flats Trail. (Courtesy of the North Carolina Collection, Wilson Library, University of North Carolina at Chapel Hill.)

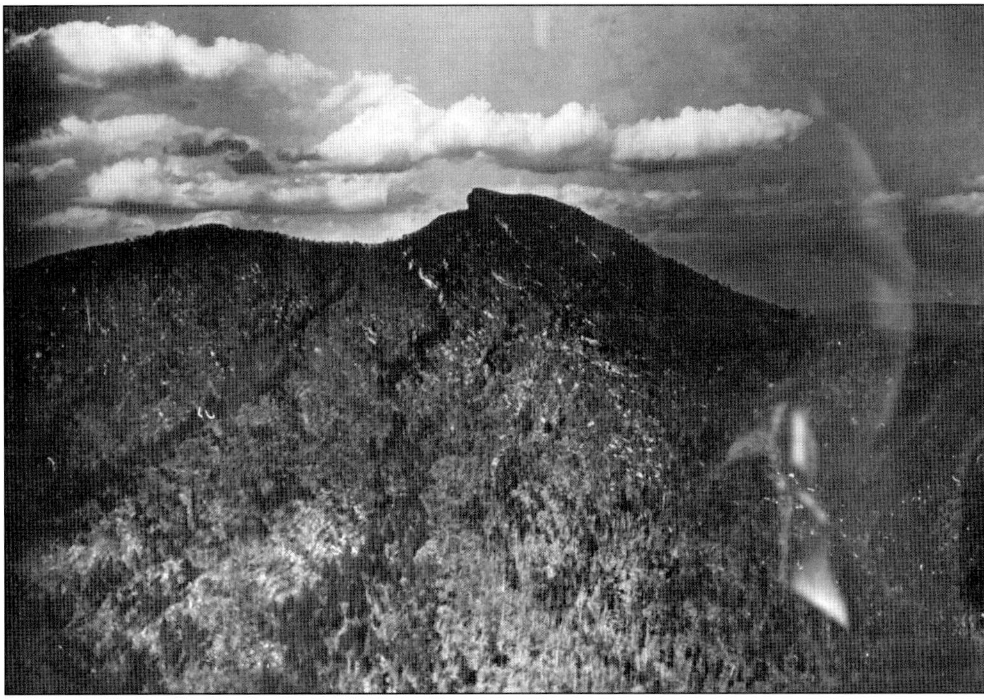

"HAWKSBILL FROM WISEMAN'S VIEW." Frank Bicknell took this view of Hawksbill from the popular Wiseman's View on the west rim of the Linville Gorge facing between Hawksbill and Table Rock Mountain. The view is named for Lafayette "Uncle Fete" Wiseman who grazed his cattle nearby in the 1800s. He contributed to the lore of the Brown Mountain Lights, which are seen on fall nights on a ridge seven miles away, with his story of the faithful slave seeking his dead master by lantern. (Courtesy of the North Carolina State Archives.)

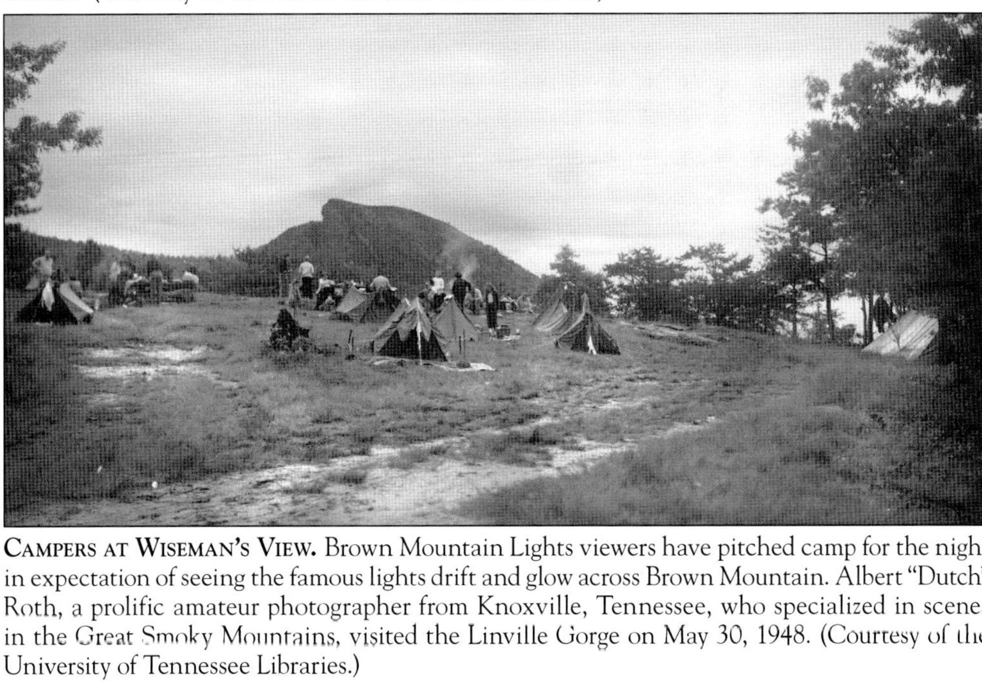

CAMPERS AT WISEMAN'S VIEW. Brown Mountain Lights viewers have pitched camp for the night in expectation of seeing the famous lights drift and glow across Brown Mountain. Albert "Dutch" Roth, a prolific amateur photographer from Knoxville, Tennessee, who specialized in scenes in the Great Smoky Mountains, visited the Linville Gorge on May 30, 1948. (Courtesy of the University of Tennessee Libraries.)

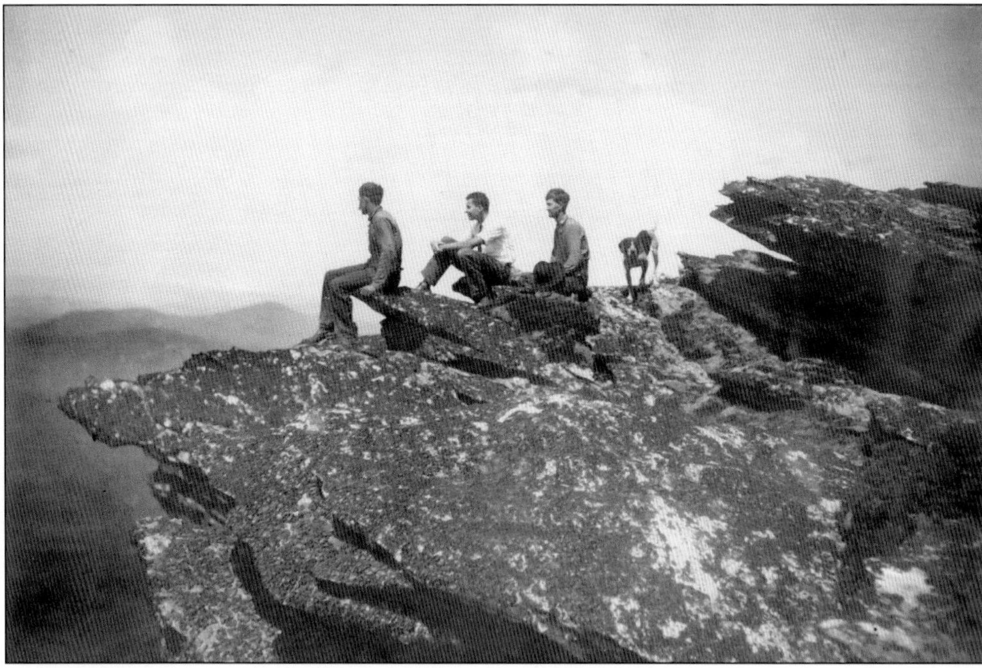

"**Top of Hawksbill, Stokes Aldridge, William, Bo [sic].**" This group shot was made by Frank Bicknell on June 17, 1912. William is one of the Hossfelds, and Bo is Boe Franklin. Boe appears later in connection with a 1943 army aircraft wreck (see page 120). (Courtesy of the North Carolina State Archives.)

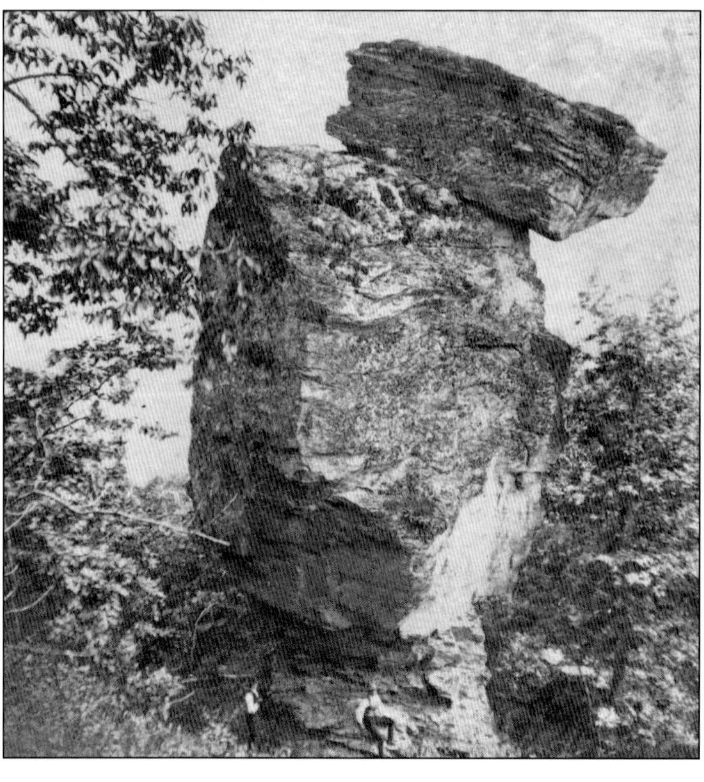

"**Devil's Cap or Ginger Cake.**" This 70-foot-tall formation is more commonly called "Sitting Bear." It lies on Jonas Ridge about a mile north of Hawksbill. The first fully authenticated ascent of the rock was made by three climbers (Steve Longeneker, John Lawrence, and Will Fulton) in September 1968. (Courtesy of the North Carolina Collection, Wilson Library, University of North Carolina at Chapel Hill.)

Sitting Bear Rock. J. Alex Mull's photograph, made in the 1970s, shows Sitting Bear with unusual clarity. The woman posing at the base provides an idea of the scale of the rock. (Courtesy of the Friends of Linville Gorge.)

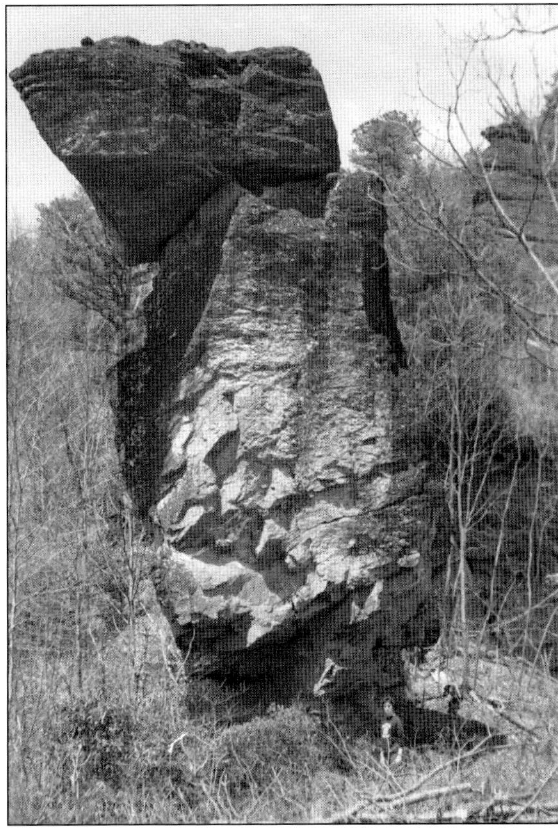

Profile of the Sitting Bear. This photograph taken by Mull from Forest Road 210 shows the famous rock in the position that gave it its name. (Courtesy of the Friends of Linville Gorge.)

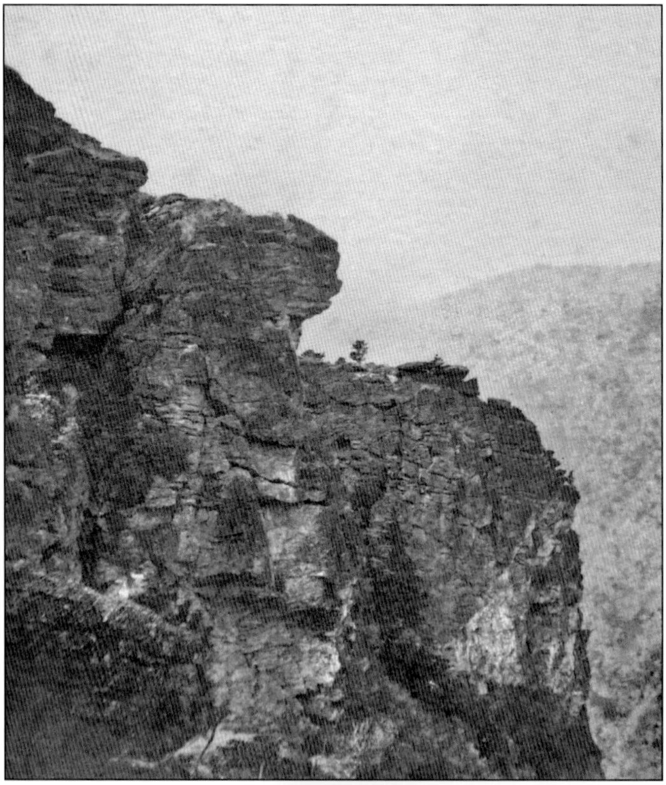

"PRECIPICE, 1,000 FEET HIGH." Rufus Morgan lugged his bulky 5-inch-by-7-inch camera out to the cliffs south of Table Rock Mountain to take the following series of views of the stark crags known as the Chimneys and the North Carolina Wall. (Courtesy of the North Carolina Collection, Wilson Library, University of North Carolina at Chapel Hill.)

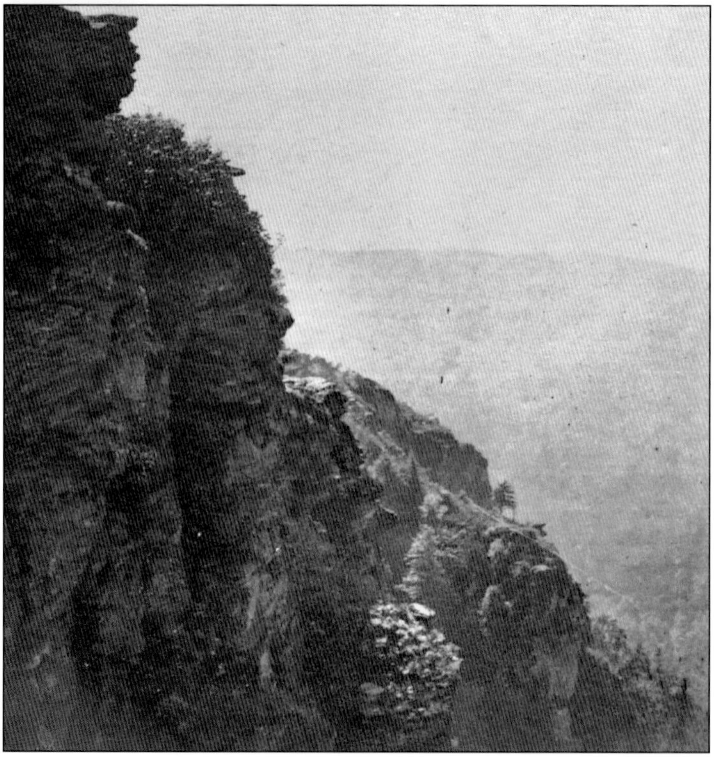

"APPROACHING THE CHIMNEYS." Morgan captures the hardy growth in this area of the Linville Gorge. Laurel, rhododendron, and Table Mountain pine with a variety of grasses, ferns, and mosses endure here. Peregrine falcons have been successfully introduced to these crags. (Courtesy of the North Carolina Collection, Wilson Library, University of North Carolina at Chapel Hill.)

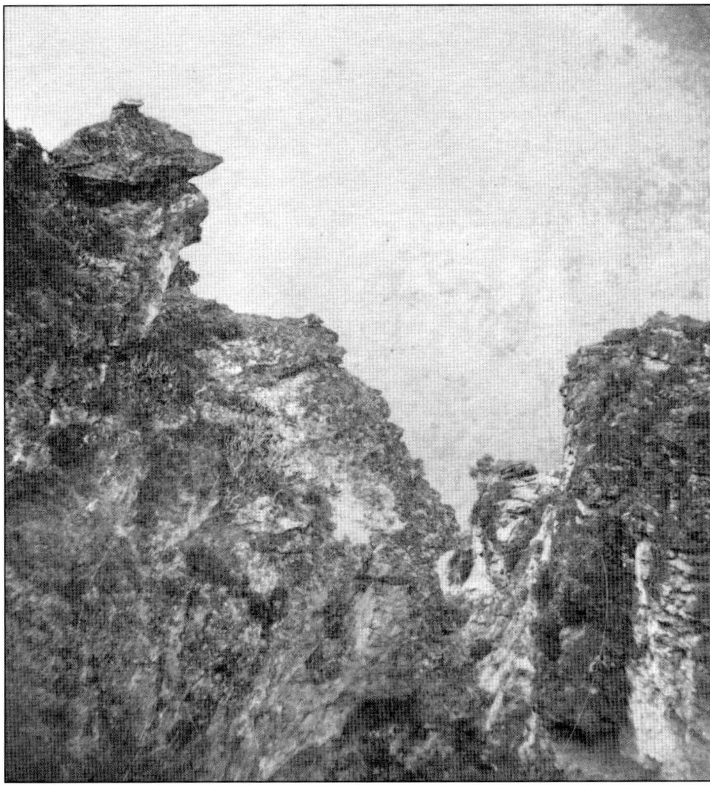

"Among the Chimneys." The formation on the left suggests the origins of this area's name. The rock is metasandstone and quartzite and is thickly covered with grey lichen. (Courtesy of the North Carolina Collection, Wilson Library, University of North Carolina at Chapel Hill.)

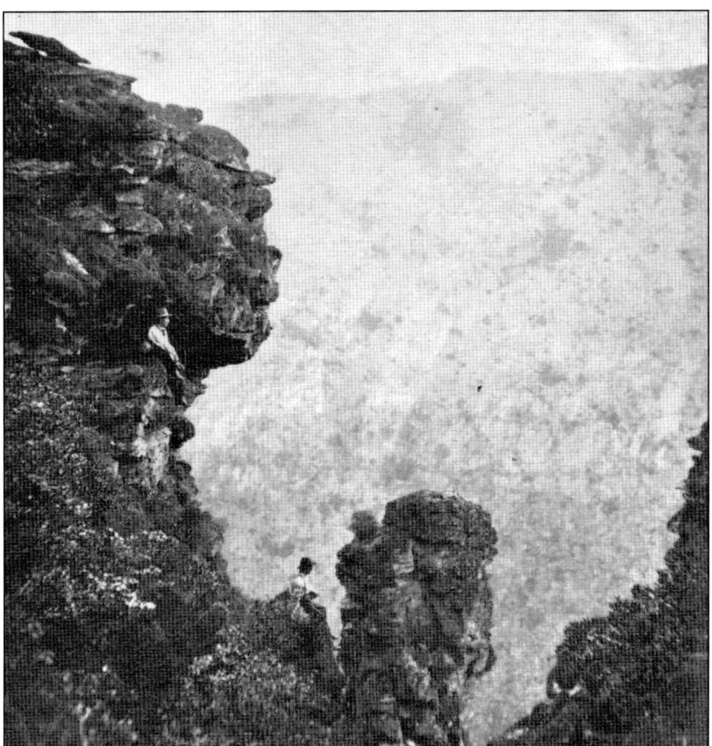

"The Old Man's Head." Morgan has again posed two of his companions in the picture to add scale to the view. Again we see what has been called a "chimney" in the center. In the distance are the west Linville Gorge cliffs known as "the Gold Coast." (Courtesy of the North Carolina Collection, Wilson Library, University of North Carolina at Chapel Hill.)

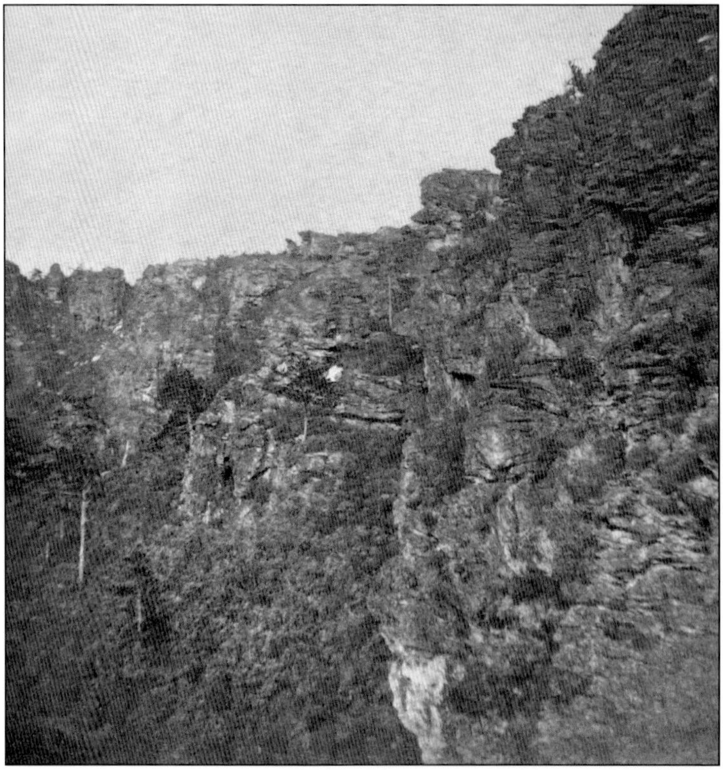

"THE CLIFFS." This view by Morgan depicts the North Carolina Wall (3,200 feet), which is about half-a-mile long with cliffs averaging 500 feet. It offers many challenges to rock climbers. (Courtesy of the North Carolina Collection, Wilson Library, University of North Carolina at Chapel Hill.)

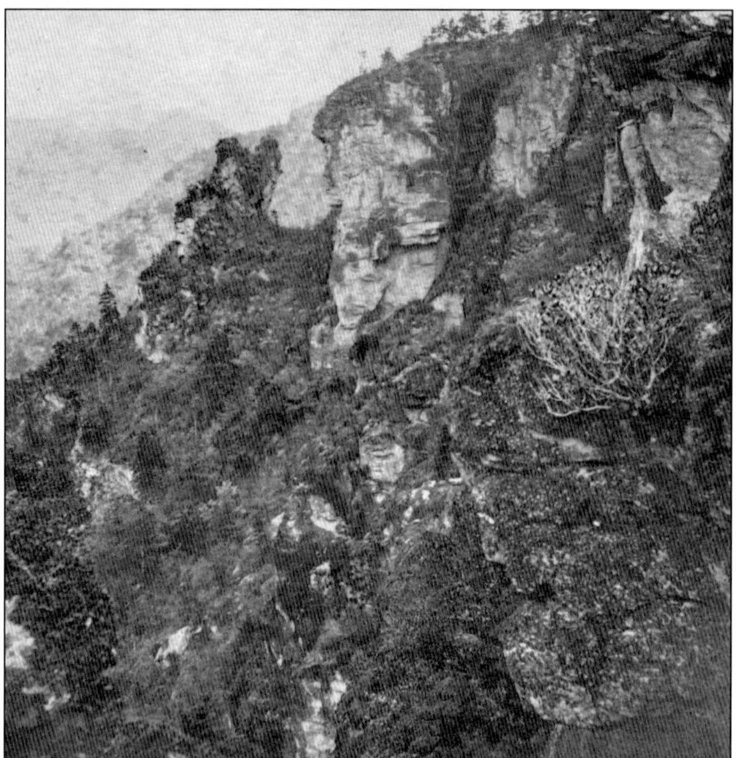

"CASTLE COVE." Morgan's view of the North Carolina Wall facing north includes the formation called "the Camel" as well as faint profiles of Table Rock Mountain and Hawksbill in the distance. (Courtesy of the North Carolina Collection, Wilson Library, University of North Carolina at Chapel Hill.)

"The Old Castle." These rock bluffs and spires are especially popular among rock climbers. (Courtesy of the North Carolina Collection, Wilson Library, University of North Carolina at Chapel Hill.)

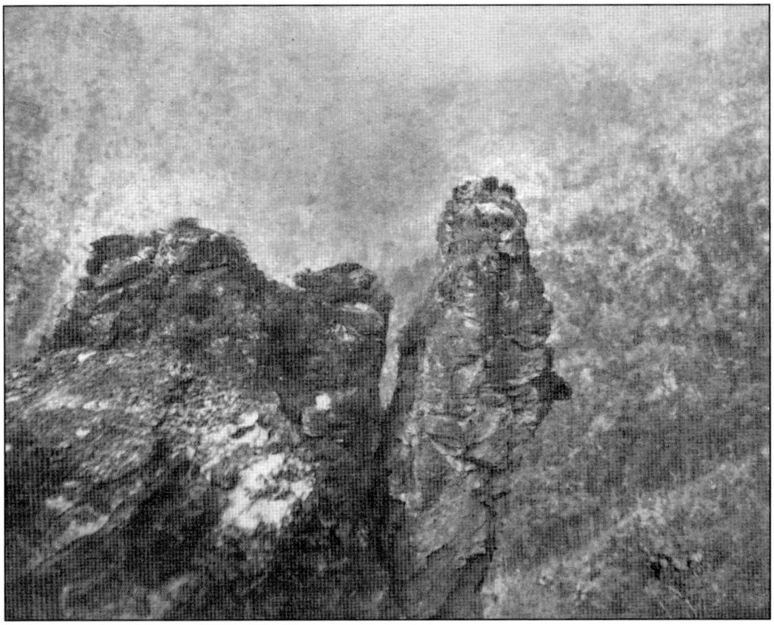

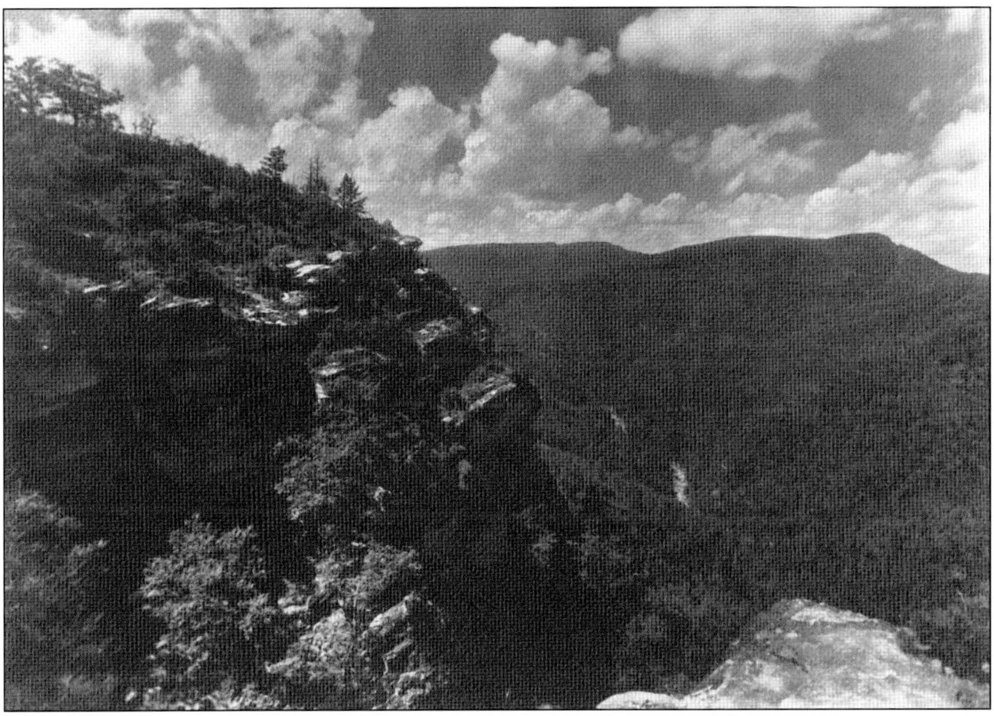

From Wiseman's View Northward. Bayard Wootten pioneered the role of women in the male-dominated world of professional photography, becoming one of the leading photographers of the American South. Operating from a studio in Chapel Hill from 1928 to 1954 she trekked to remote areas of western North Carolina bringing an acute artistic sensibility to her treatment of mountain people and the land. This silver gelatin print depicts the view of Linville Gorge north from Wiseman's View and has been given a matte finish. (Courtesy of the North Carolina Collection, Wilson Library, University of North Carolina Chapel Hill.)

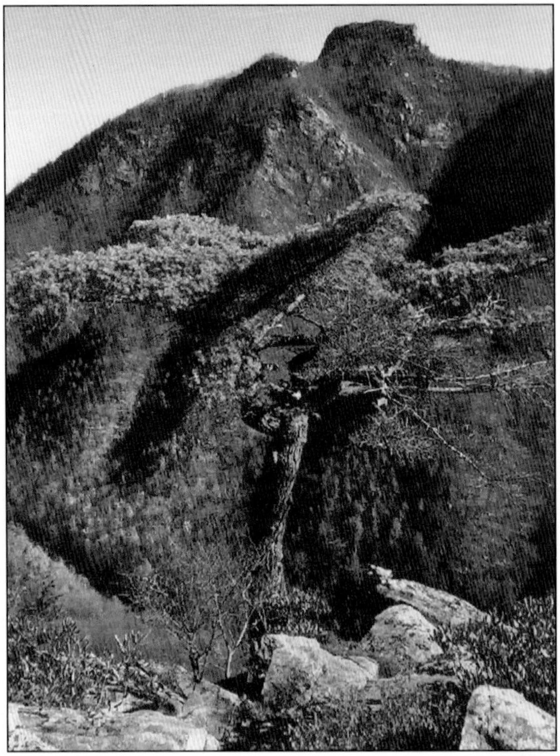

Table Rock from Hacker's Point. Table Rock Mountain assumes a wholly different aspect in this view made from a point on the Rock Jock Trail south of Wiseman's View on Linville Mountain. Little Table Rock and its cliff faces are visible here. The picture was taken on January 29, 2007. (Courtesy of the Friends of Linville Gorge.)

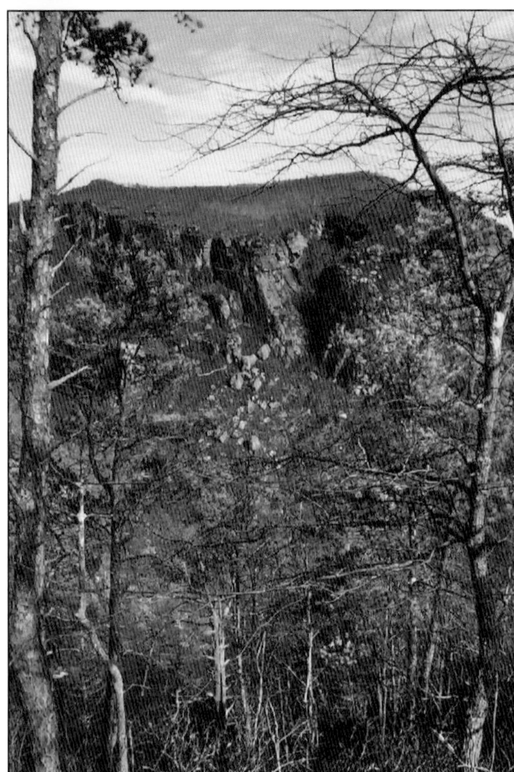

North Carolina Wall and Amphitheatre. The massive wedge-shaped canyon on the southern end of the North Carolina Wall is known as the "Amphitheater." Like the rest of the wall, this is a favorite among climbers. The Mountains-to-Sea Trail, running from Clingman's Dome in the Smokies to Jockey's Ridge on the Outer Banks, passes just above this area. (Courtesy of the Friends of Linville Gorge.)

Four

Linville Gorge
"The Deep Wood's Woven Shade"

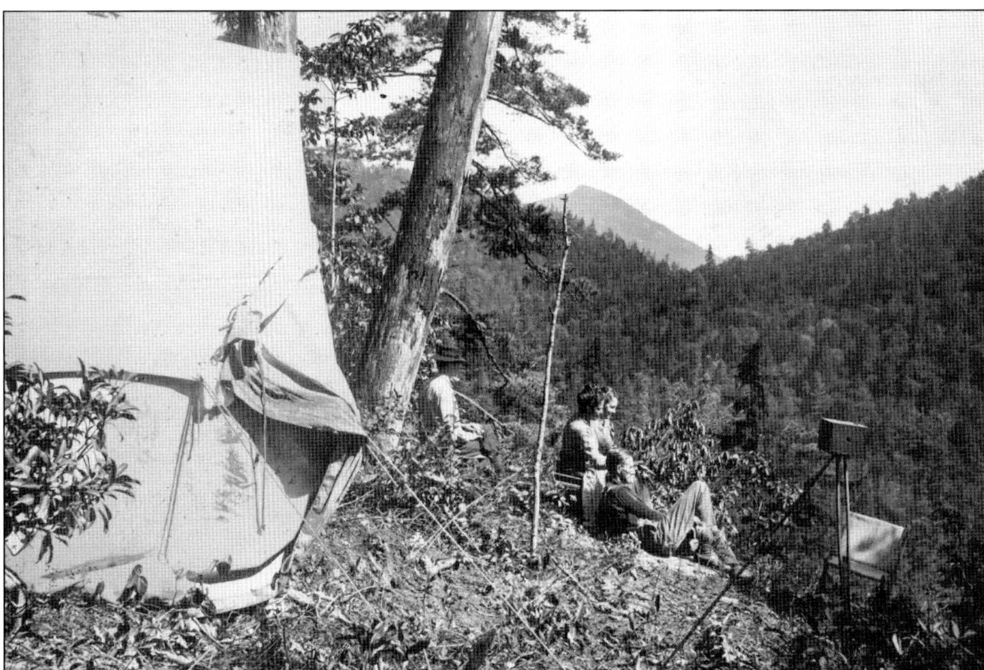

"**Newell Camp at Gooseneck.**" The Newell party has pitched camp on a rise overlooking the gooseneck bend in the river below Bynum's Bluff. Frank Bicknell also included a camp chair and a camera in this view he took on August 16, 1909. Hawksbill rises in the distance. (Courtesy of the North Carolina State Archives.)

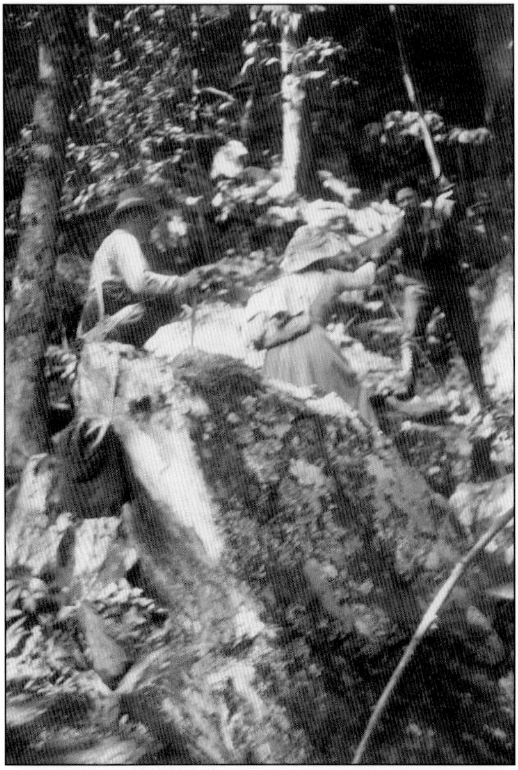

"Climbing Out Via Connelly's Cove Trail." The Conley Cove Trail descends 930 feet in 1.4 miles on the west side of Linville Gorge, which is located less than a mile south of Wiseman's View. It is named for planter William Connley. Bicknell's photograph on May 24, 1912, indicates how strenuous movement in the Linville Gorge can become. Bicknelly's caption and the U.S. Forest Service give alternate spellings of the proper name Connley. (Courtesy of the North Carolina State Archives.)

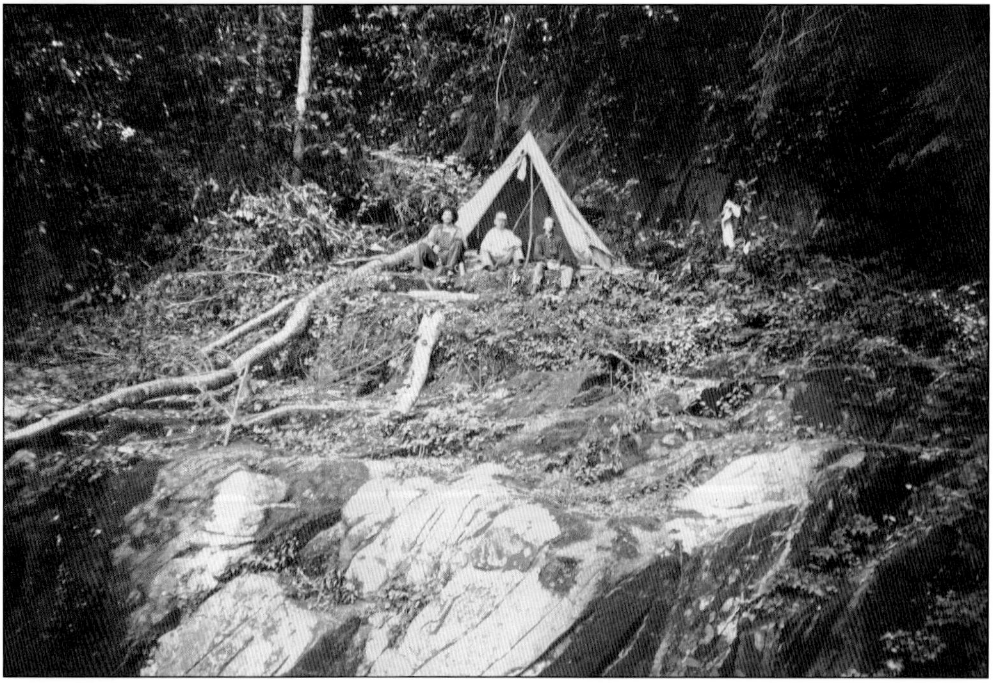

"Camp Peterson, Bynum's Bluff." The campsite shown here was named for Bicknell's fishing companion. Posing before the tent are Turner Vance, C. B. Carpenter, and Tommy Dellinger on May 26, 1911. (Courtesy of the North Carolina State Archives.)

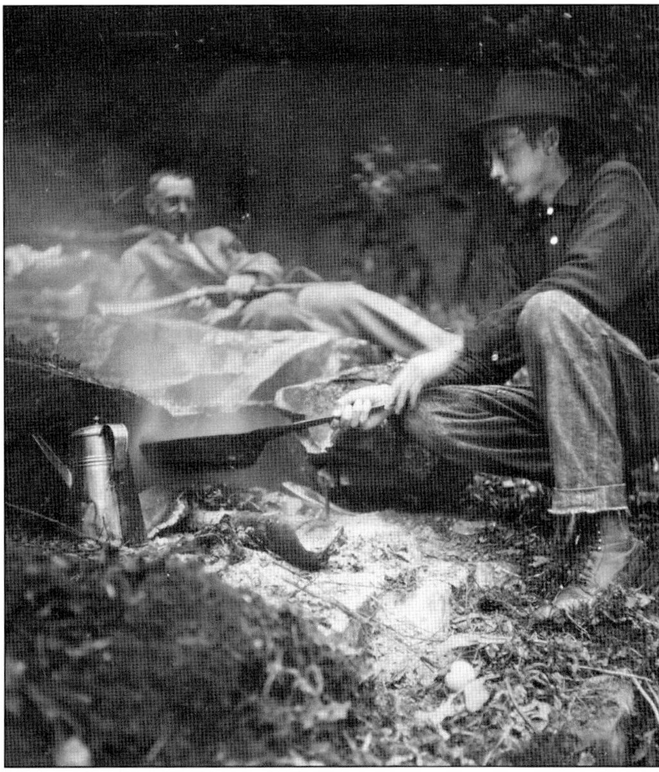

"TOMMY DELINGER, THE COOK, AND G. H. PETERSON." Seventeen-year-old Tommy Dellinger (born in 1894) was an expert at catching Linville River trout with a horsehair snare and panfrying his catch. During his lifetime, he amassed an amazing collection of over 12,000 American Indian artifacts and knew the Linville Gorge intimately. He is shown here on May 27, 1911. (Courtesy of the North Carolina State Archives.)

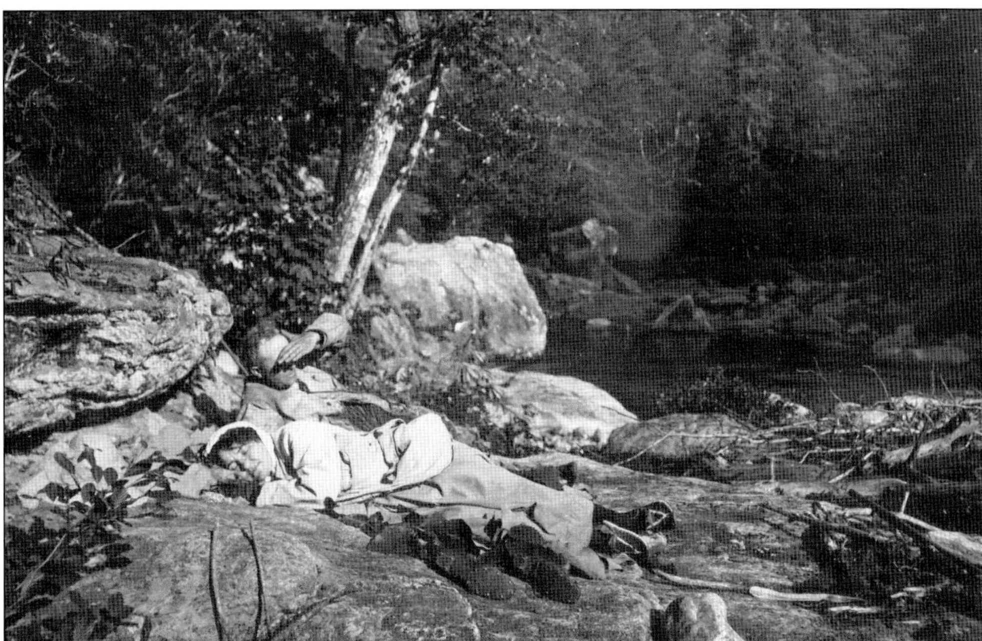

"A SOLID ROCK BED THE NIGHT BEFORE THE BABEL TOWER GORGE TRIP. FIRE ALL NIGHT FOR WARMTH." C. B. Carpenter might have taken this picture of the Bicknell's bedded down for the night without a tent on May 31, 1912. The month of May can be extremely chilly in Linville Gorge. (Courtesy of the North Carolina State Archives.)

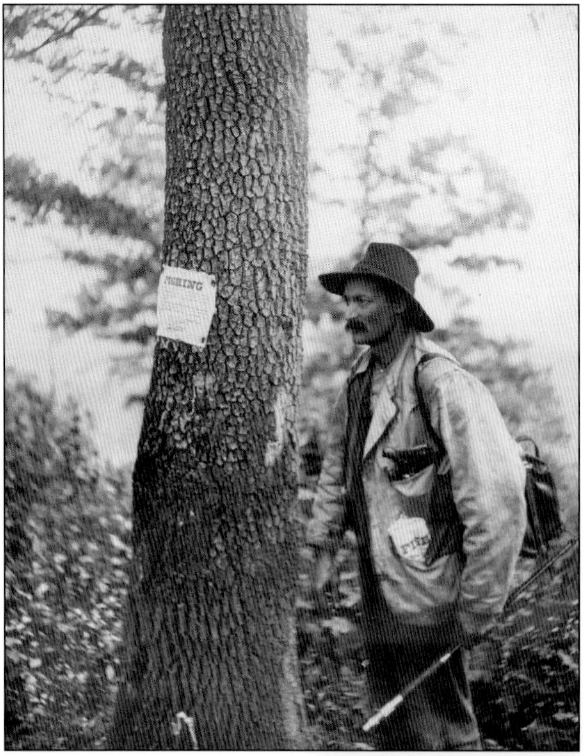

"The Late Turner Vance, Faithful Guide and Fish Warden, At Bynum's Bluff after First Trip." Turner Vance posts fishing regulations along the Bynum's Bluff Trail on the Linville Gorge's west side on September 14, 1910. He carries a roll of flyers in one pocket and a revolver in another. Sadly he was killed by an outraged husband. (Courtesy of the North Carolina State Archives.)

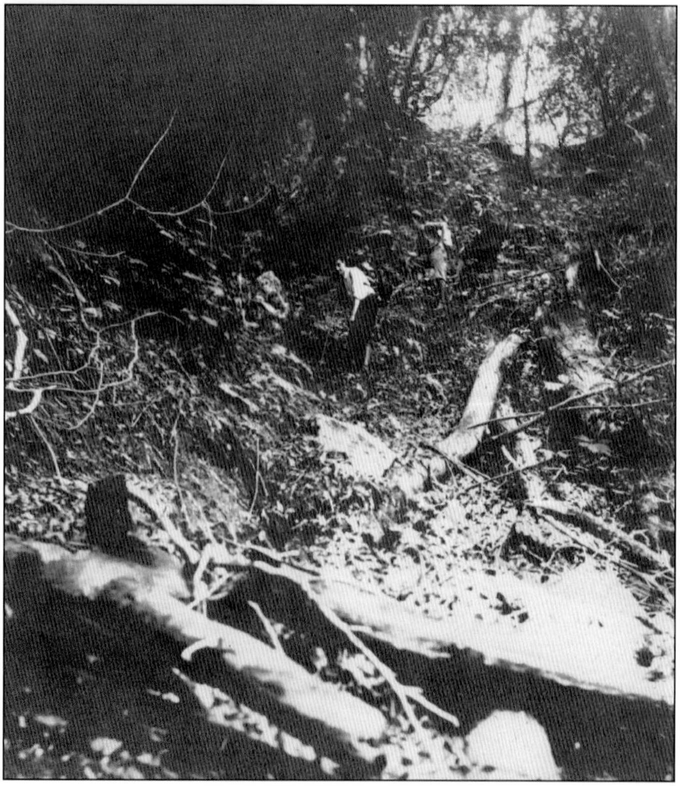

"Sliding down Linville Mountain into the Linville River Gorge." D. R. Beeson's party left Johnson City, Tennessee, on the Clinchfield Railway, debarking at the Ashford (Linville Falls) Station on July 3, 1914. Instead of taking the old Winding Stair Road (now U.S. 221) up the mountain through Linville Falls, they bushwhacked over Linville Mountain behind the station and descended to the river on the other side. (Courtesy of East Tennessee State University.)

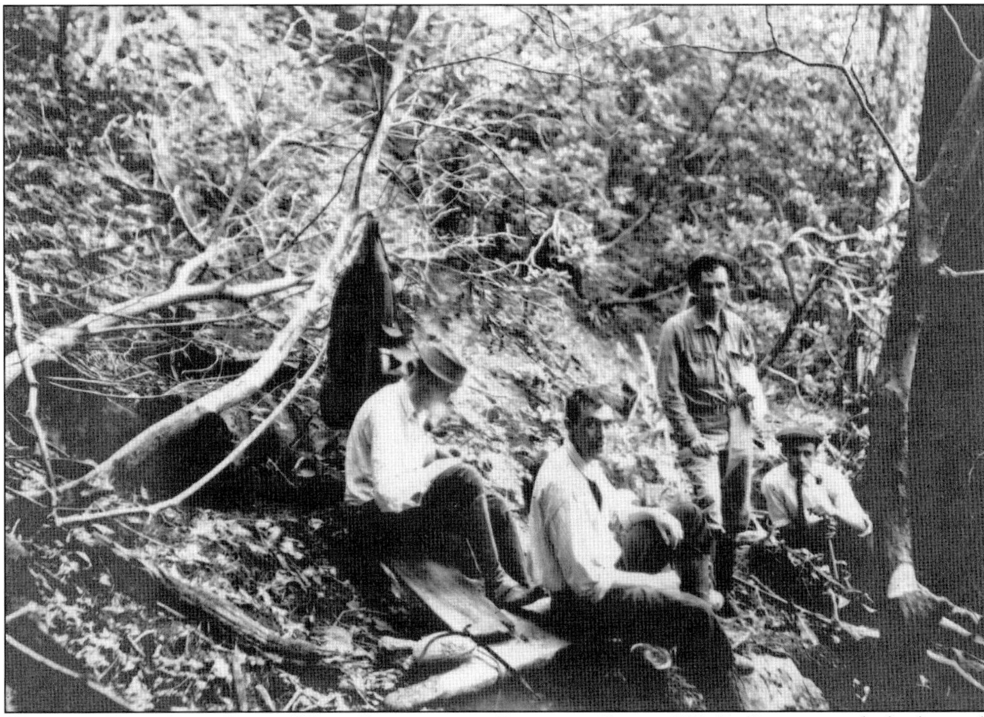

"Dinner First Day Out—West Bank of the Linville River." D. R. Beeson includes himself in this group picture with friends C. Hodge Mathes, Buford Mathes, and Schoen as they rest before the next day's climb up to Table Rock Mountain from the river. When was the last time someone wore a tie into the wilderness? (Courtesy of East Tennessee State University.)

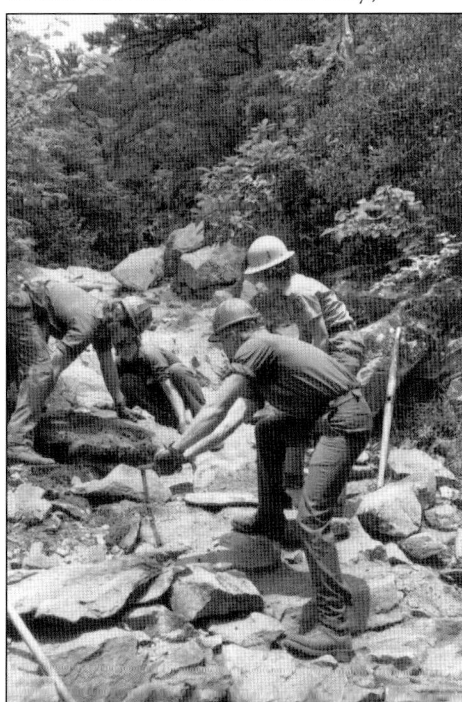

U.S. Forest Service Trail Crew. This trail crew of young men is rerouting the access trail leading to the summit of Table Rock Mountain from the parking lot at the rock's southern side. Properly constructed and maintained grades, switchbacks, and rain bars and ditches are essential for mountain trails. U.S. Forest Service Adopt-a-Trail volunteers maintain the trail system in Linville Gorge, performing thrice-annual seasonal walk-throughs to trim vegetation, remove blown-down timber, clean out rain bars, and remove litter. (Courtesy of the U.S. Forest Service, Grandfather Ranger District.)

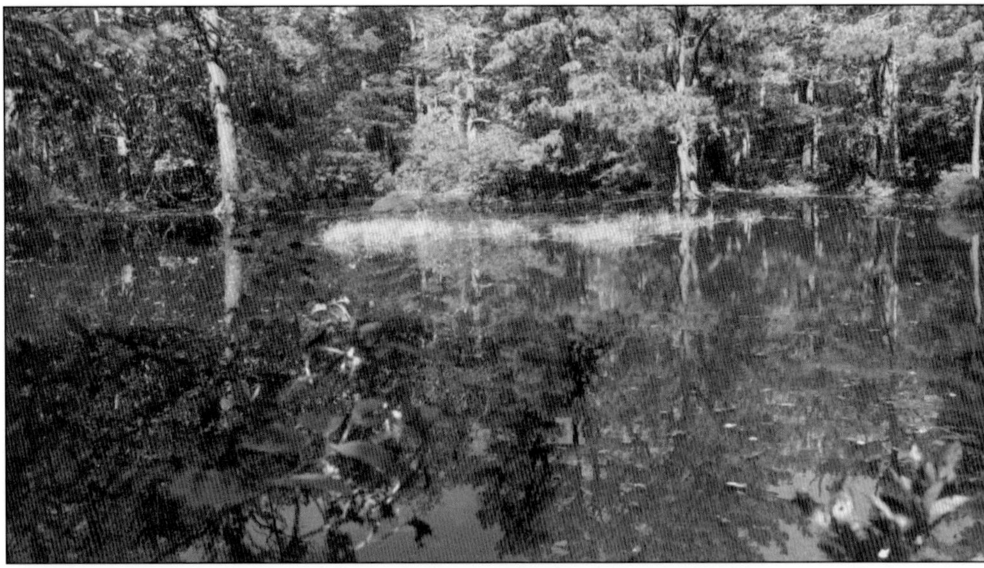

"**Natural Pond on Shortoff Mountain in Linville Gorge Wilderness.**" This pond is a well-known natural landmark on the Mountains-to-Sea Trail as it crosses the top of Shortoff Mountain between the bottom of Linville Gorge and the Chimneys to the north. It is affected by recent drought conditions and at times becomes a marsh. (Courtesy of the U.S. Forest Service, Grandfather Ranger District.)

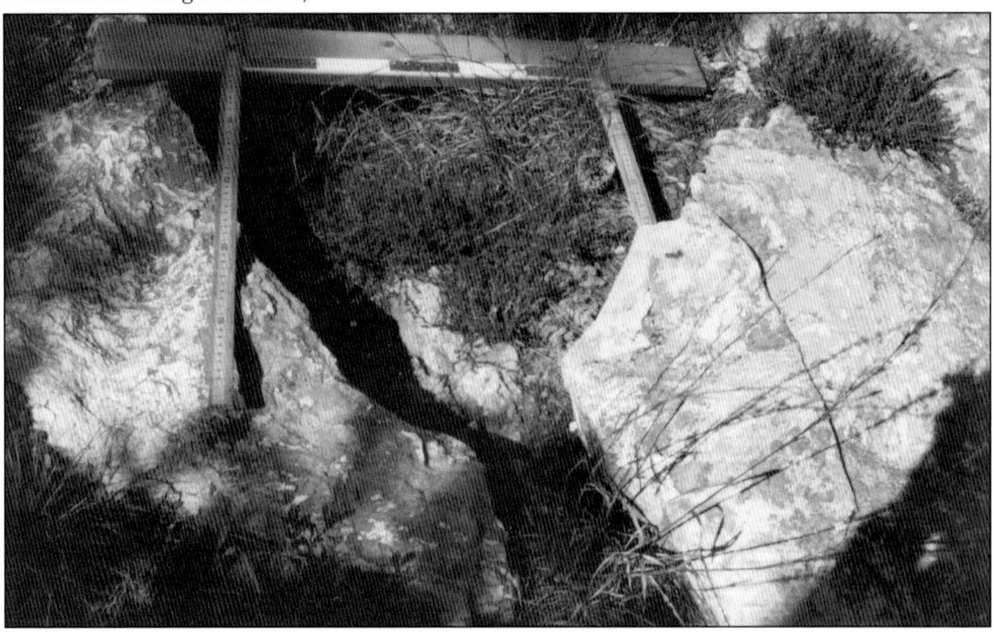

"**Endangered Species Mountain Golden Heather.**" Botanist Thomas Nuttall found this small, golden-blossomed shrub on the rim of Linville Gorge in 1816. Two years later, he named it *Hudsonia montana*. Once thought extinct, a small number of colonies still survive under a Critical Habitat designation. Like the Table Mountain pine, *Hudsonia montana* is a fire-adapted species, meaning that controlled burns by the U.S. Forest Service assist in reseeding. Still poachers and careless visitors threaten the survival of this rare plant. (Courtesy of the U.S. Forest Service, Grandfather Ranger District.)

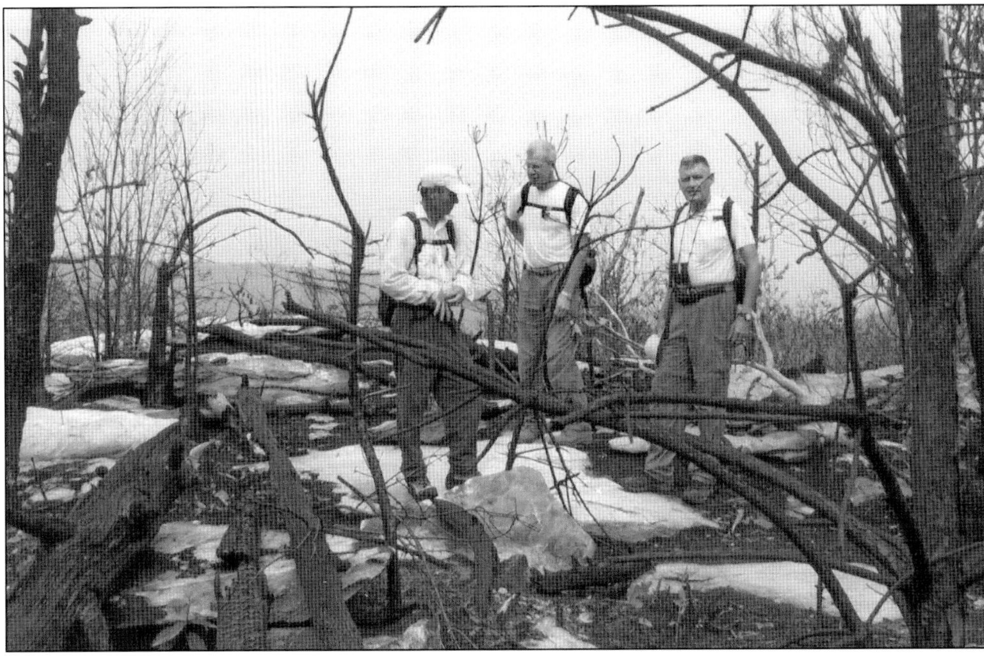

Forest Fire Damage. In November 2000, some 6,000 acres of the Linville Gorge suffered forest fire damage. Fires starting on April 25 and June 8, 2007, damaged thousands of acres in the Shortoff and Dogback Mountain areas. Untended campfires and lightning strikes are the major cause of fires. Jonathan Cox photographed (from left to right) David Martin, Allen Hyde, and Toby Collins amid the blackened timber on the northwest end of Shortoff Mountain on August 30, 2007. (Courtesy of Allen Hyde.)

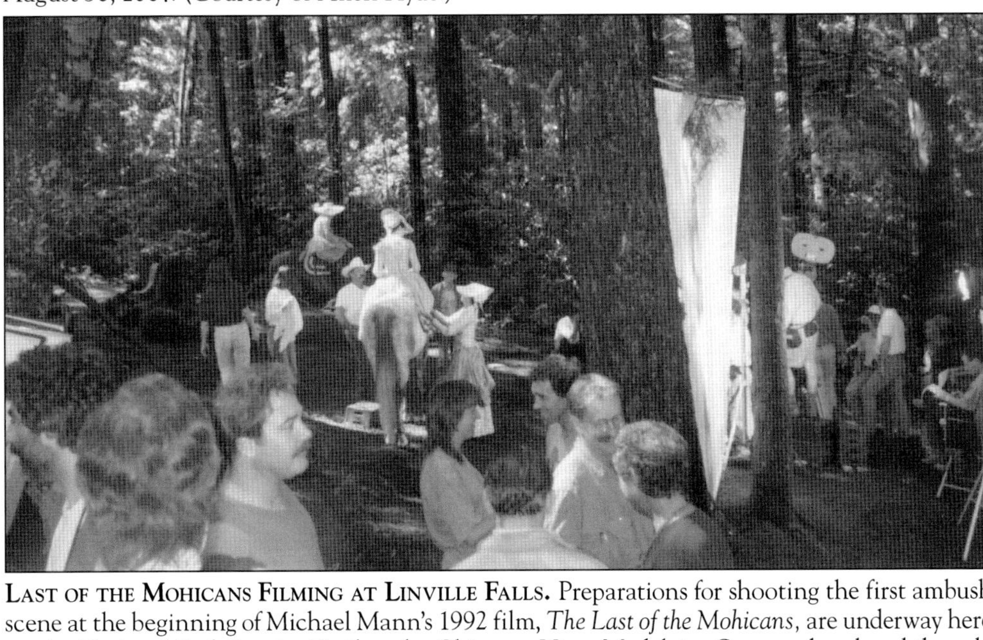

Last of the Mohicans Filming at Linville Falls. Preparations for shooting the first ambush scene at the beginning of Michael Mann's 1992 film, *The Last of the Mohicans*, are underway here on the National Park Service Trail to the Chimney View. Madeleine Stowe, who played the role of Cora Munro, is on one horse, and costar Jodhi May as Alice Munro is on the other. (Courtesy of the U.S. Forest Service, Grandfather Ranger District.)

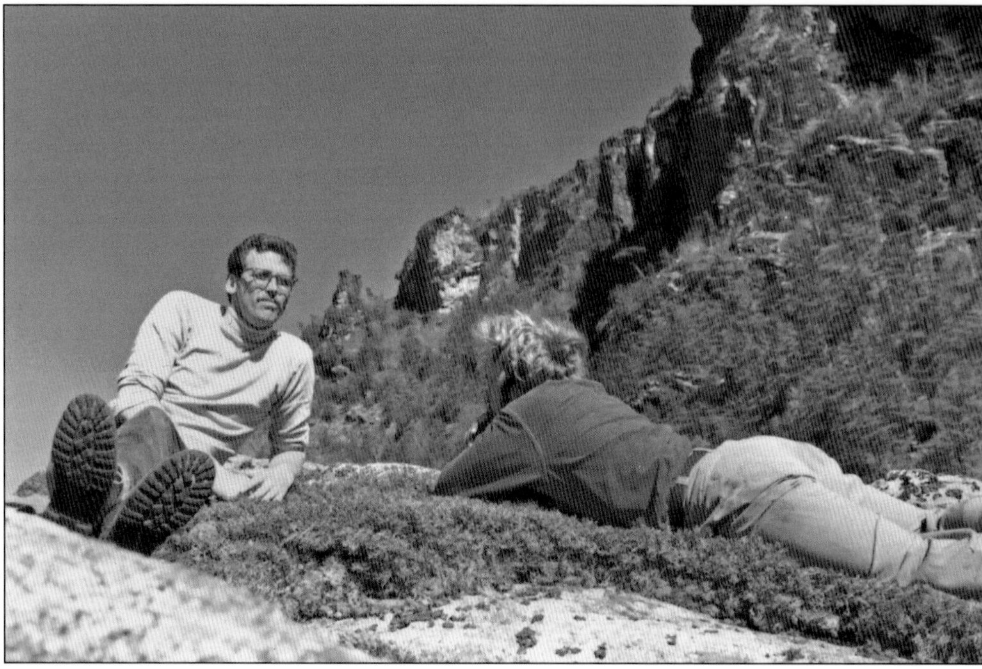

"Jed Williamson and George Cron on Sphinx Rock." Here two early climbers in the Linville Gorge below the North Carolina Wall have made it to the top of the massive freestanding rock about halfway down the eastern slope of the Linville Gorge. Also known as "Mashburn's Pinnacle" after early 1960s climber and Outward Bound instructor Dave Mashburn, the rock is a landmark feature in the wilderness. Between the men's heads, the spire known as "the Camel" can be seen (see lower photograph on page 67). (Courtesy of Mike Fischesser.)

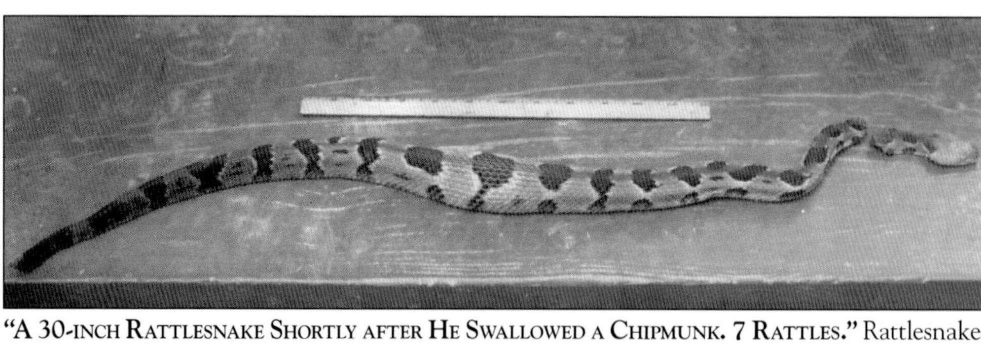

"A 30-inch Rattlesnake Shortly after He Swallowed a Chipmunk. 7 Rattles." Rattlesnakes are becoming increasingly more rare as they are commonly destroyed on sight by hikers. Snake attacks are very rare, and biologists advise leaving the creatures alone. Allen Hyde killed this timber rattler in his yard near the Linville Gorge in August 2007. (Courtesy of Allen Hyde.)

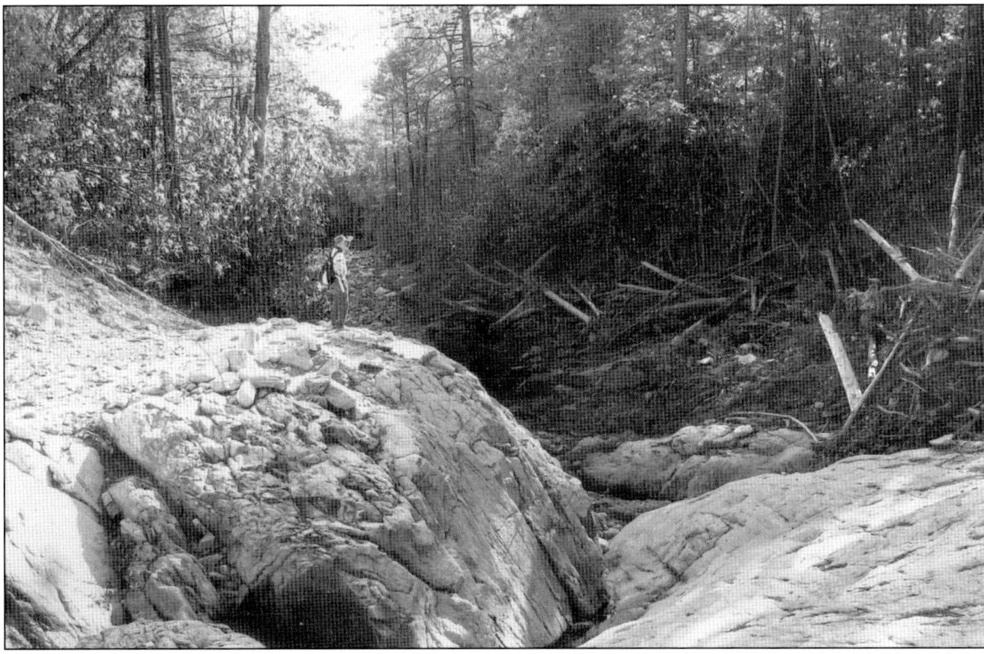

"AVALANCHE GULLY BELOW THE CHIMNEYS." Torrential rains from Hurricane Frances (2004) washed out a section of the Blue Ridge Parkway south of Linville Falls and also caused this serious slide on the Mountains-to-Sea Trail section through the Chimneys. Mud and boulders have crashed far down the slope below the trail. The photograph, made on October 28, 2007, is by Toby Collins. (Courtesy of Allen Hyde.)

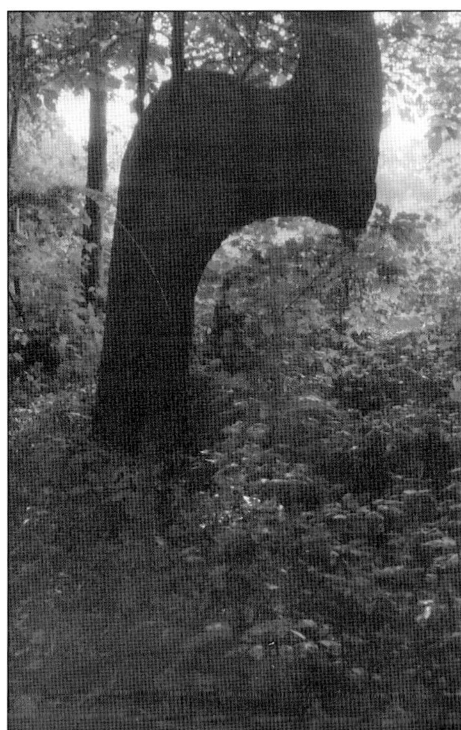

"INDIAN SIGN TREE." Geologist Raymond E. Janssen of Evanston, Illinois, claimed in July 1941 that he had solved the riddle of strangely bent trees. He said they are Native American directional signs. Formed by distorting the natural growth of young trees, the trees display a right-angled bend in their trunks some 2–5 feet above ground. Skeptics claim that fallen trees or stones weigh down saplings and that the growths are accidental. (Courtesy of Allen Hyde.)

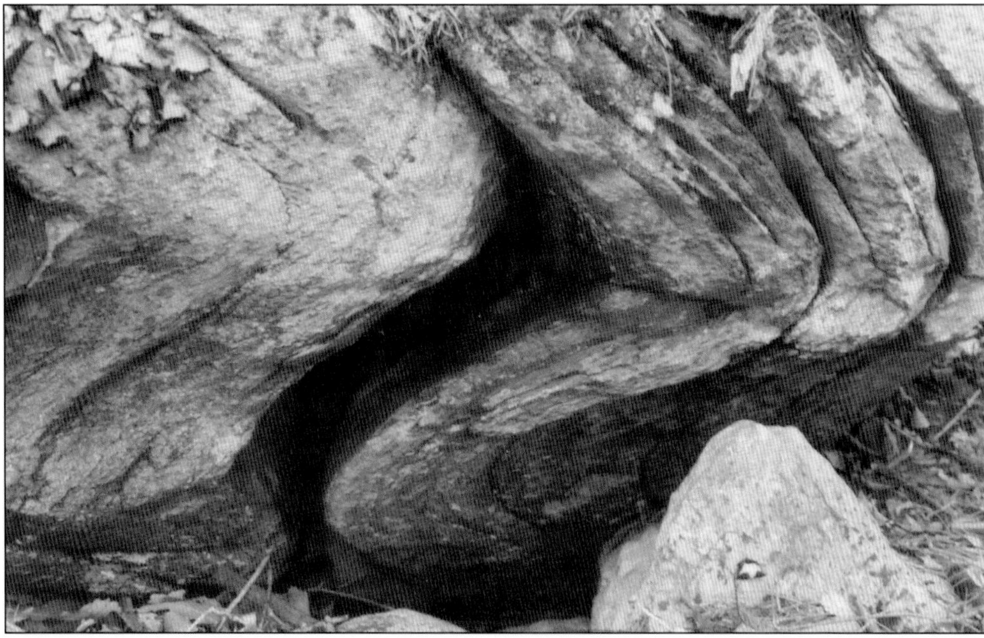

"The Folded Rock." Dramatic evidence of the heat and compression that formed the geology of the Linville Gorge is revealed in this picture of what's commonly called the "folded rock" located in the Mountain Park neighborhood of Gingercake Acres on Jonas Ridge. (Courtesy of Allen Hyde.)

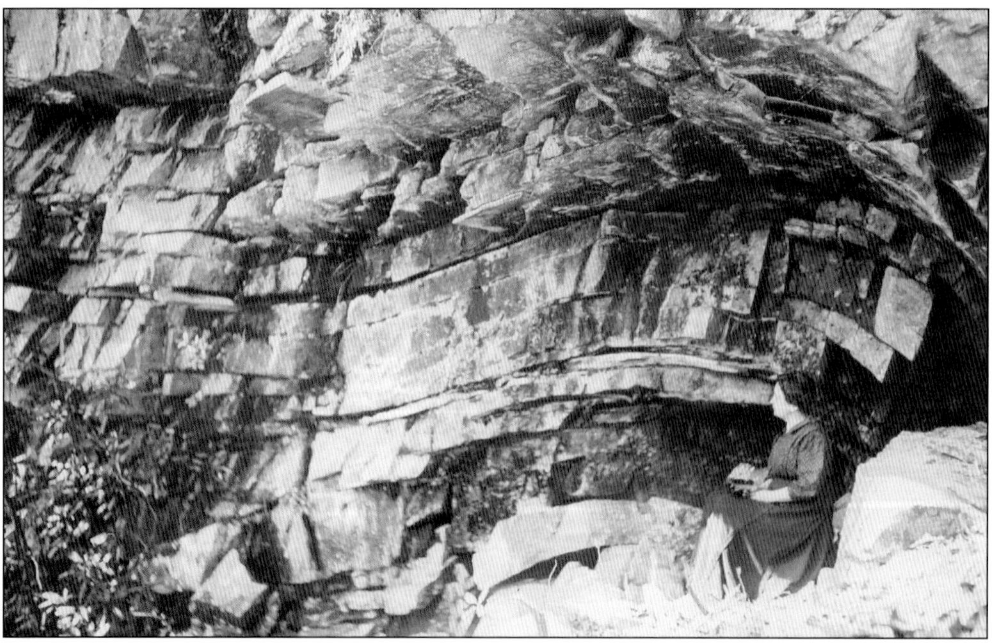

"Natural Arch, Volcanic Upheaval Near Pine Gap." Jessie Bicknell sits beside this well-known example of folded rock on the Pine Gap Trail, the northernmost trail on the Linville Gorge's eastern side. Her husband, who took her picture on April 14, 1910, was wrong in his geology; continental collision not volcanic activity compressed the rock into this wave-like pattern. (Courtesy of the North Carolina State Archives.)

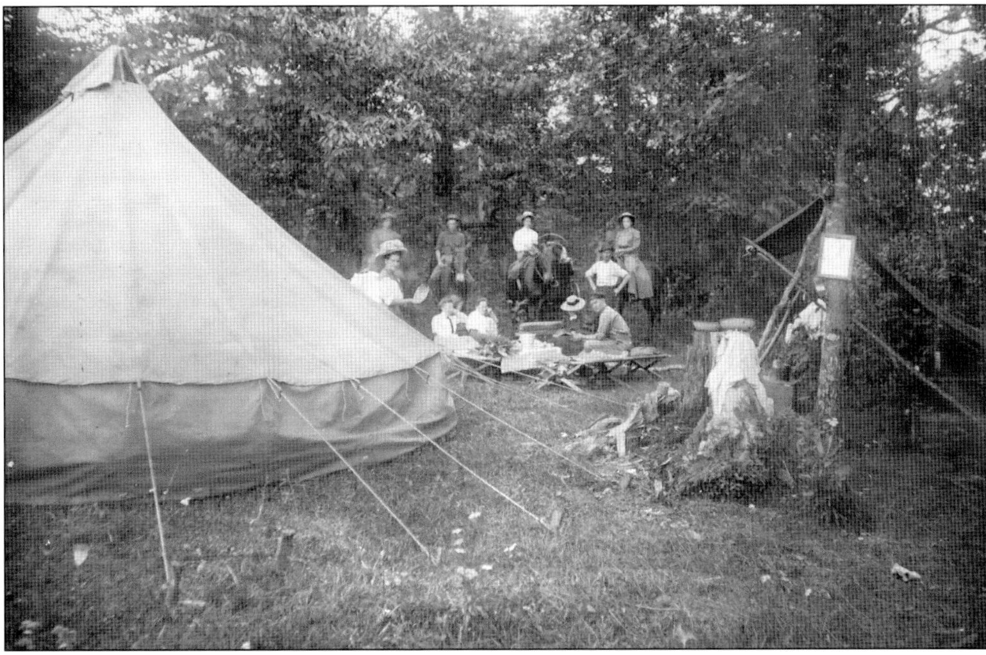

"THE DALLAS CAMP AT THE TOP OF THE MOUNTAIN." Frank Bicknell visited and photographed this camping party from Dallas, North Carolina, in 1910. They are probably camped on Linville Mountain just off the Kistler Memorial Highway (Old 105). (Courtesy of the North Carolina State Archives.)

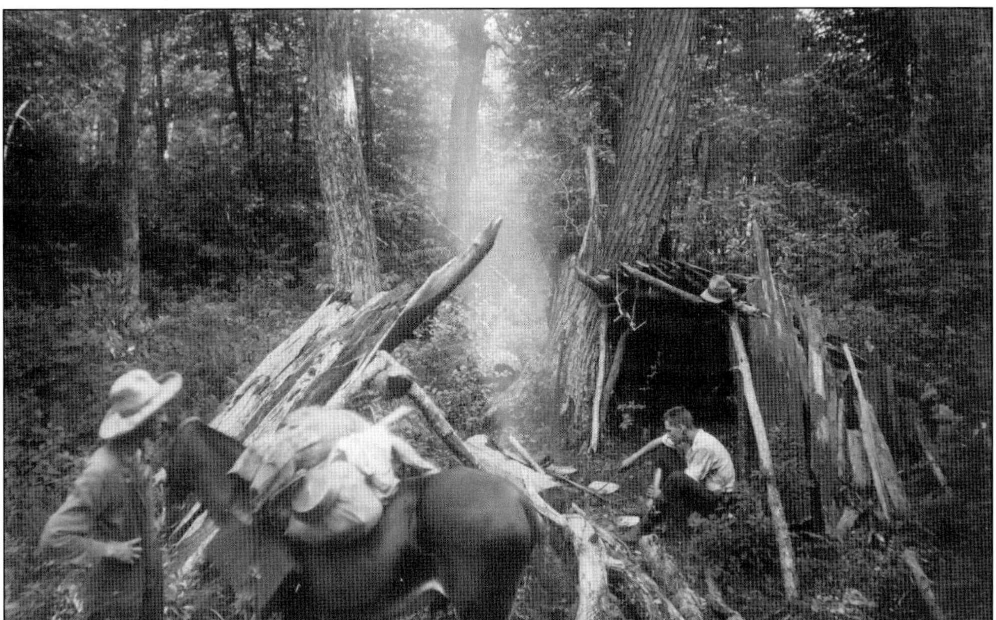

"WILLIAM HOSSFELD, COMMODORE BROWNING IN CAMP IN CHESTNUT COVE." Frank Bicknell photographed these members of a surveying expedition at their makeshift shelter on Dobson's Knob on September 8, 1911. Dobson's Knob (3,440 feet) lies outside the Linville Gorge area overlooking the farms and pastures in North Cove. (Courtesy of the North Carolina State Archives.)

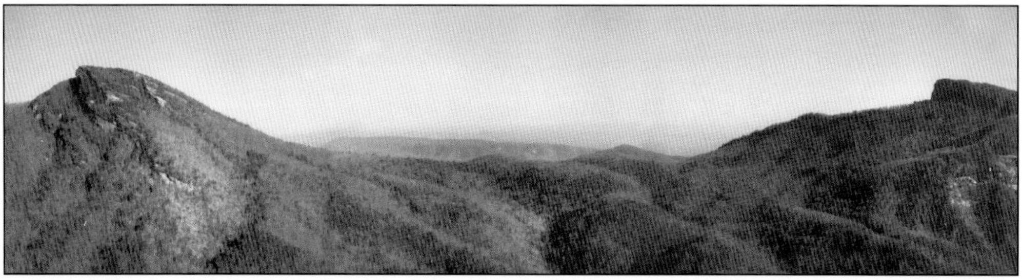

"Panorama from Wiseman's View." Allen Hyde made this panoramic view of Jonas Ridge from the observation balcony at Wiseman's View. To the left rears Hawksbill Mountain and to the right is Table Rock Mountain. Brown Mountain is the level ridge in the distance between the two. In the saddle between the peaks, the Spence Ridge Trail descends 1.7 miles to Linville River and the U.S. Forest Service footbridge. Hyde visited on December 9, 2006. (Courtesy of Allen Hyde.)

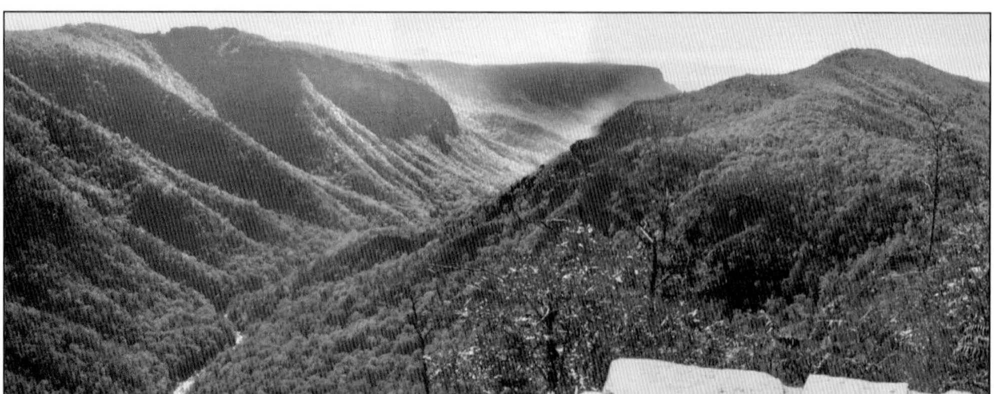

"Looking South from Wiseman's View." This panoramic view taken on October 31, 2007, includes, from left to right, the Chimneys, the North Carolina Wall, and Shortoff Mountain on the Linville Gorge's eastern side. South of Wiseman's View on the west lies Dogback Mountain (3280 feet). (Courtesy of Allen Hyde.)

Five

THE DOMESTIC WILD
"MAN AND HIS WORKS"

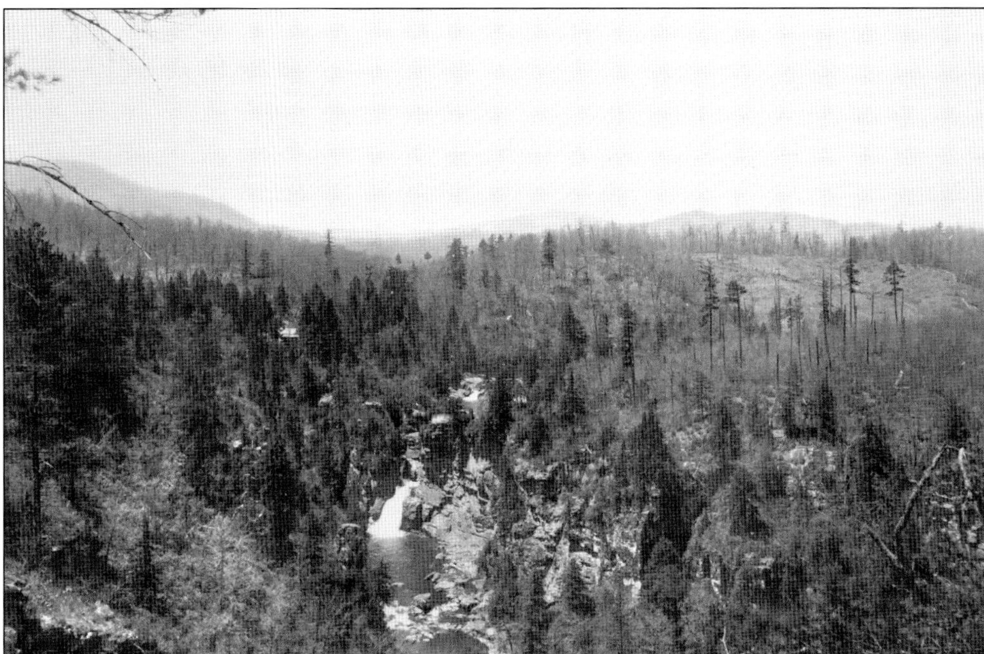

"FROM ERVIN'S VIEW (VIRASALTA) COTTAGE ABOVE AND LEFT OF FALLS." The little white cottage stood above the Linville Falls for over 60 years before the National Park Service had it removed in 1951. The cottage appears as a small white square in the trees and to the left of the falls. Notice the clear cut on the right of the waterfall. Bicknell owned a sawmill on the Linville River, above the present-day parkway picnic area. Ervin's should be Erwin's, for the view was not named for Hossfeld Sr.'s partner W. C. Ervin but for the surveyor of Old Route 105. *Vira salta* is Spanish for "it turns, leaps," which is a fitting place name. Salta is also a provincial capital in northwestern Argentina, a country where Frank Bicknell served as an agricultural expert. (Courtesy of the North Carolina State Archives.)

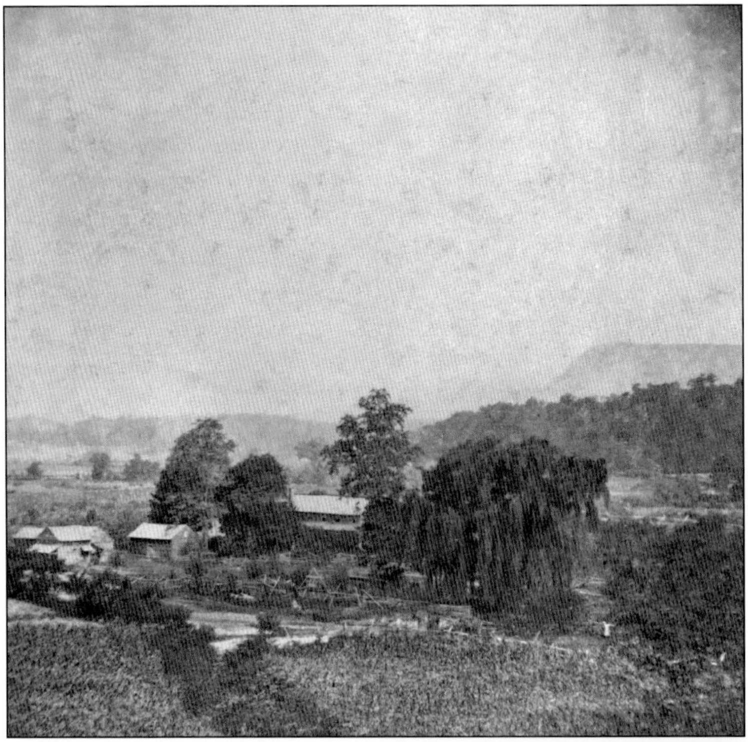

"Linville Farm below Shortoff." This farm, photographed by Rufus Morgan around 1873, was part of the Fonta Flora community, named so because of the rich bottomlands there. Fonta Flora was famed for its horse racing and gambling. Today the area lies under the waters of Lake James, created by Duke Power Company in 1926. (Courtesy of the North Carolina Collection, Wilson Library, University of North Carolina at Chapel Hill.)

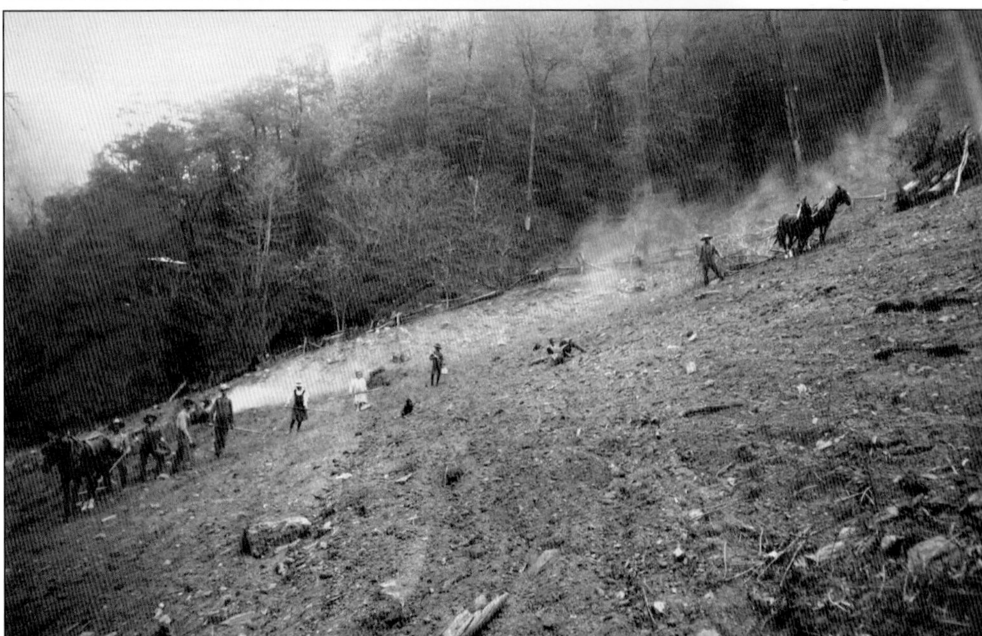

"A Mountainside Corn Planting." Frank Bicknell visited this family planting corn on the slope of Humpback Mountain (4179 feet) on May 3, 1910. Humpback (which local author Shepherd M. Dugger preferred to call by the more euphonious Native American name *Sunnalee* or "morning') extends to the Linville Falls village area. Today the Blue Ridge Parkway runs along its eastern edge. (Courtesy of the North Carolina State Archives.)

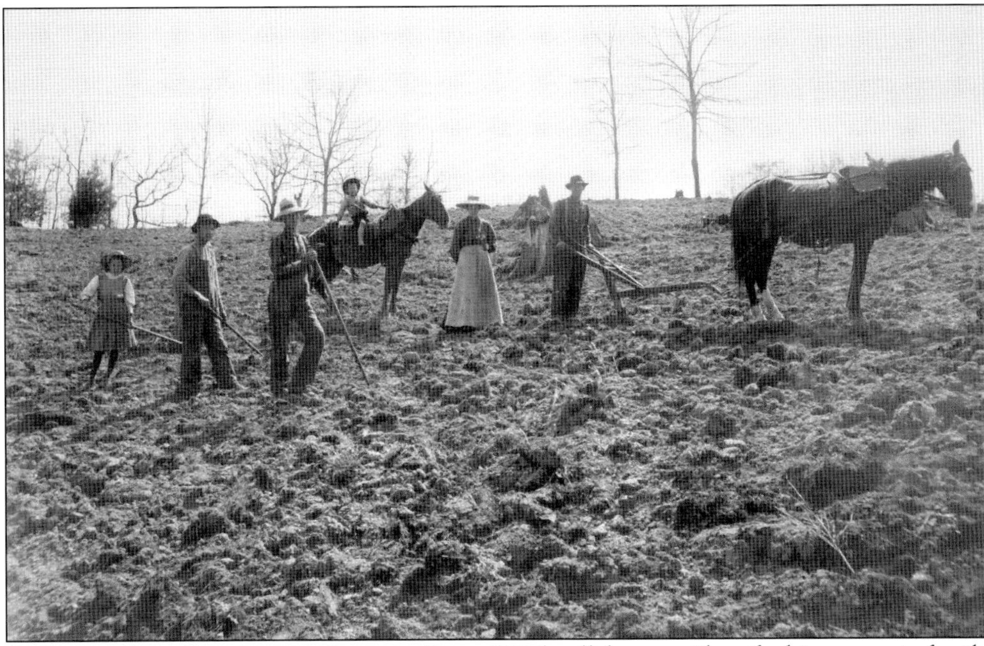

"A FAMILY CORN PLANTING AT LINVILLE FALLS." Bicknell does not identify this mountain family, all the members of which have turned out for spring planting. He photographed the group two days after taking the picture on the bottom of the previous page; it is probably the same group working on a level part of Humpback. (Courtesy of the North Carolina State Archives.)

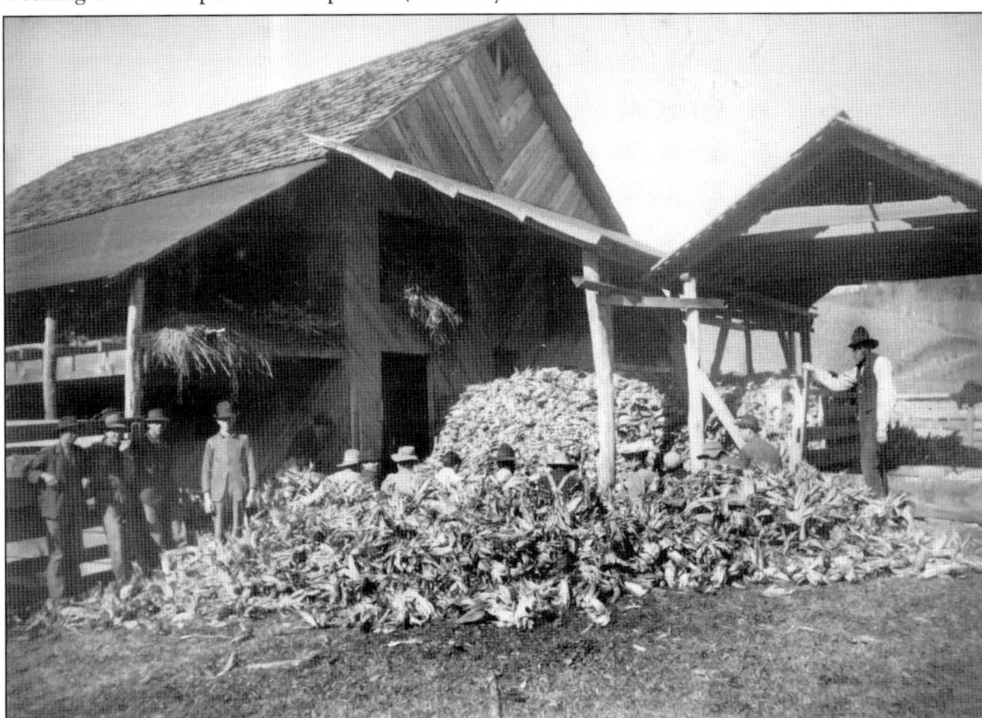

"CORN SHUCKING AT GUS CHILD'S." Members of the Child family and their friends gather at the barn to shuck corn on November 9, 1910. (Courtesy of the North Carolina State Archives.)

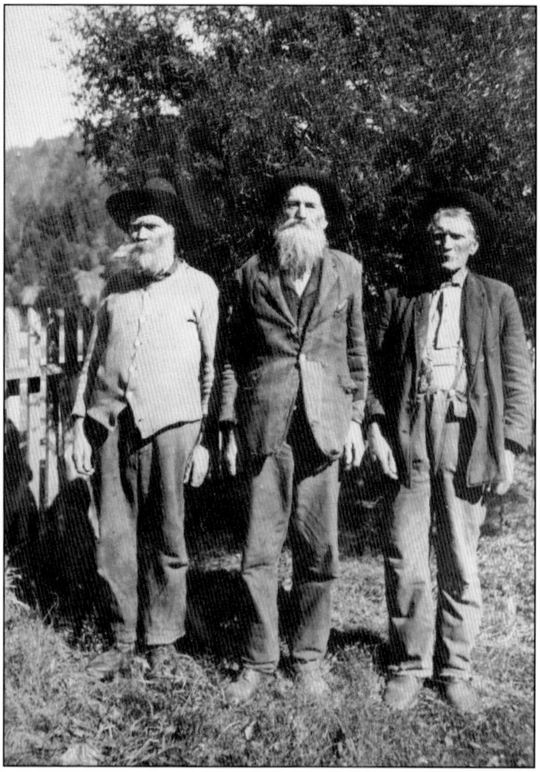

"TOM WISE, JOHN WISE, NEWT WISE." Bicknell photographed the Wise brothers as they gathered for a corn shucking at John Wise's farm in October 1911. All three were Confederate army veterans and had seen action at the Battle of Gettysburg. (Courtesy of the North Carolina State Archives.)

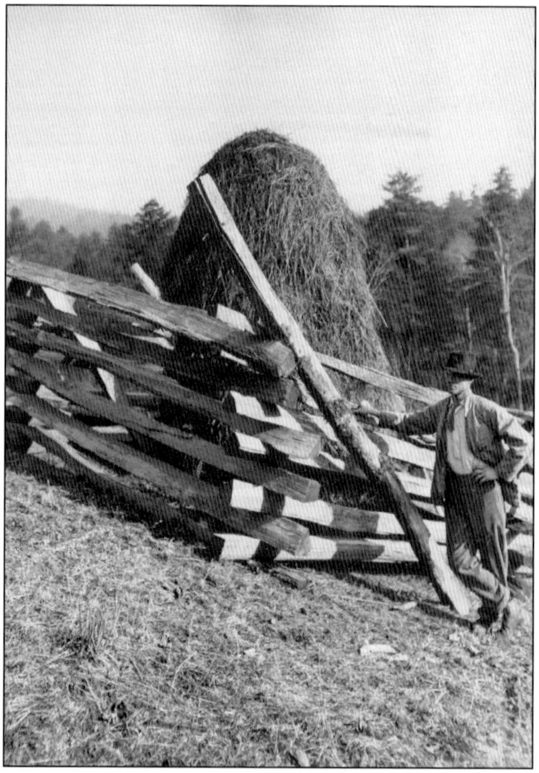

"HAYSTACK ON LINVILLE MOUNTAIN." Frank Bicknell recorded this haystack and a man identified only as "G. J. B." in harvest season, 1909. (Courtesy of the North Carolina State Archives.)

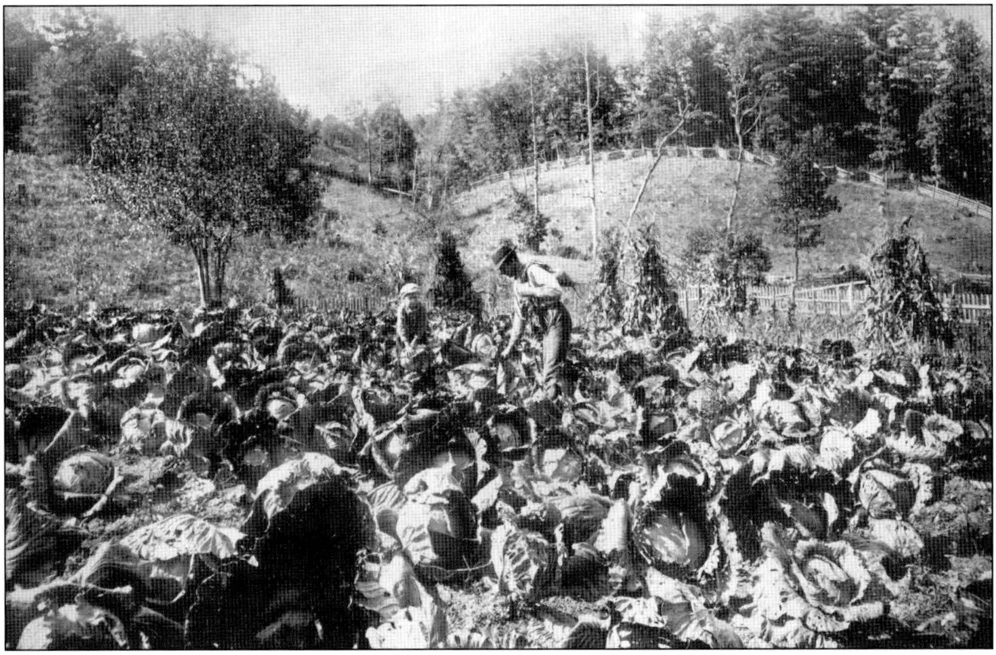

"ADEE WISEMAN'S CABBAGE." Cabbage, corn, pole beans, and potatoes made up the typical vegetable crops in the farms around the Linville Falls and Linville Gorge at the beginning of the 20th century. Today Christmas trees provide the greatest cash crop, as Frazer firs flourish in the climate of the area. Bicknell visited this cabbage patch on October 1, 1910. (Courtesy of the North Carolina State Archives.)

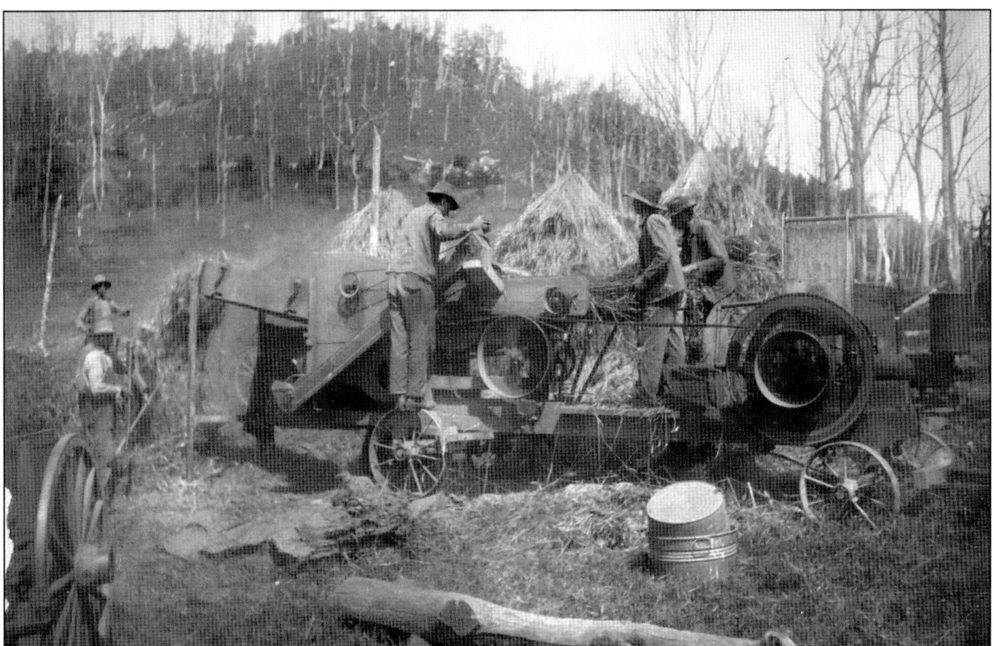

"THRASHING RYE ON THE BLUE RIDGE." Farm laborers on the Wise Farm use a motor-driven mechanical thresher for the rye crop. (Courtesy of the North Carolina State Archives.)

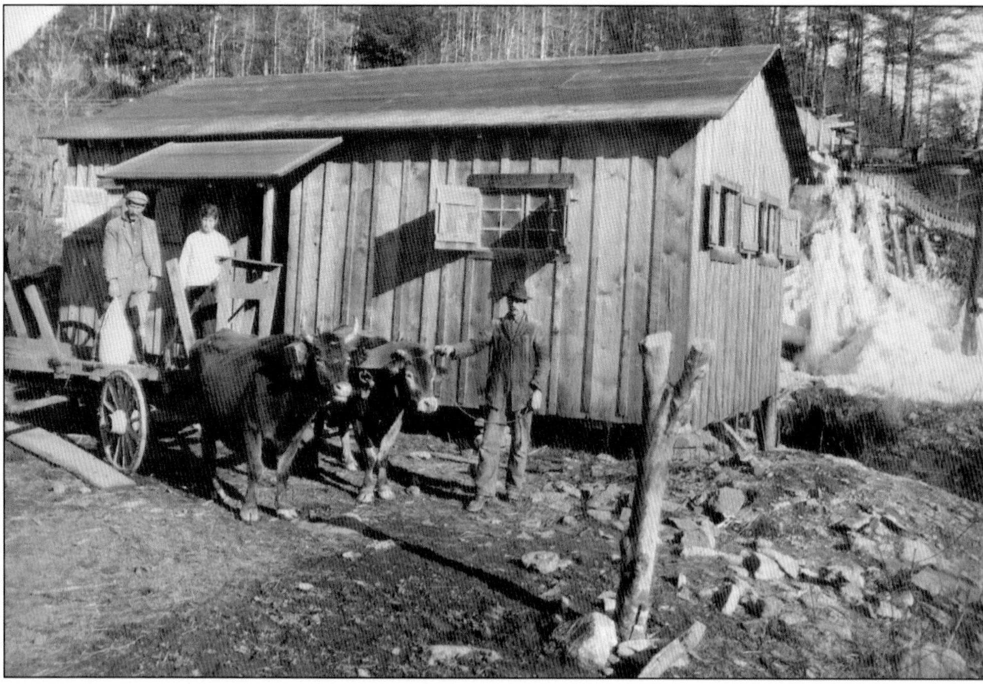

"Camp Creek Grist Mill." Bicknell owned and operated a sawmill near this tributary creek of the Linville River. The creek was named after the Camp brothers of Chicago, Illinois, who ran a logging operation there in the early 1900s. Bicknell photographed the gristmill on New Year's Day, 1920. (Courtesy of the North Carolina State Archives.)

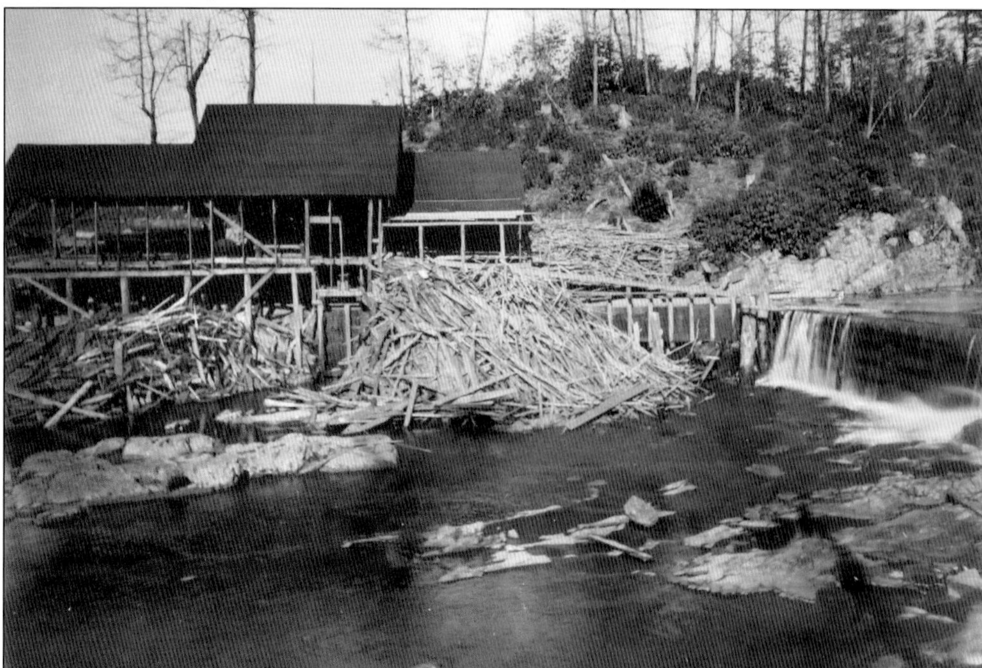

"Sawmill from across Linville River." Bicknell photographed his sawmill on the Linville River the same day he took the gristmill picture above. (Courtesy of the North Carolina State Archives.)

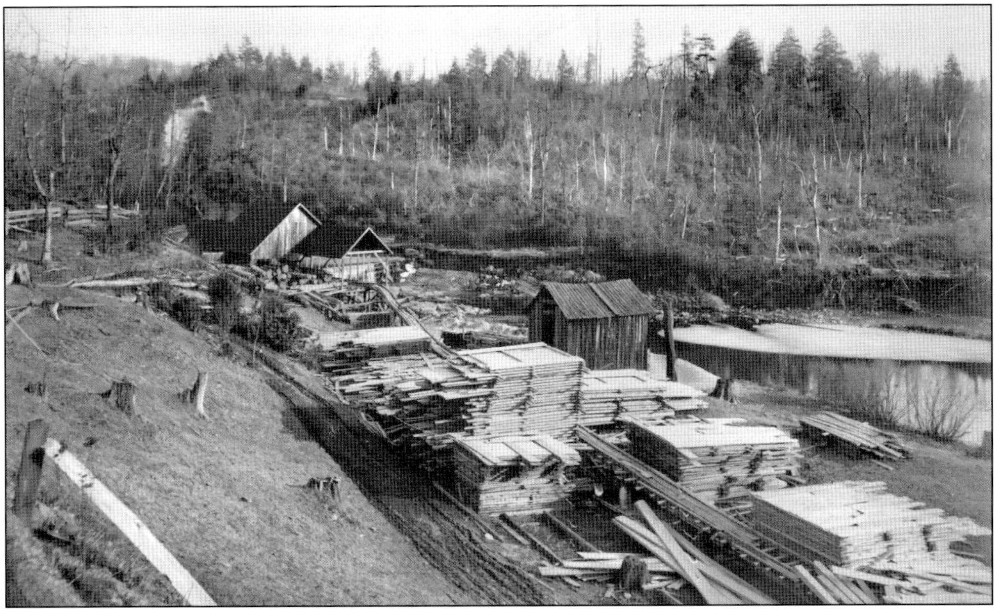

"SAWMILL AND LUMBER YARD FROM LOG ROAD." Taken the same day as the image on the bottom of page 100, this photograph records more of the sawmill property and the ice on the Linville River. Bicknell contributed wood from this mill to the building of the first church in Linville Falls, which was destroyed by fire and later rebuilt. (Courtesy of the North Carolina State Archives.)

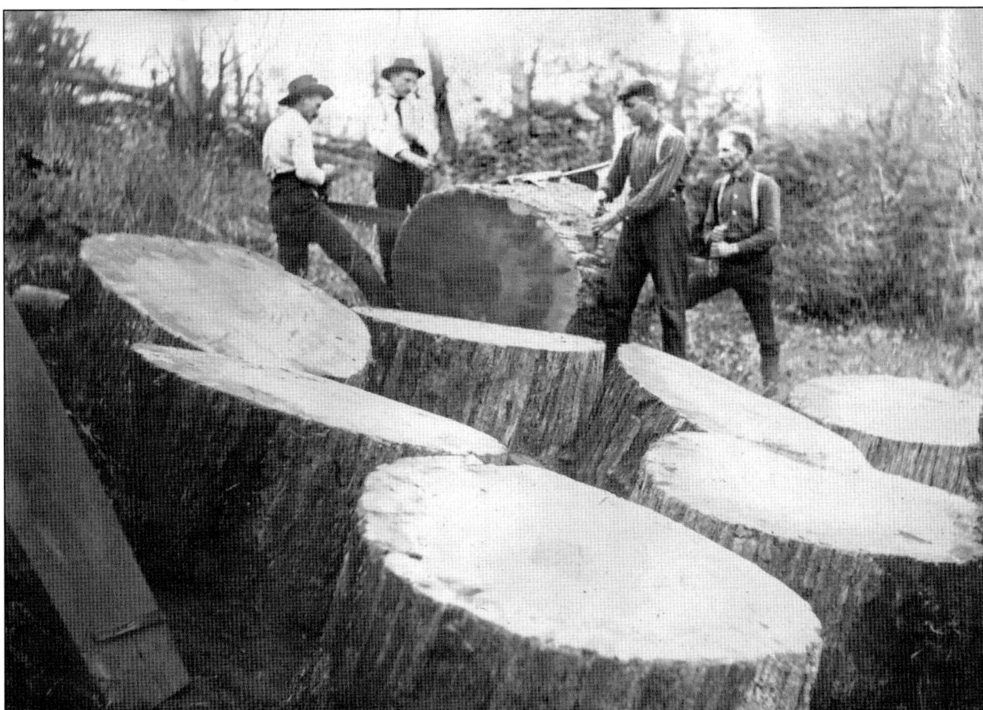

"SAWING UP THE BIG LOG." These men are sawing up "a great red oak tree girdled and killed to clear land" in an undated photograph by Frank Bicknell. Bicknell adds that the tree is to be used for firewood. (Courtesy of the North Carolina State Archives.)

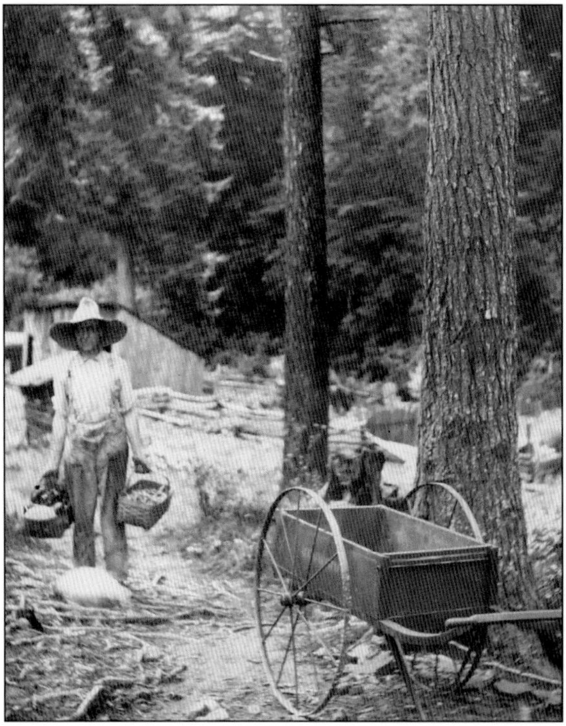

"FARMER BICKNELL." Jessie Bicknell probably took this photograph of her husband carrying the fruits of his labors. The Bicknell garden was located near the cottage above the Upper Falls. Frank Bicknell was a farming specialist with the U.S. Department of Agriculture, publishing articles and raising record-sized crops such as his giant lima beans. (Courtesy of the North Carolina State Archives.)

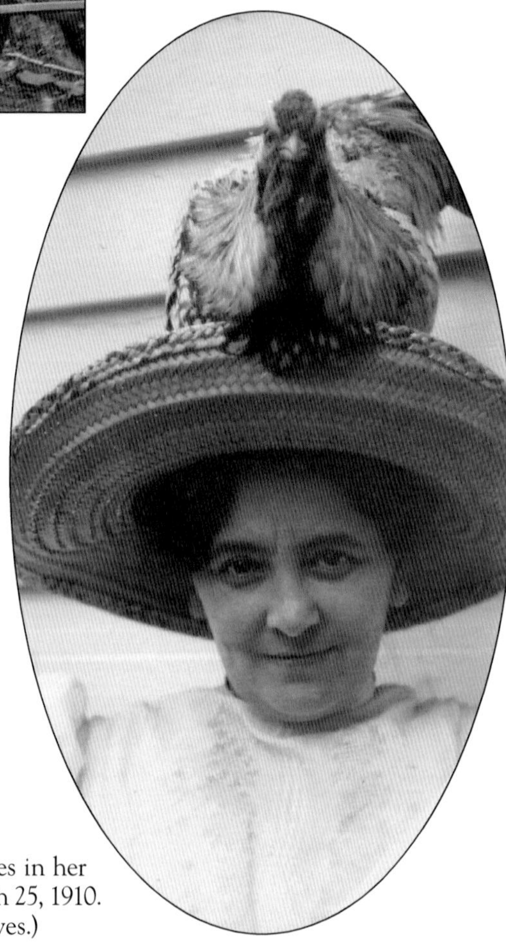

"THE CHANTICLER HAT." Jessie Bicknell poses in her feathered hat for her husband, Frank, on March 25, 1910. (Courtesy of the North Carolina State Archives.)

"Old Gus." In this undated photograph, probably taken by Jessie Bicknell, Frank poses with his rooster. (Courtesy of the North Carolina State Archives.)

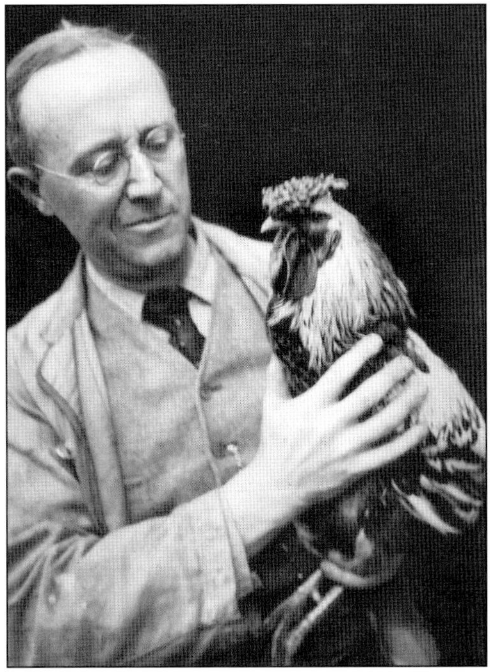

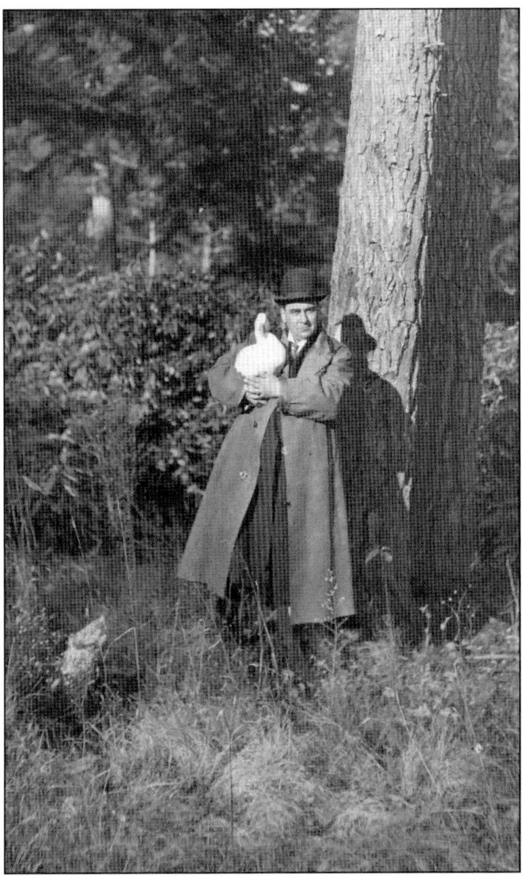

"George Vaupel and Launcelot." Fred "Fritzt" Hossfeld Sr.'s brother-in-law, George Vaupel, poses here in a derby hat with the Bicknell's pet goose. (Courtesy of the North Carolina State Archives.)

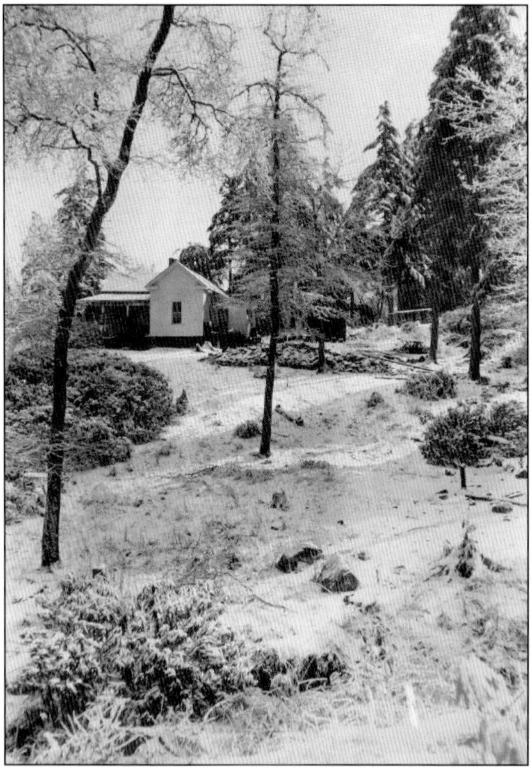

"The Cottage Amid Sleet and Snow." The Bicknell cottage was constructed by the Morganton Land Improvement Company in 1890 as a model for other chalet-style houses. It rested on a brick foundation on a small knoll overlooking the Upper Falls. (Courtesy of the North Carolina State Archives.)

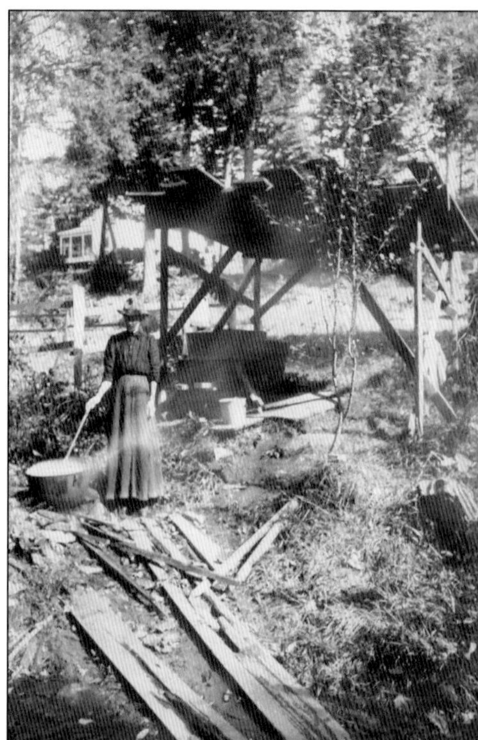

"Mrs. Pitman at Wash House." The Bicknells allowed a local woman named Pitman to operate an outdoor laundry near the cottage. Frank Bicknell's photograph is undated. (Courtesy of the North Carolina State Archives.)

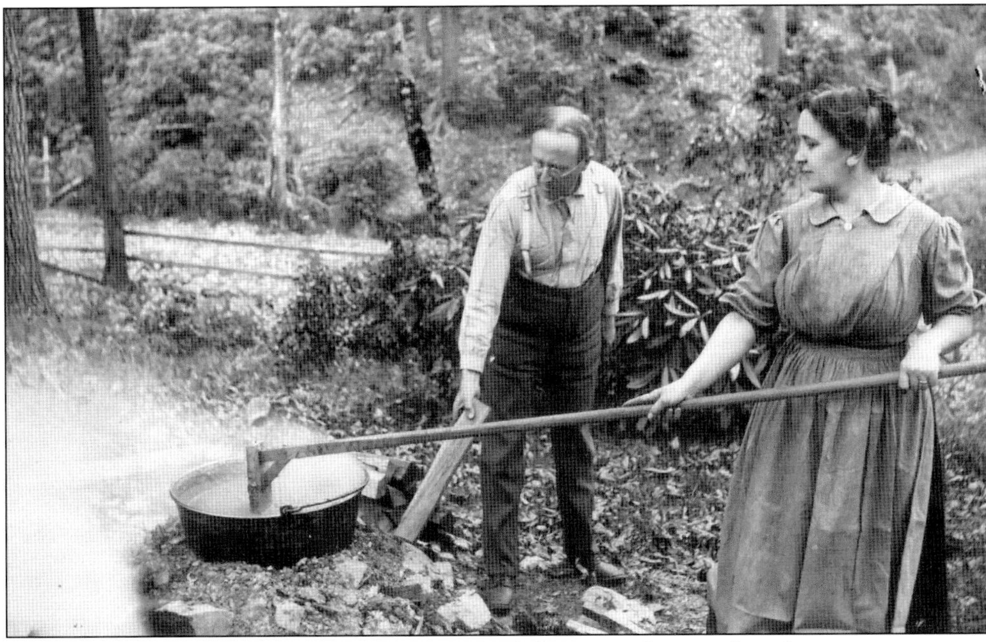

"MAKING APPLE BUTTER IN BRASS KETTLE." Apple butter–making is a lengthy process, so several hands turned up to help Jessie stir the preserve. Frank photographed the work on October 27, 1909, near the cottage at the Linville Falls. (Courtesy of the North Carolina State Archives.)

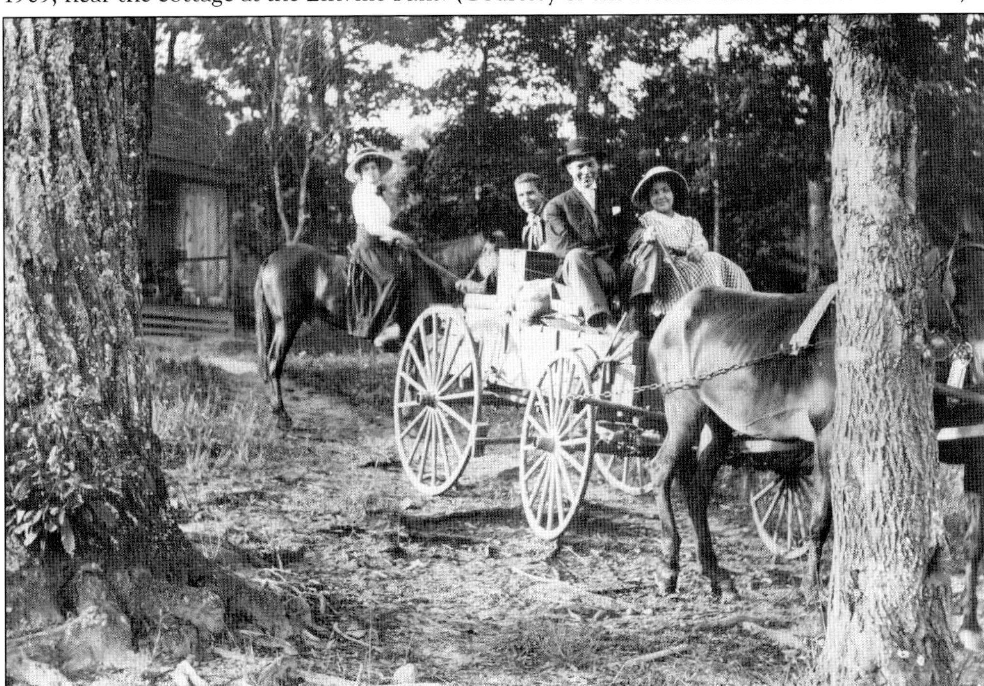

"THE HOSSFELD'S HOME." As owner, with W. C. Ervin, of the Realty Loan Guaranty Company, Fred Hossfeld Sr. lived with his family in Morganton. They would visit a summer residence in the Linville Falls area. Frank Bicknell visited the family and took this picture on August 10, 1909. (Courtesy of the North Carolina State Archives.)

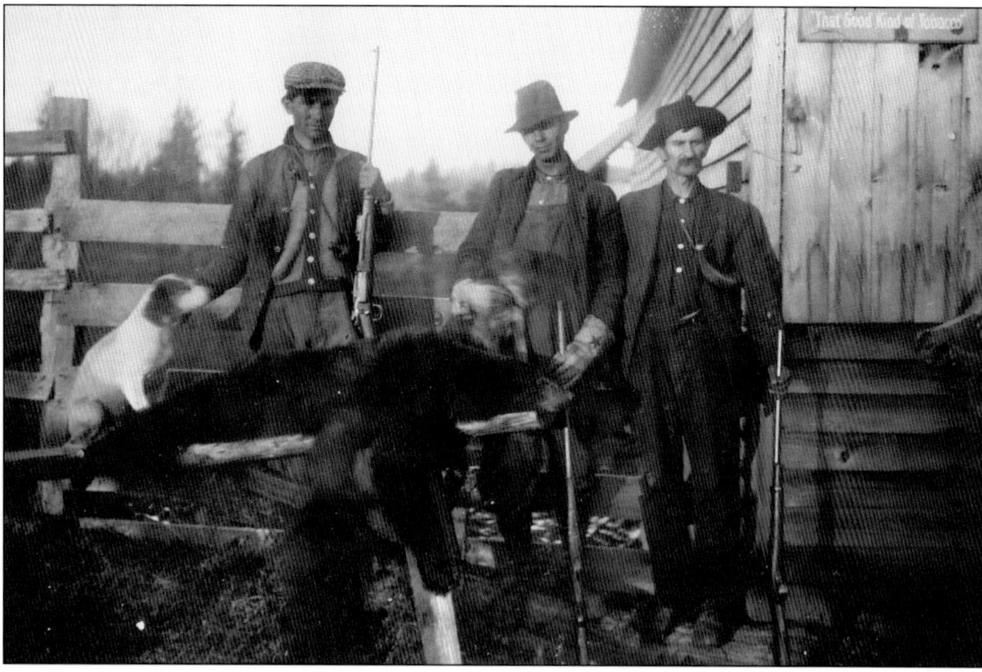

"MITCH BURLESON, ADAM WISEMAN, AND COMMODORE BURLESON." Mitch Burleson is on the left and Commodore Burleson is on the right in this picture of successful bear hunters in Linville Gorge made by Frank Bicknell on November 25, 1911. (Courtesy of the North Carolina State Archives.)

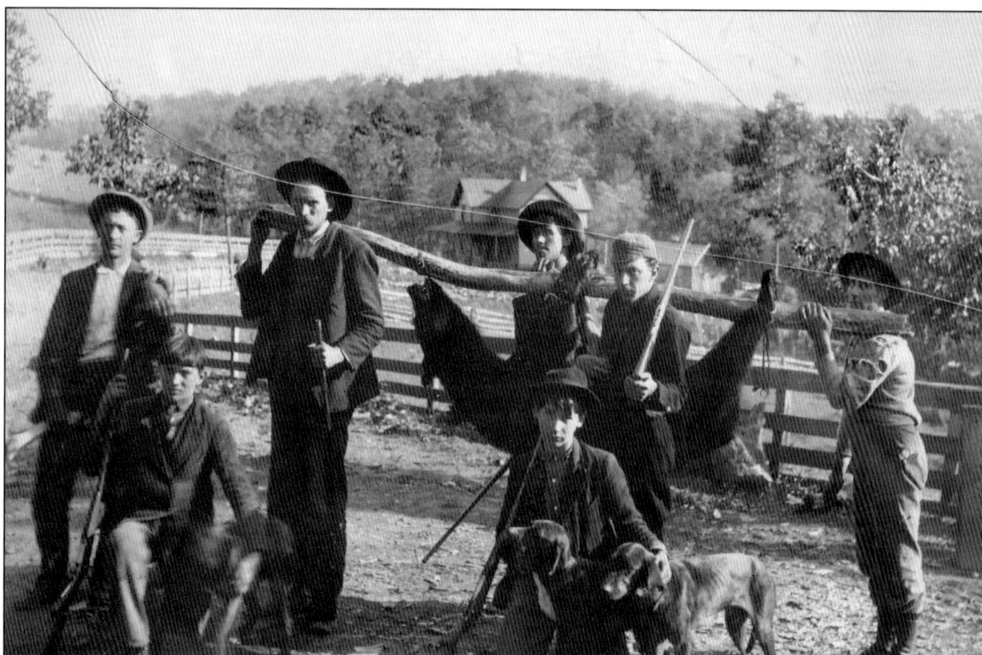

"BRINGING IN THE LARGEST BLACK BEAR." Frank Bicknell photographed these hunters and their record-sized bear on October 16, 1909, but he did not record the size or weight of the animal. (Courtesy of the North Carolina State Archives.)

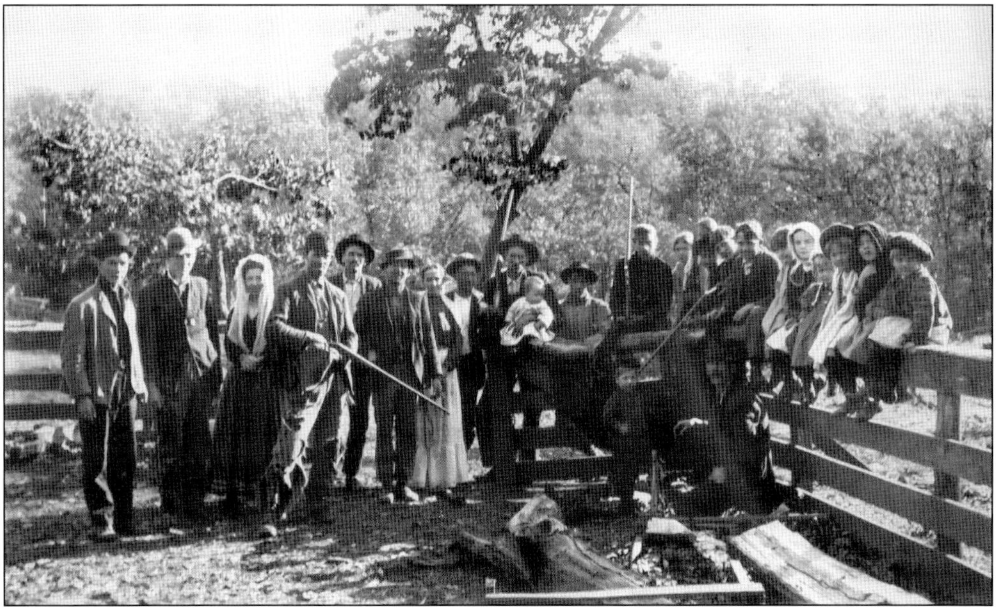

"THE ENTIRE POPULATION TURNED OUT TO SEE THE BEAR." Frank Bicknell photographed the crowd of Linville Falls villagers who turned out to see the large bear on October 16, 1909. (Courtesy of the North Carolina State Archives.)

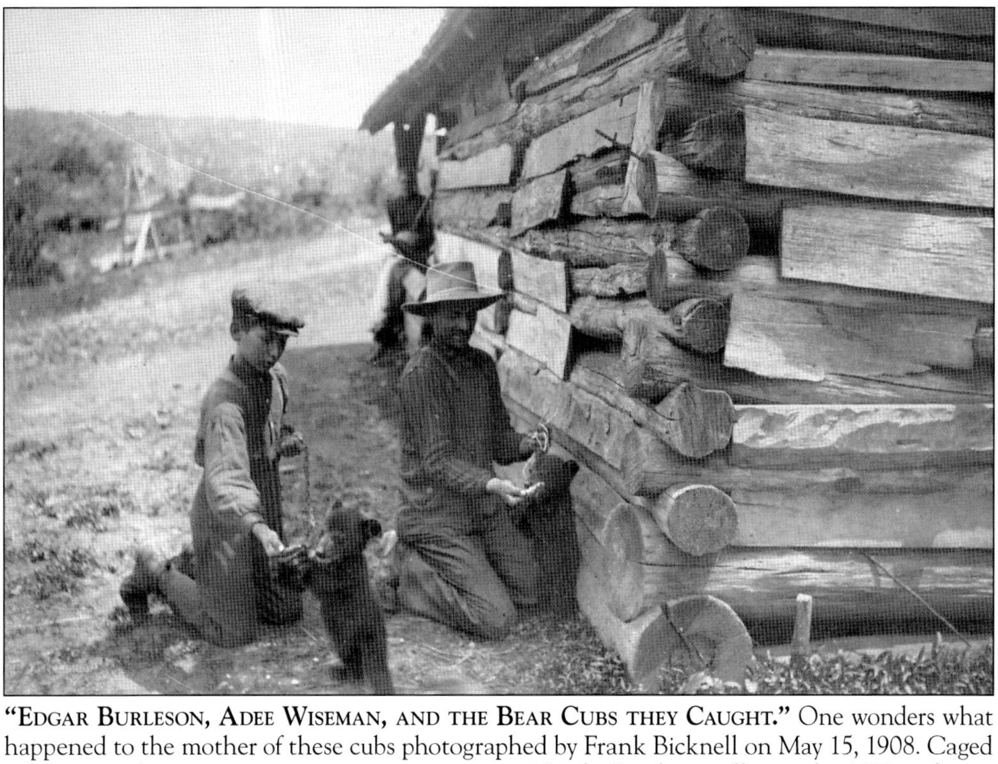

"EDGAR BURLESON, ADEE WISEMAN, AND THE BEAR CUBS THEY CAUGHT." One wonders what happened to the mother of these cubs photographed by Frank Bicknell on May 15, 1908. Caged cubs were a frequent tourist attraction in western North Carolina well into the 1970s, when a halt was put to the practice because of the inhumane living conditions suffered by the animals. (Courtesy of the North Carolina State Archives.)

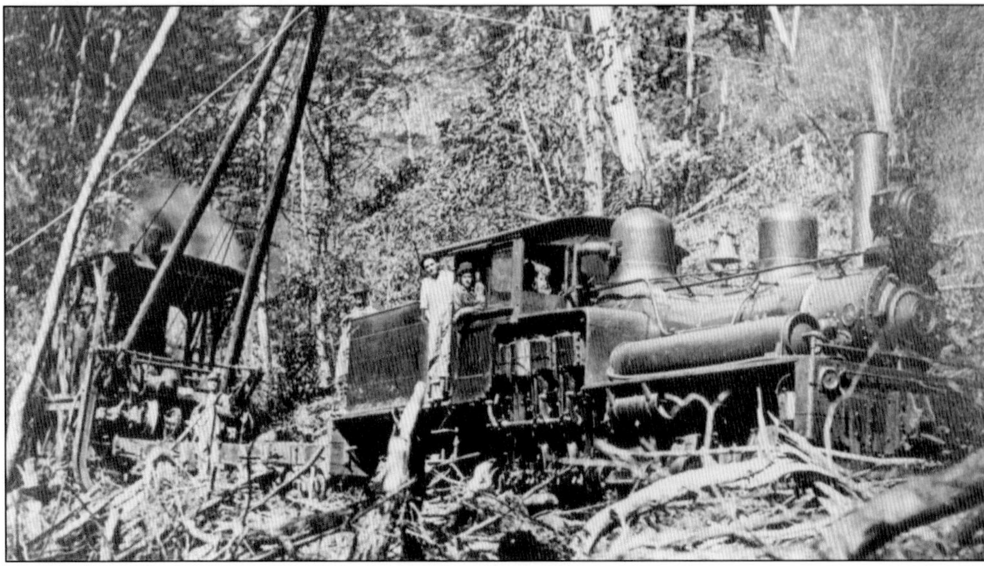

Linville River Railway Shay Engine No. One during Work. The Camp brothers of Chicago began the Linville River Railway around 1896. Later, William M. Ritter assumed control of the line for his own logging operation. Timber from the Jonas Ridge and Linville Falls areas at the head of the gorge was hauled to the mills in Pineola. Ephraim Shay invented this logging locomotive especially for difficult terrain. Built in Lima, Ohio, this engine still exists in Virginia. (Courtesy of East Tennessee State University.)

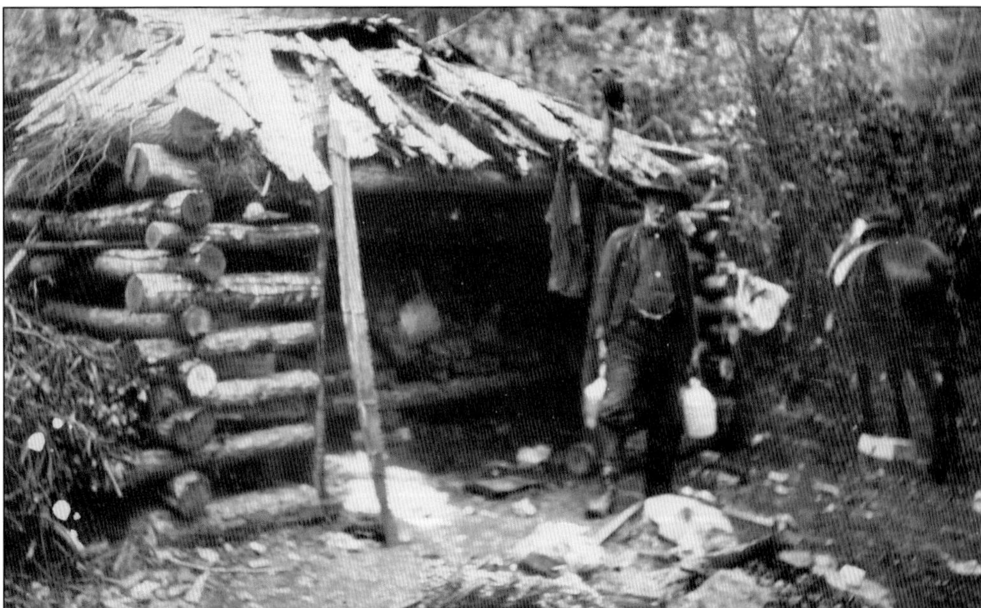

"Galax Puller's Shelter, Linville Mountain." Galax (*Galax aphylla*), with its glossy 3–4-inch-wide leaves, which turn a reddish brown in winter, is a popular floral decoration and still picked in the mountains for sale. Pickers tie the leaves off in bundles of 10, filling bags as they move through the woods in and around the Linville Gorge. J. Stokes Penland, depicted here on April 23, 1908, was proprietor of the Penland Hotel (see page 111, top image). (Courtesy of the North Carolina State Archives.)

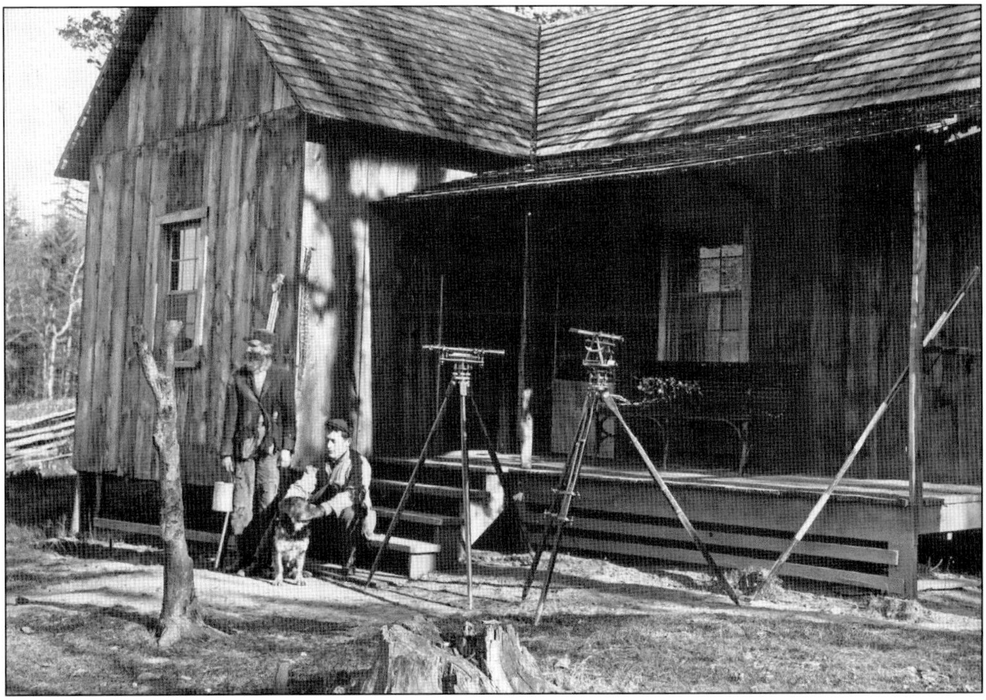

"BEN WATROUS AND HENRY HOLTCLAW AT SURVEYOR'S COTTAGE." Frank Bicknell accompanied a surveying party into the woods, probably on Linville Mountain, in October 1909. (Courtesy of the North Carolina State Archives.)

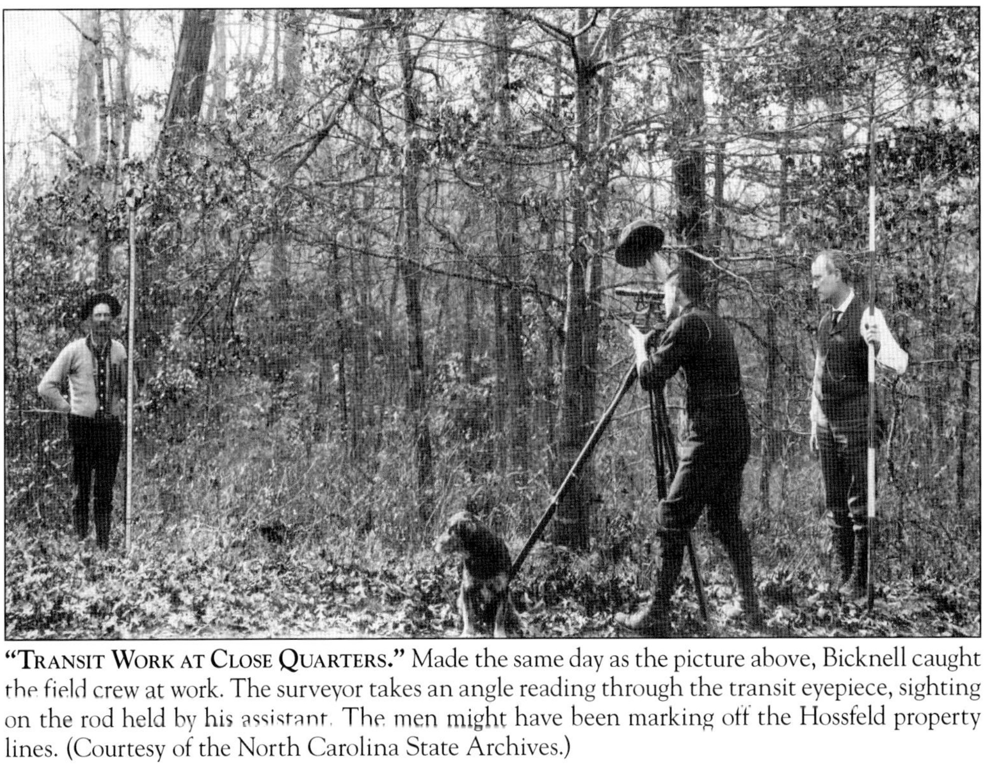

"TRANSIT WORK AT CLOSE QUARTERS." Made the same day as the picture above, Bicknell caught the field crew at work. The surveyor takes an angle reading through the transit eyepiece, sighting on the rod held by his assistant. The men might have been marking off the Hossfeld property lines. (Courtesy of the North Carolina State Archives.)

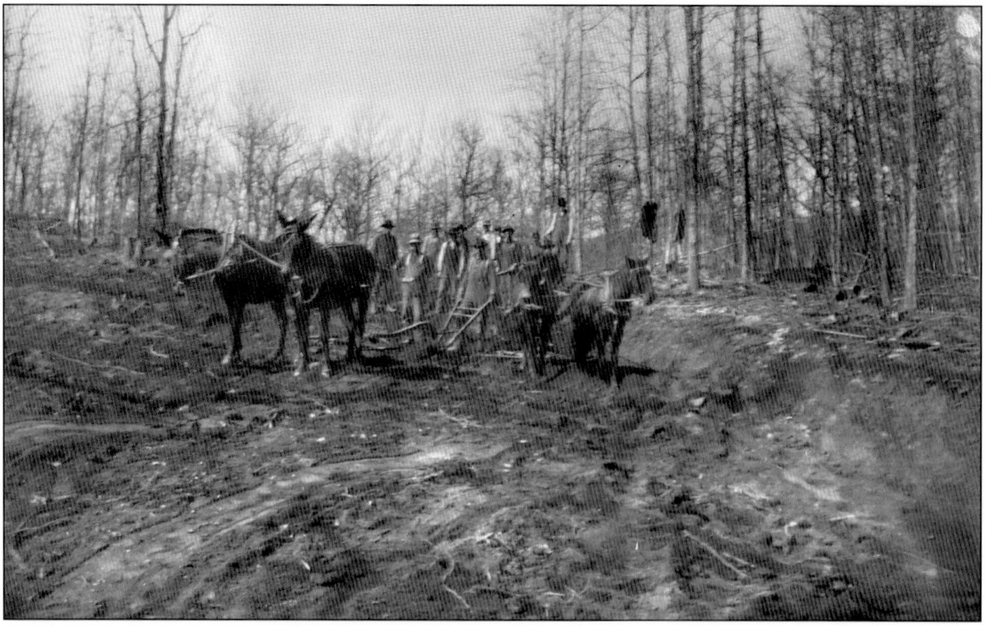

"Building Crest of the Blue Ridge Highway." Col. Joseph Hyde Pratt, head of the North Carolina Geological and Economic Survey, proposed a scenic highway to boost tourism in the state. Work began in 1913, and by the time World War I caused the project to be abandoned, a portion of the highway between Altapass and Pineola was completed. The Appalachian Highway Company was chartered by the state to construct the road from Marion, Virginia, to Tallulah Falls, Georgia. Today's parkway follows the old roadbed between mileposts 317.6 and 318.7. Bicknell visited the site on February 14, 1913. (Courtesy of the North Carolina State Archives.)

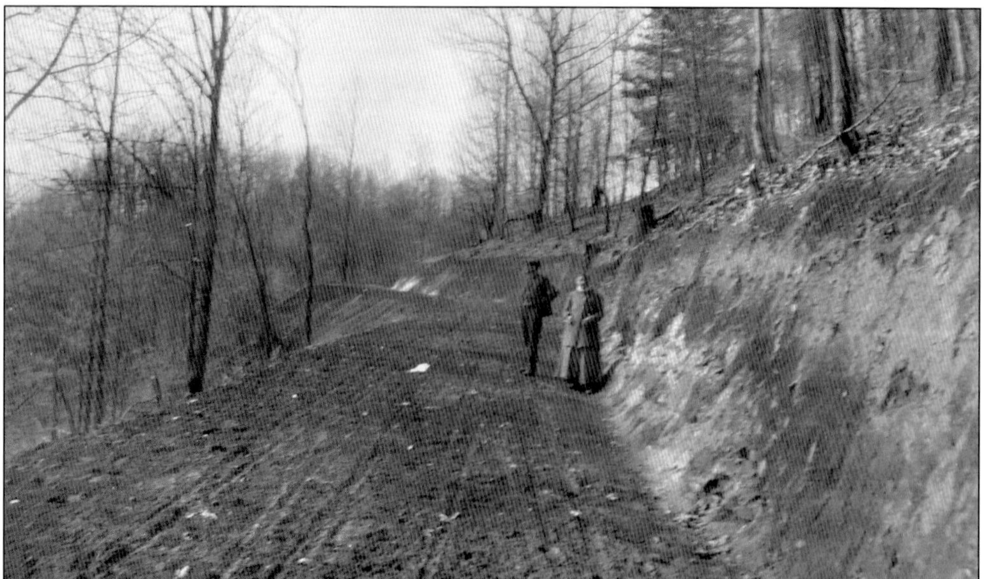

"C.B.C. and Mrs. Mace on Blue Ridge Highway." These unidentified visitors to the highway project were photographed the same day as Bicknell took the view above of the workers. Construction of today's Blue Ridge Parkway began in September 1935. (Courtesy of the North Carolina State Archives.)

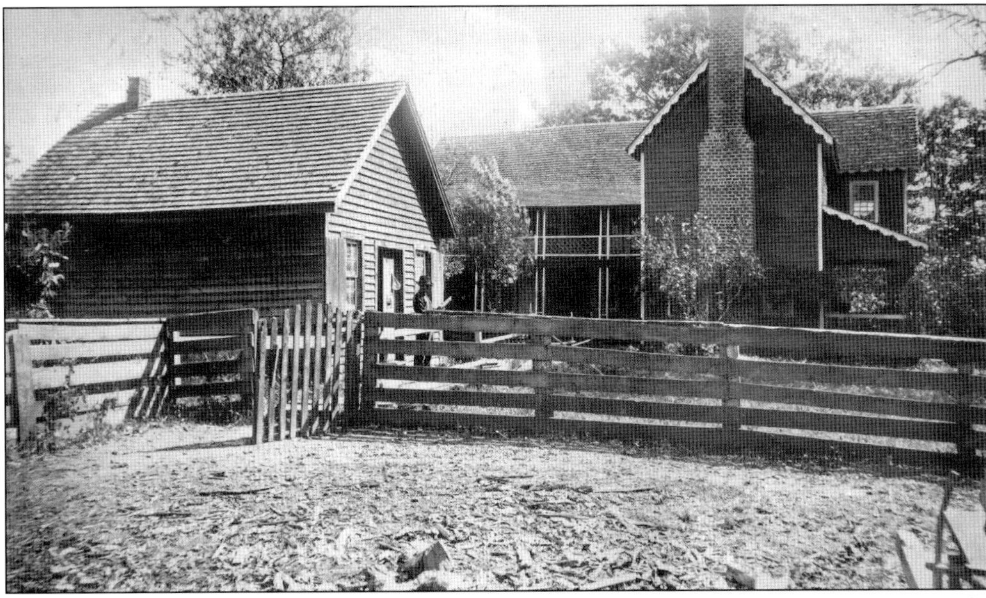

"POST OFFICE AND PENLAND'S." Built by Theodore Franklin and his brothers in the 1870s, the two-story white-framed house was bought by Stokes Penland when Theodore's wife died and was run as a highly successful boardinghouse for Linville Falls and Linville Gorge visitors. Called the Penland Hotel and Boardinghouse, it offered eight rooms and had a well rope and bucket running from the second-story porch through the first floor into the well for the convenience of guests on both floors. The structure beside it is Linville Falls's first post office building. Bicknell visited in 1910. Both structures still stand and are being renovated. (Courtesy of the North Carolina State Archives.)

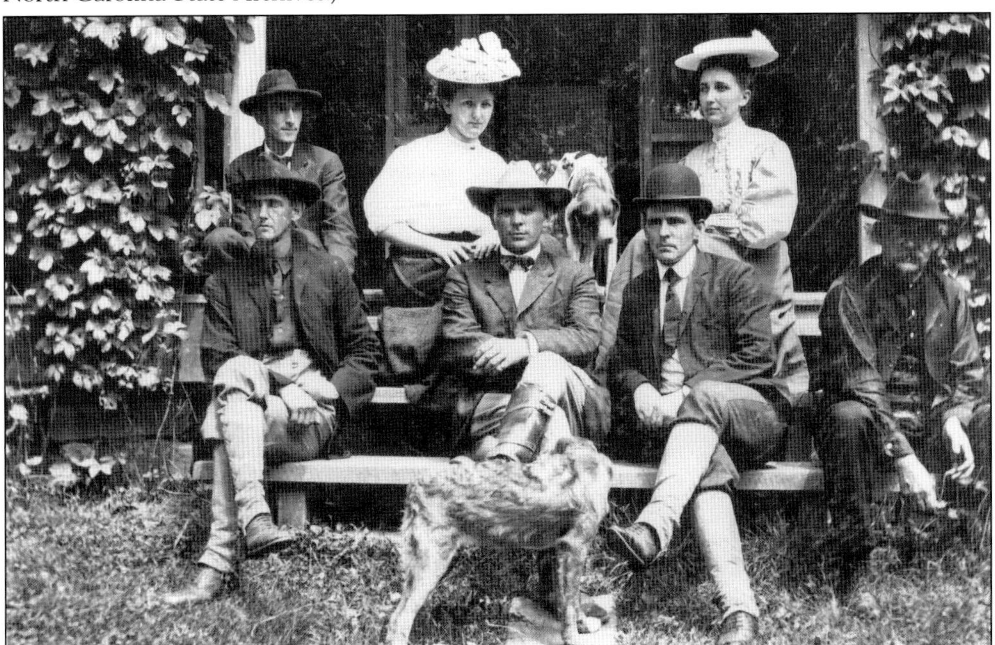

"PARTY AT PENLAND HOTEL." William Cary Hattan visited the Penland Hotel and photographed this party of tourists sitting on the front steps. (Courtesy of East Tennessee State University.)

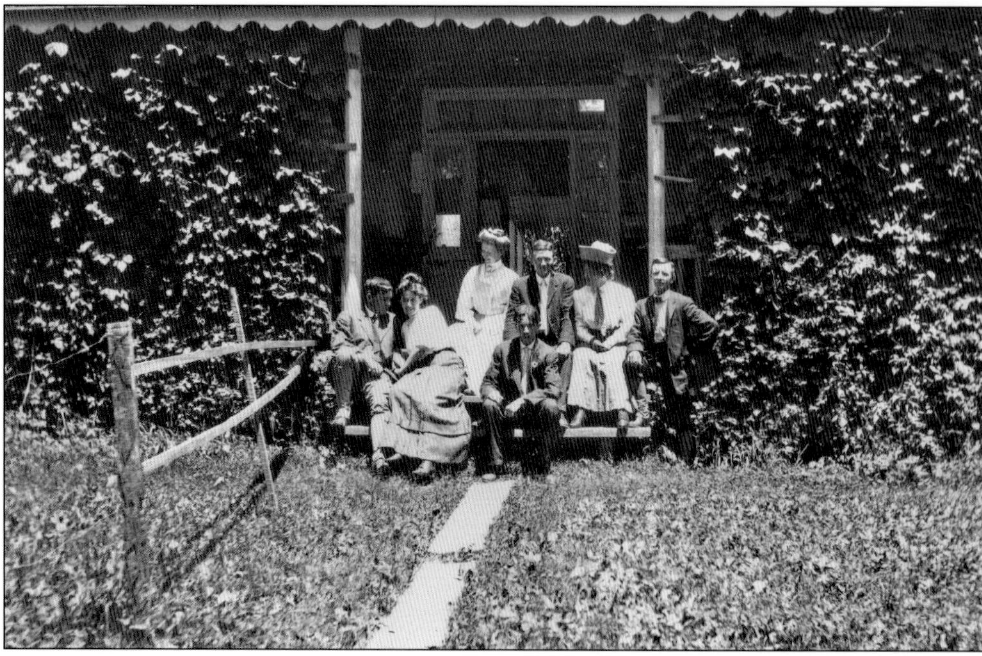

"HOTEL LINVILLE FALLS." Clinchfield Railroad chief engineer William Hattan took this group portrait of Linville Falls visitors in 1906. Though he titled the shot "Hotel Linville Falls," the building is the Penland Hotel. (Courtesy of East Tennessee State University.)

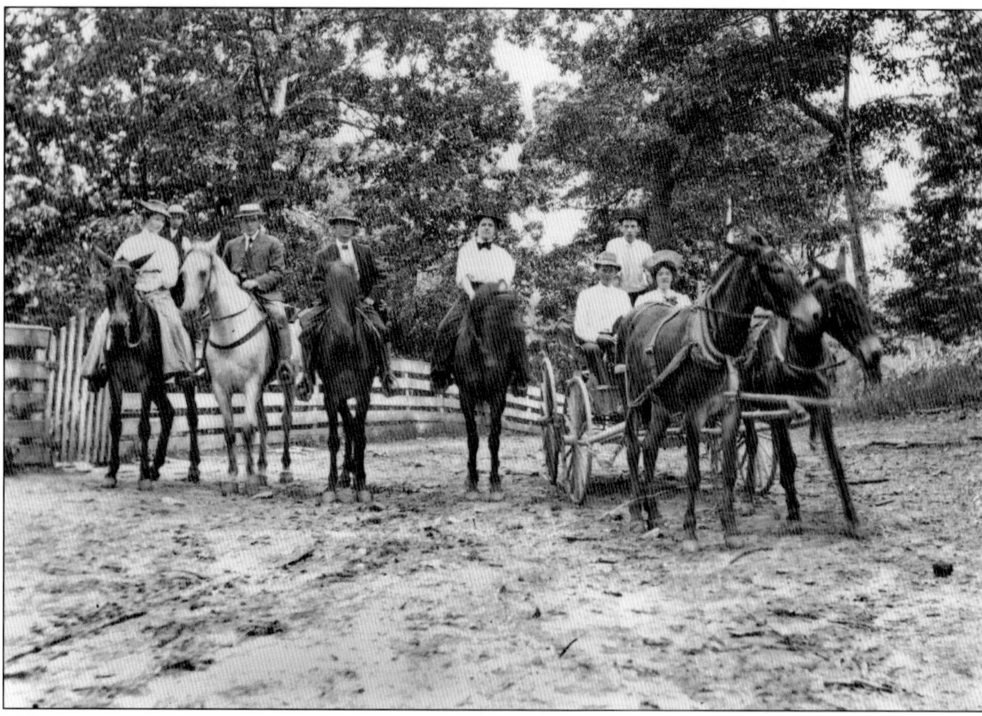

"TRIP TO LINVILLE FALLS, 1908." This sightseeing party, photographed by Hattan, poses in the road (Highway 183) in front of the Penland House. On the left, a woman and boy share a horse. (Courtesy of East Tennessee State University.)

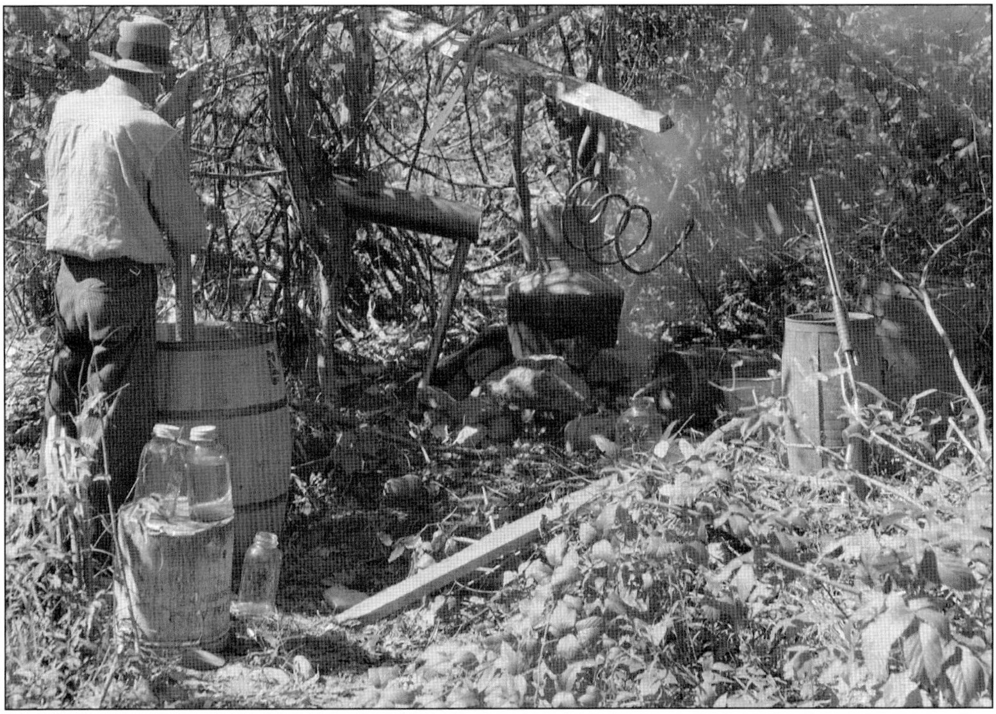

Moonshiners at Work. Bayard Wootten, Rufus Morgan's daughter, naturally kept this location a secret. It could very well represent an illicit distillery in Linville Gorge, for many locals are reputed to have operated there, and pieces of equipment still turn up in the area, including metal drums and copper pipe for example. Concealment and clear running water were of prime importance to moonshiners. (Courtesy of the North Carolina Collection, Wilson Library, University of North Carolina at Chapel Hill.)

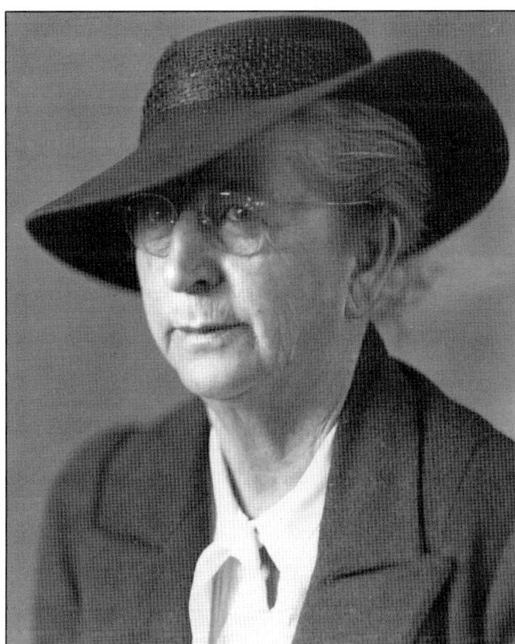

Bayard Wootten. This portrait of Bayard Wootten in a hat and peak-lapel jacket was made in the 1950s. Like her father, Wootten took scenic photographs of the Linville Gorge. (Courtesy of the North Carolina Collection, Wilson Library, University of North Carolina at Chapel Hill.)

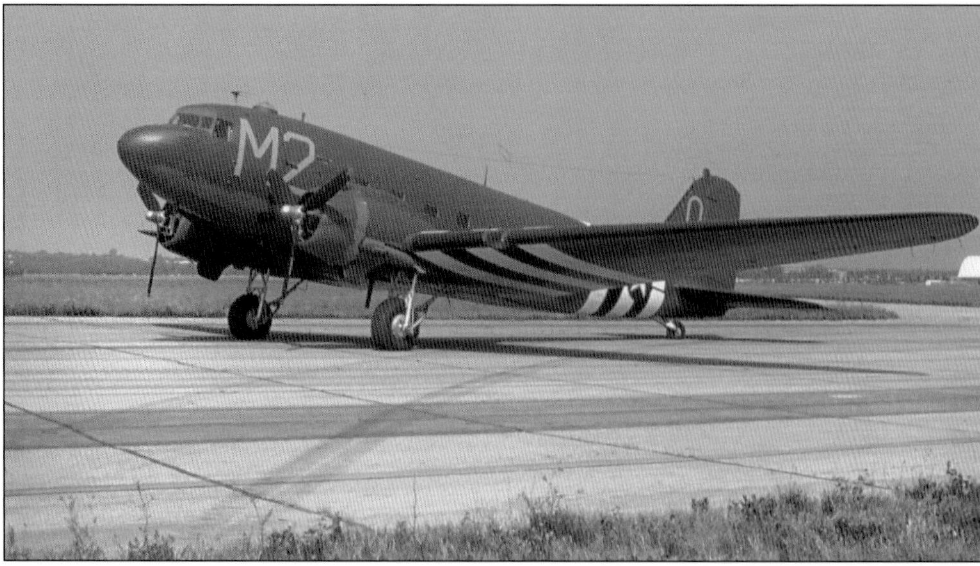

Douglas C-47D "Skytrain." On May 15, 1943, a foggy afternoon, a C-47D like the one shown here crashed into Gingercake Mountain on Jonas Ridge, killing all 18 airmen aboard. The impact sheared the wings off the plane, hurling the two engines far up the slope. The men were recent graduates of the army glider pilot training at Maxton air base and were en route to Cincinnati, Ohio, on leave before participating in the D-day invasion of Europe. After removing the remains of 17 of the men, the army sealed off the area and blew up the engines. (Courtesy of the U.S. Air Force Museum.)

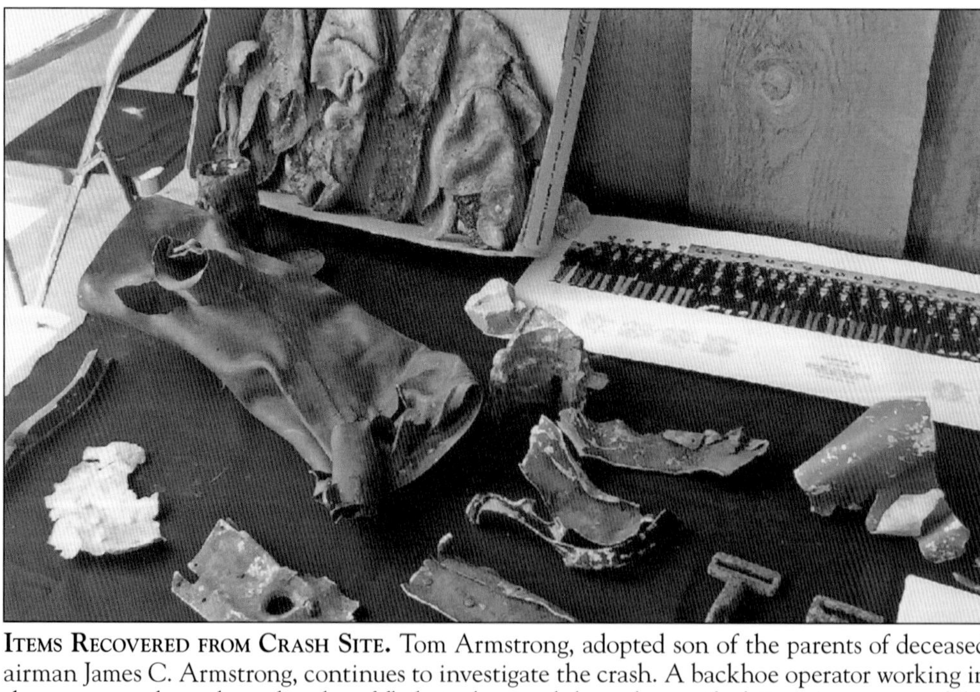

Items Recovered from Crash Site. Tom Armstrong, adopted son of the parents of deceased airman James C. Armstrong, continues to investigate the crash. A backhoe operator working in the area turned up a buried cache of flight jackets and shoes; he notified Tom Armstrong of the discovery. In the display here, the shoes can be seen with a graduation photograph of the glider pilots and some engine parts. (Courtesy of the Friends of Linville Gorge.)

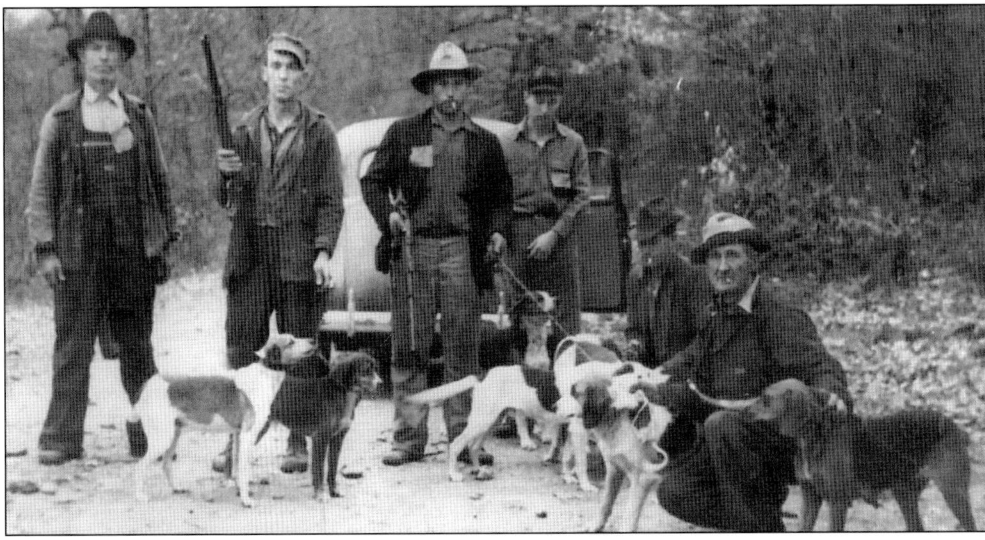

Boe Franklin. The first person on the scene of the crash was Boe Franklin, who lived in a shack about 200 yards from the site. Franklin said he heard the plane hit the rock then a second explosion as the nearly full gas tank exploded. Franklin also said the intense heat kept him from approaching the burning wreckage, but local LeRoi Rose, a child at the time, recalls seeing Boe dousing the bodies with water. The elevation at the crash site is 3,615 feet, and the U.S. Army Aircraft Clearance form recommends flying at an altitude of 3,500 feet. Boe Franklin squats to the right in this undated photograph of hunters. In his youth, he had accompanied the Bicknells on Linville Gorge outings. (Courtesy of LeRoi Rose.)

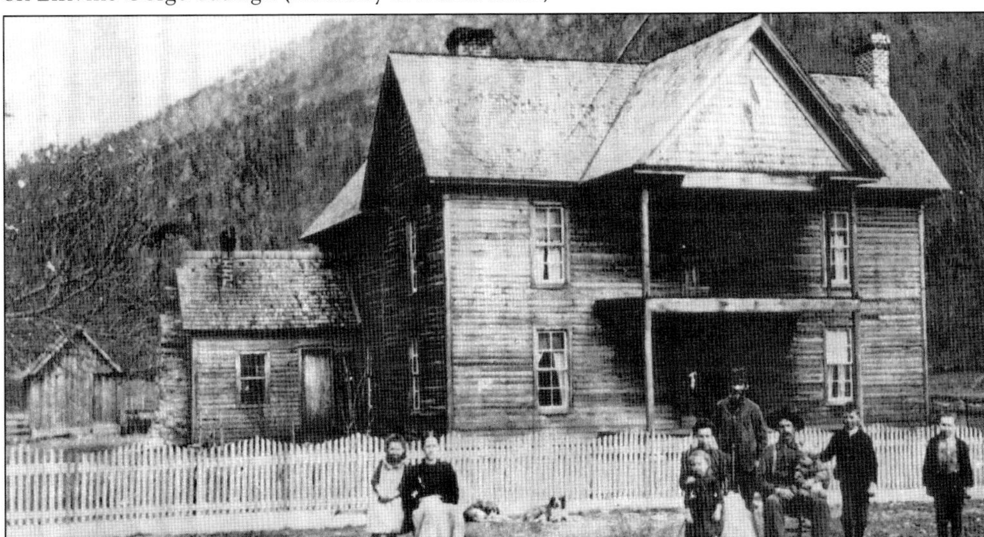

Alexander House Pre-1916. The Alexander family stands in front of the farmhouse completed by Thomas William Alexander in 1901. Of the fourth generation of Alexanders, Thomas married a young widow named Anna England Hunter in 1892. The couple lived in an old log house until Anna told Thomas that if he wanted any more children (they had four) he would just have to build her a bigger house. Shortoff Mountain, in the background, appears to be forested on its southern end, where now sheer rock cliffs stand. Has a major landslide altered the face of the rock? The question continues to be debated among Burke County residents. (Courtesy of Forest Dula.)

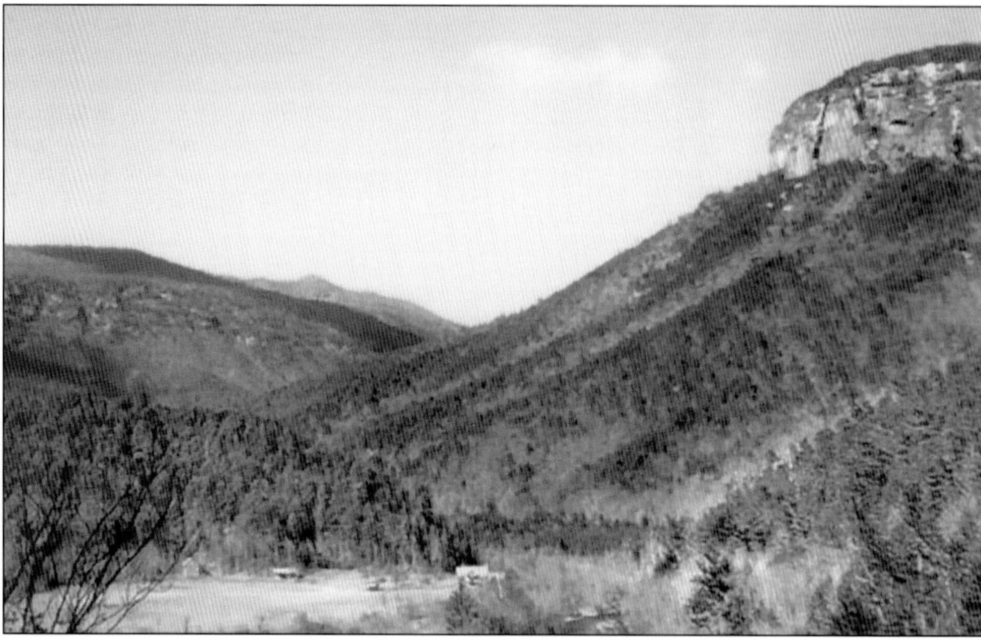

Alexander House in 1952. This picture made in 1952 shows the old farmstead to the left of the Linville River. For years, the place was a shelter for hikers and hunters heading north into the Linville Gorge. According to Carl Fleming, the old house burned down around 1962. (Courtesy of Carl Fleming.)

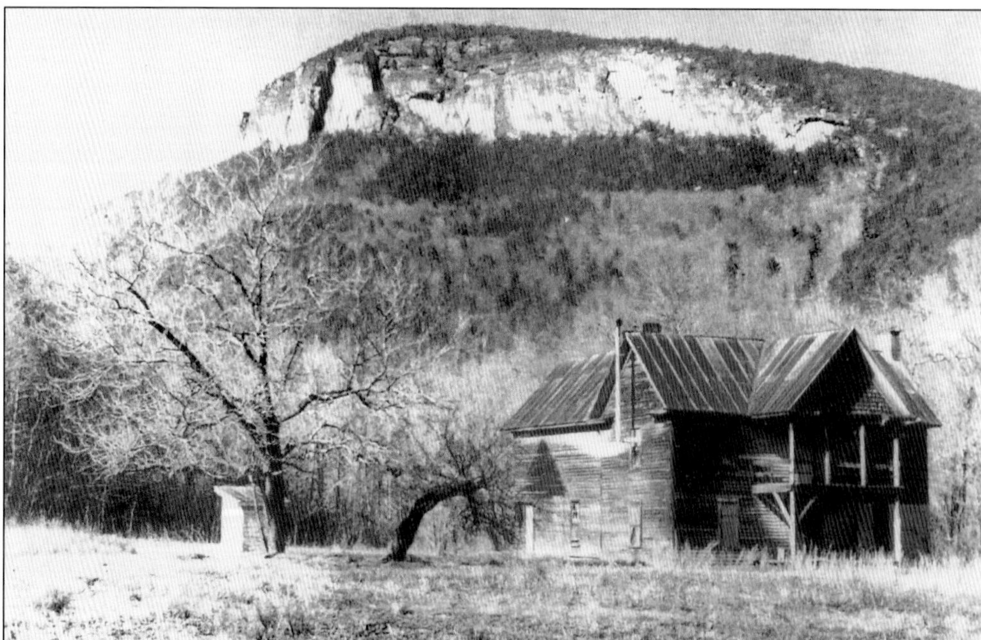

Alexander House in 1960s. Abandoned to the elements, the old house served as a hunting lodge in its final years, until it was accidentally destroyed by fire. Today the land is a 218-acre private hunting preserve whose northern edge borders the southern end of the Linville Gorge Wilderness Area. (Courtesy of C. Lewis Paschall.)

"Pine Gap, Mountain Road." For untold centuries, this path across the top of Linville Mountains served to bring Native Americans and later settlers into the Blue Ridge and the Linville Falls area. Drovers herded cattle up and down the track for summer pasturing. Today the road is the Kistler Memorial Highway. Frank Bicknell visited on May 21, 1908, near the Pine Gap Trail head. (Courtesy of the North Carolina State Archives.)

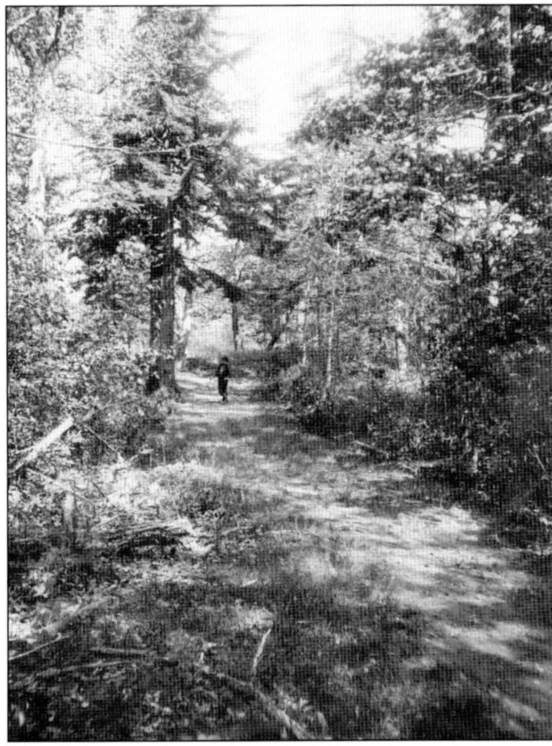

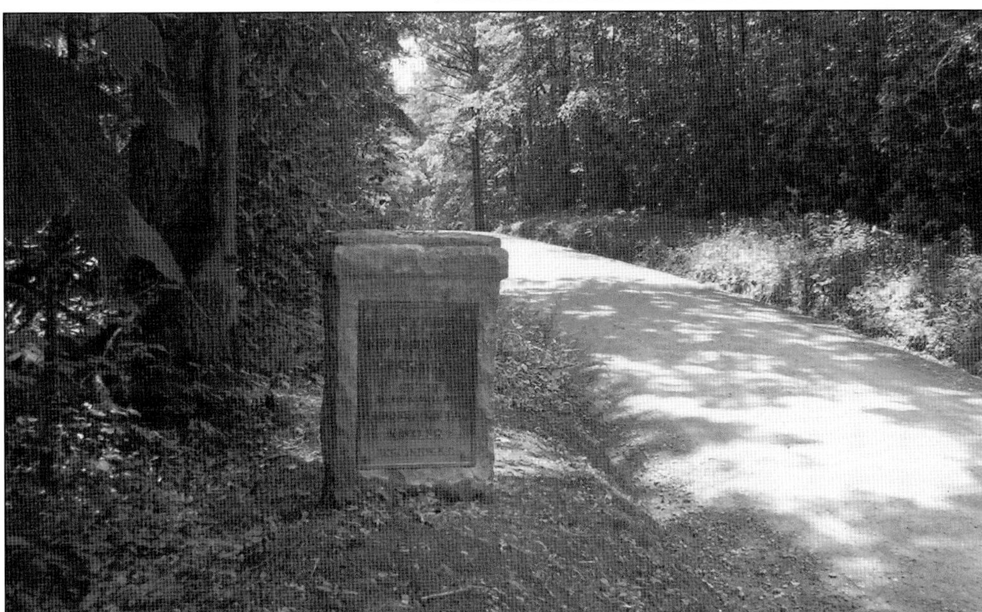

Kistler Memorial Highway. Periodically voices call for the paving of this bumpy dirt road with the grand name, but the project remains on hold. In June 2005, the 15-mile highway became part of North Carolina Scenic Byway 49, which is also called the "Pisgah Loop," running from and back to Morganton, North Carolina. The Kistler Highway connects Linville Falls to Lake James, passing six trails and the popular Wiseman's View overlook on the west side of the Linville Gorge. (Courtesy of the Friends of Linville Gorge.)

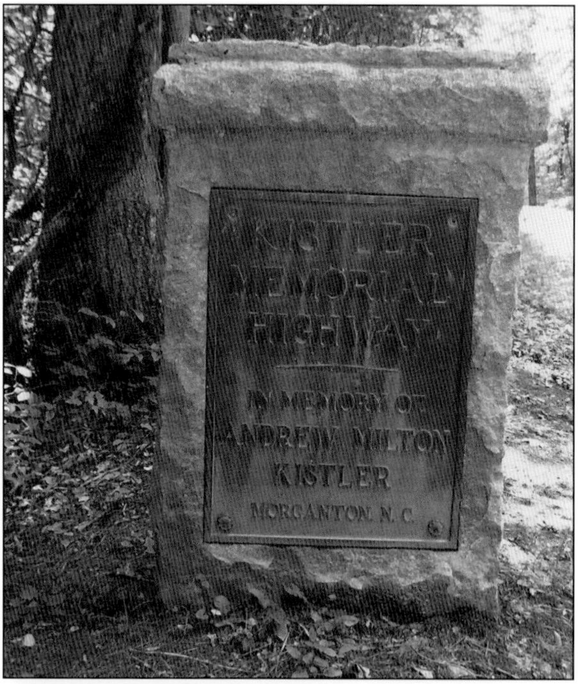

ANDREW M. KISTLER MONUMENT. Andrew M. Kistler came from a family of Pennsylvania tanners to Morganton after 1900 to promote industry and roads in Burke County. (Courtesy of the Friends of Linville Gorge.)

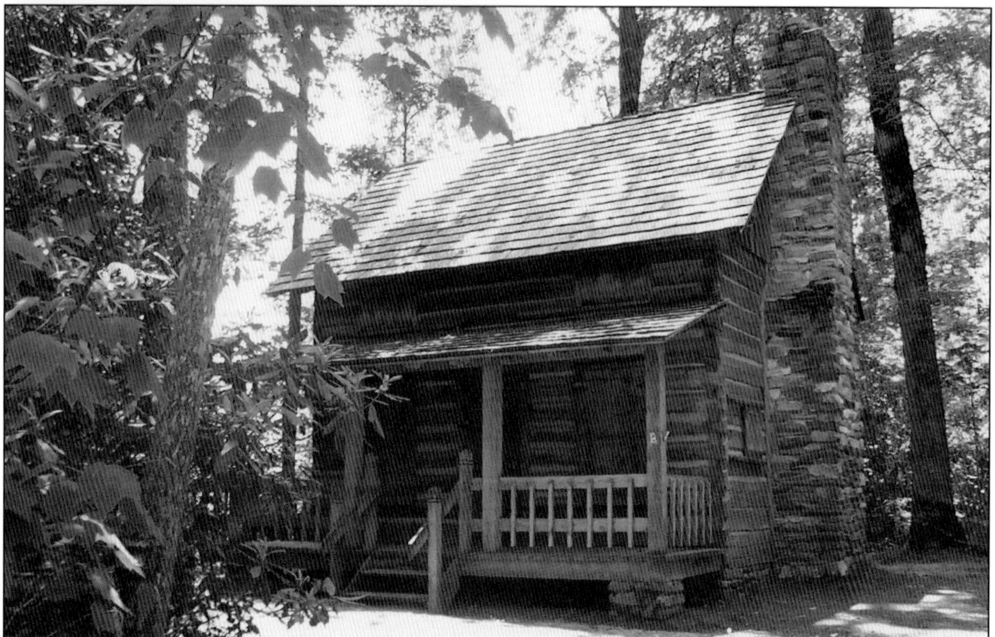

U.S. FOREST SERVICE INFORMATION CABIN. Located on the Kistler Memorial Highway, a quarter of a mile off Highway 183, the cabin is a source of maps, camping permits, and the droll wit of Hansel Singletary, a former service host. Built in 1983 by a log cabin–building class of college women under the direction of Don Chapman, the structure has hemlock interior, oak flooring, and the traditional shake roof. Assisted by members of a senior volunteers program and U.S. Forest Service workers, the women spent all summer on the project, camping at the work site. (Courtesy of the Friends of Linville Gorge.)

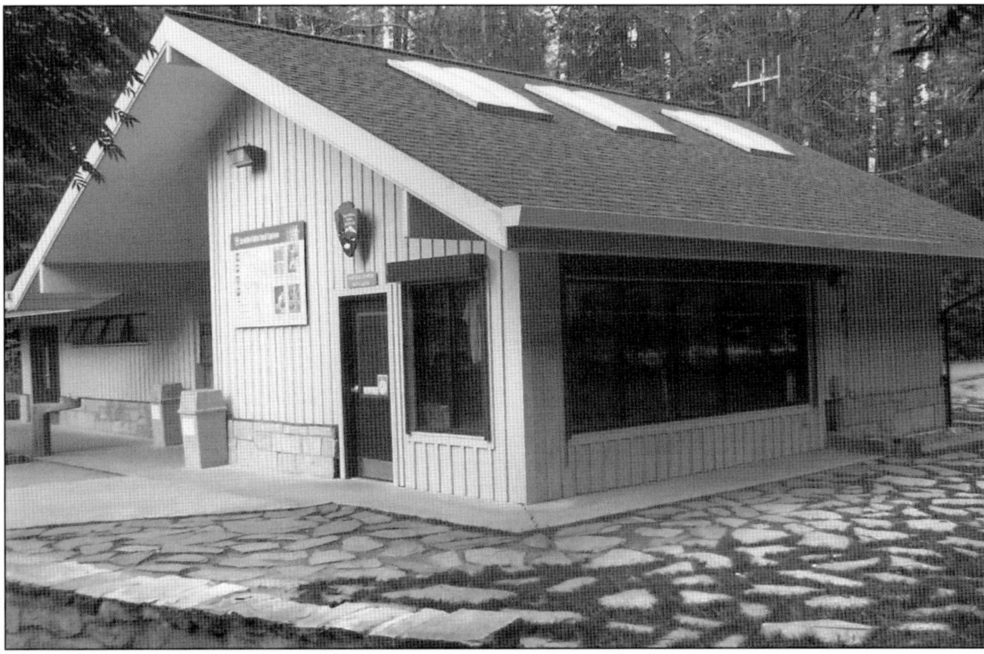

LINVILLE FALLS VISITOR CENTER. After the damage done by Hurricane Frances to the visitor center in 2005, the structure was restored and enlarged. Park service personnel and a staff of volunteers run a small shop and answer questions about the Linville Falls area here. (Courtesy of the Friends of Linville Gorge.)

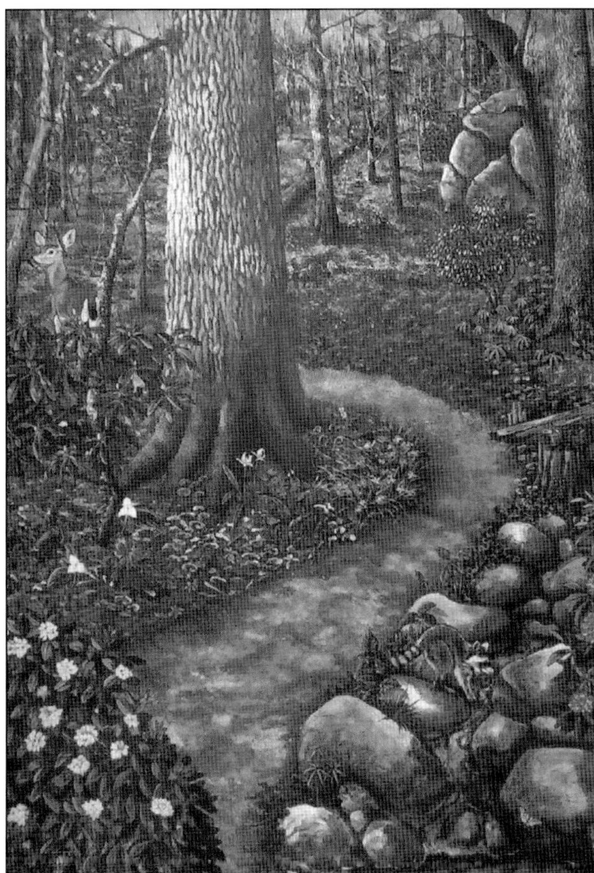

LINVILLE FALLS MURAL. Charlotte, North Carolina artist David Williams of the company Wingin It Works created this colorful mural in the visitor center. Titled *A Scene of the Forest in Spring*, it features 37 hidden animals on a typical spring day near the Linville Gorge. (Courtesy of the Friends of Linville Gorge.)

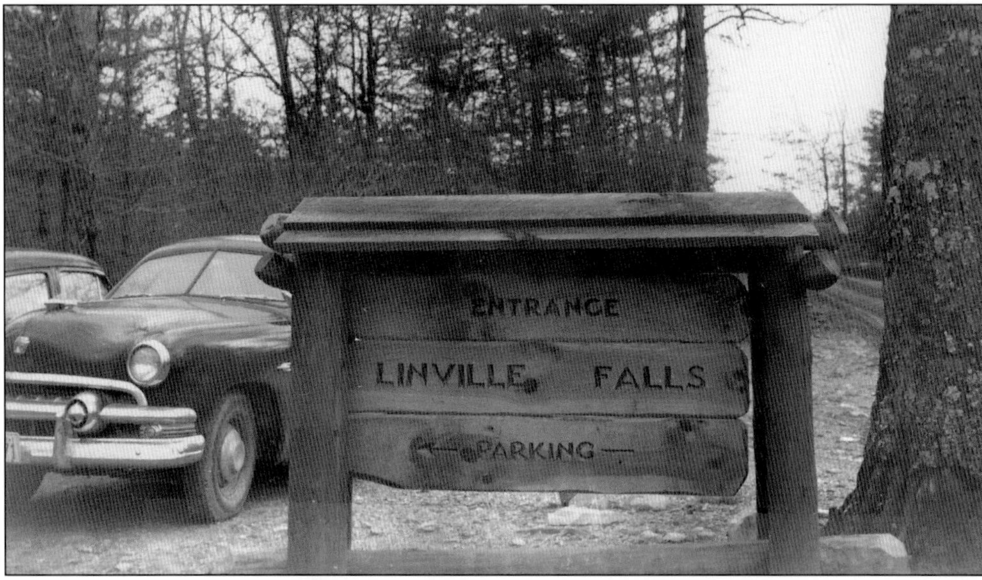

"Existing Entrance Sign [To Falls]." Park service supervisory landscape architect Edward H. Abbuehl documented the entrance sign to the Linville Falls when it had been a commercial attraction owned and managed by the Hossfelds. Abbuehl visited in February 1952. (Courtesy of the Blue Ridge Parkway Archives.)

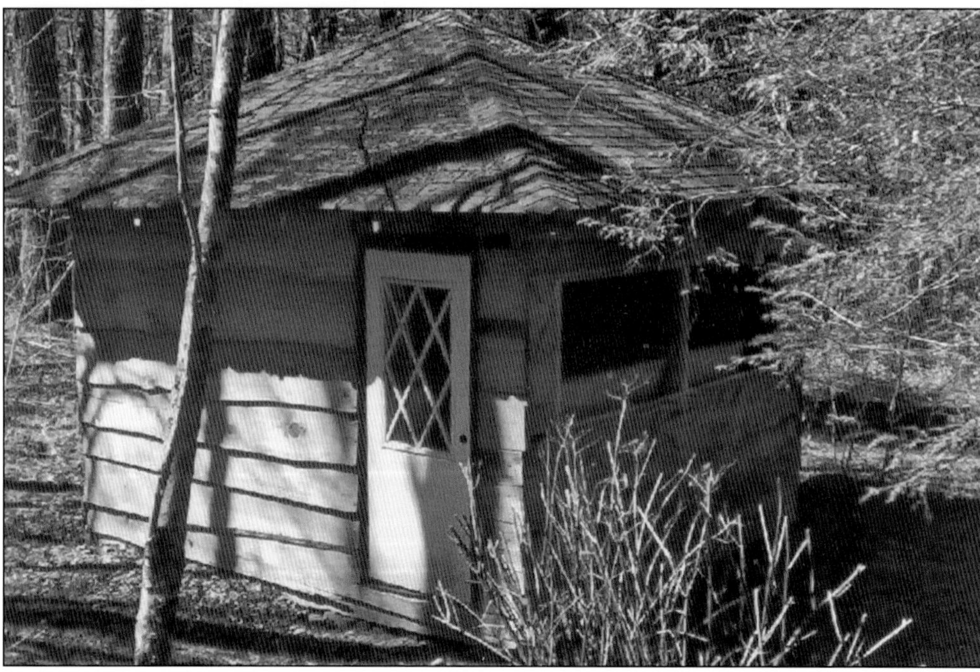

"The Old Ticket Booth." Still standing on private property near the U.S. Forest Service parking lot on the Kistler Memorial Highway, this 12-foot-by-12-foot shed served as a ticket booth and concession stand for visitors to the Linville Falls before the National Park Service acquired it for the people. Refreshments and cheap souvenirs were sold here. The sturdy window shutters could be lowered to serve as countertops. The floorboards are up to 18 inches in width and are an inch thick. Tickets to see the Great Falls probably cost 25¢. (Courtesy of the Friends of Linville Gorge.)

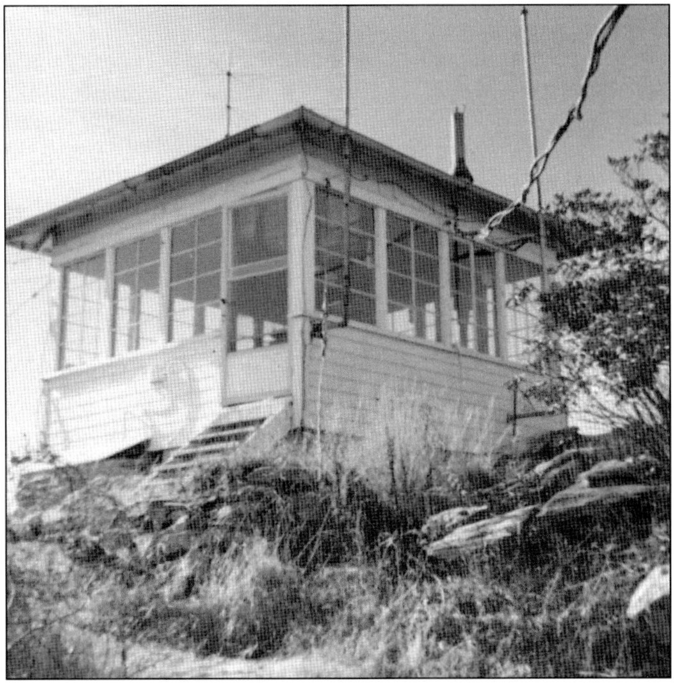

"TABLE ROCK FIRE TOWER." Located at the northernmost tip of Table Rock Mountain and active from the 1940s to the 1960s, the tower was staffed during forest fire season by a U.S. Forest Service spotter. The spotter was in radio contact with other towers, such as one on nearby Chestnut Mountain, and with district headquarters. Water was obtained from an open-sided barrel that could be lowered along a cable from the summit to a spring near the base, filled with water, then cranked back up. (Courtesy of the U.S. Forest Service, Grandfather Ranger District.)

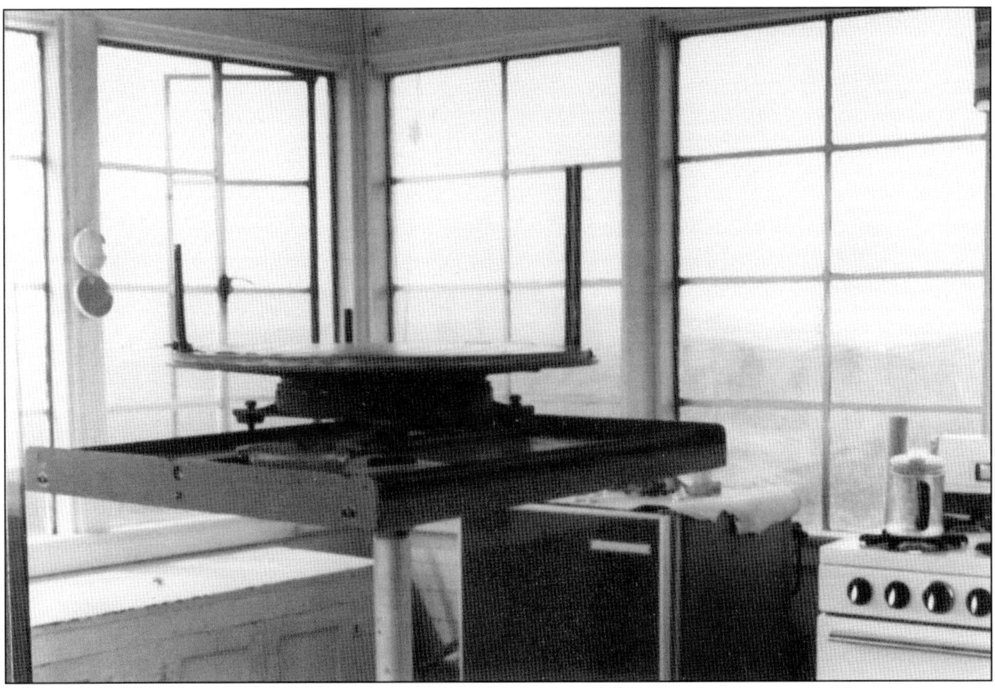

OSBORNE FIRE FINDER. William Osborne, a U.S. Forest Service employee, invented this device in 1920 to enable fire lookouts to take directional bearings on wildfires. Positioned over a topographical map oriented to the area, the spotter uses two sighting apertures, which slide freely around the rim, and points them at the smoke to determine the fire's direction. Other spotters in towers do the same thing. All the bearings are then used to pinpoint the fire's exact location. (Courtesy of the U.S. Forest Service, Grandfather Ranger District.)

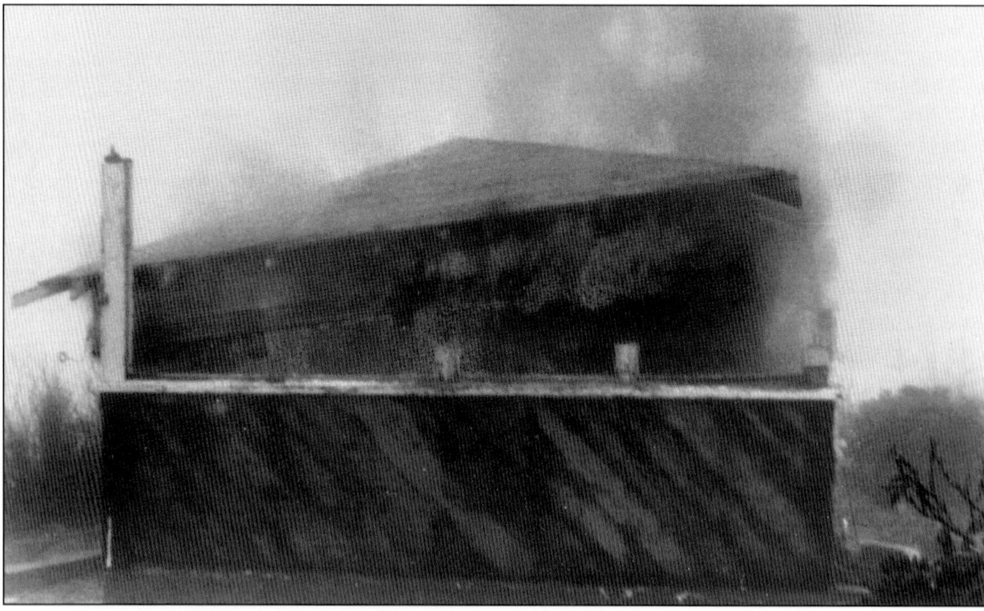

Table Rock Fire Tower in Flames. Fire towers gradually became obsolete in the Pisgah National Forest. This one was burned as a training exercise by members of the U.S. military sometime in the 1980s. Today all that remains are part of the foundation and a massive iron pin, which was once used to anchor the tower in powerful winds on Table Rock Mountain. (Courtesy of the U.S. Forest Service, Grandfather Ranger District.)

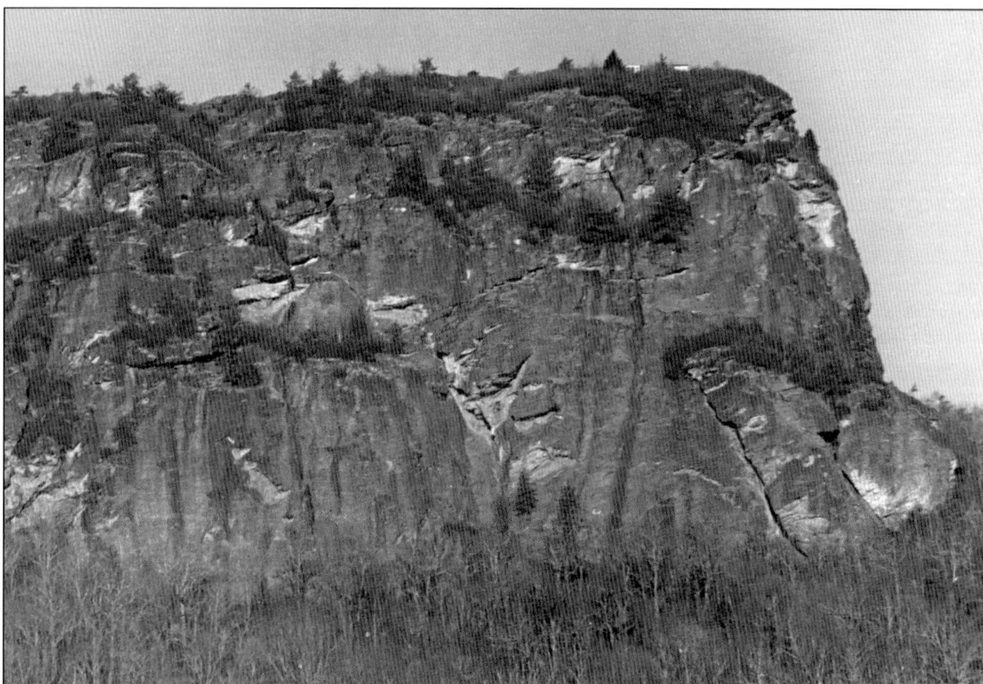

Forest Service Buildings. This 1970s photograph of Table Rock Mountain taken from the south shows the location of the U.S. Forest Service fire tower and a small shed behind it before the structures were removed. (Courtesy of Mike Fischesser.)

First Ascent of Bumblebee Buttress. Climbers Bob Mitchell and Bob Gillespie made the first ascent of this cliff on the North Carolina Wall (on the east side of Linville Gorge, below the Chimneys) in 1970. They encountered a mountain laurel in bloom covered with bees—hence the name. Bob Gillespie is seen here. Rock climbing in the Linville Gorge was still fairly new then, especially in this particular area. (Courtesy of Mike Fischesser.)

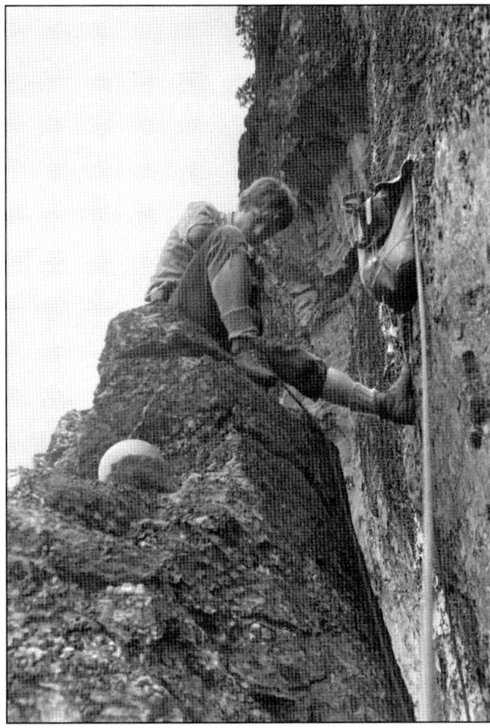

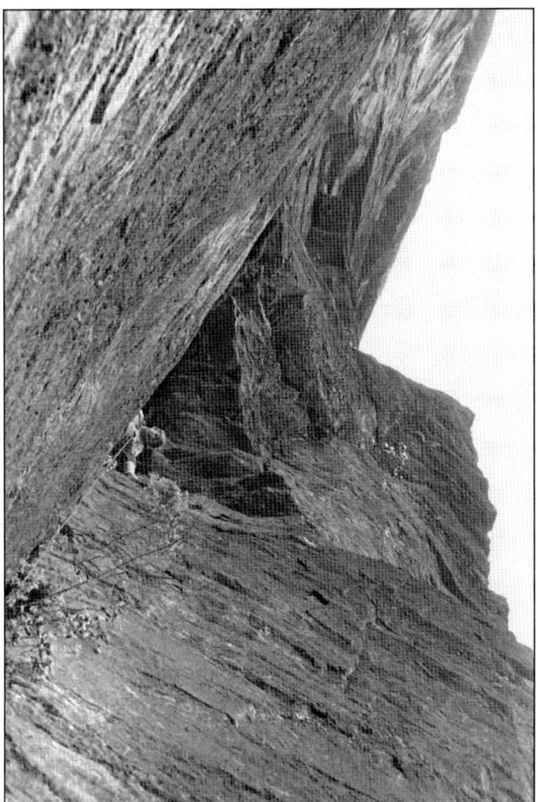

Bumblebee Buttress, 1970. Here Bob Gillespie is belaying (taking up slack in) a safety line attached to fellow climber Bob Mitchell, who has paused in his climb to photograph Gillespie above him. (Courtesy of Mike Fischesser.)

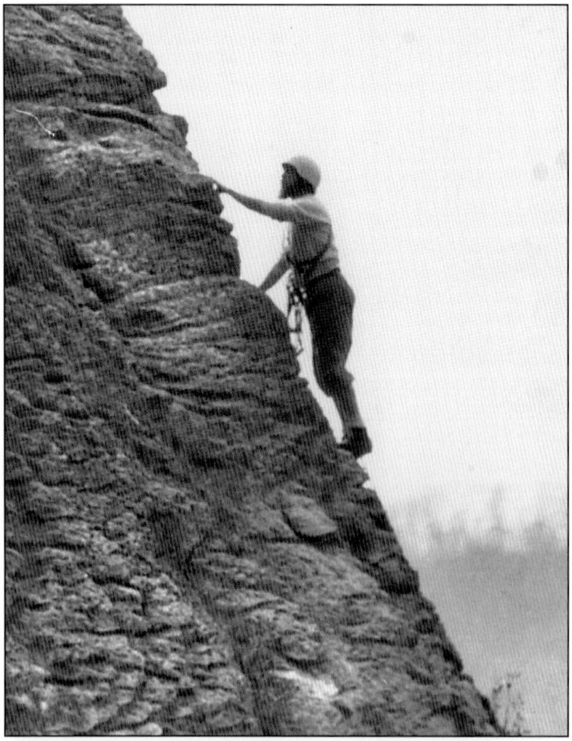

BRAD SHAVER ON CLIMB. Brad Shaver of Asheville, North Carolina, was an ardent climber, an Outward Bound student, and owner of the first climbing gear outlet, Mountaineering South, in the southeastern United States. In October 1970, he fell to his death while descending Dunagiri (7,066 meters), one of the high peaks in the Garhual Himalayas in the northern Indian state of Uttarakhand. (Courtesy of Mike Fischesser.)

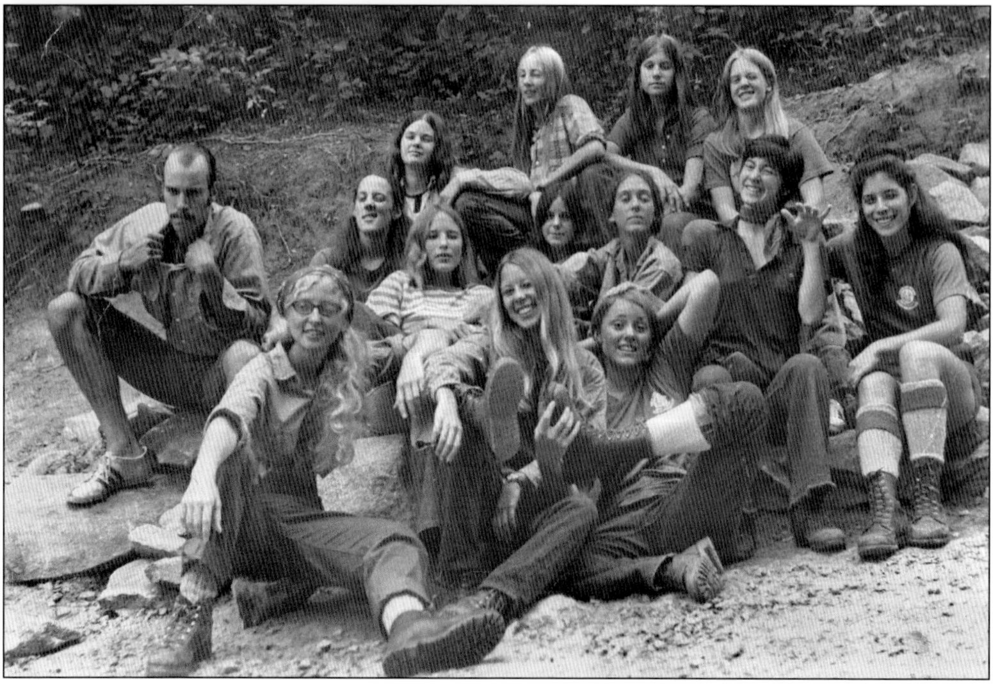

ARLENE USTIN AND GARY BUCHNER WITH GIRLS CREW. The North Carolina Outward Bound School at Table Rock Mountain graduated its first class of women in 1971. Instructor Arlene Ustin on the far right recalls the solidarity of the young women, who once stayed up all night convincing a fellow student not to quit the course. (Courtesy of Mike Fischesser.)

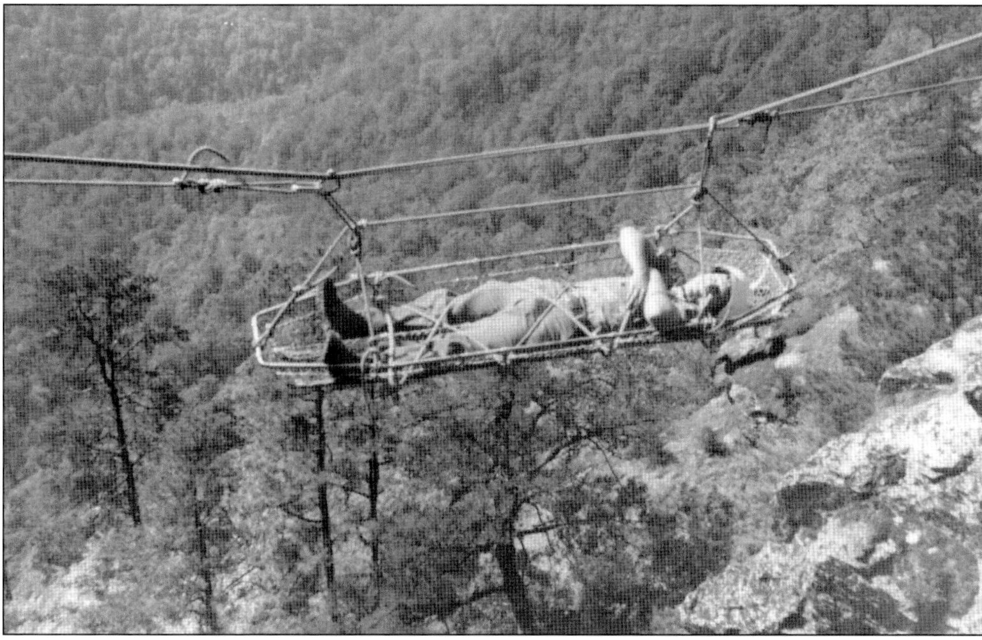

Tyrolean Traverse in the Chimneys. In search-and-rescue training classes held by Outward Bound, students learn how to transport injured people out of the wilderness. Here an "injured climber" is moved along a fixed line by rescuers who also have secured the wire basket to safety lines. The class is training in the Chimneys in 1968. (Courtesy of Mike Fischesser.)

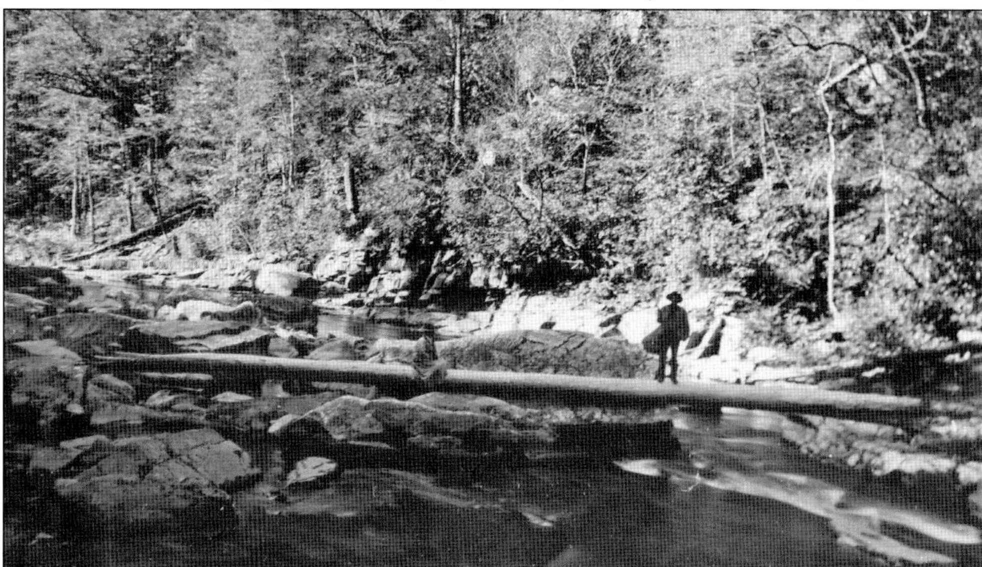

Makeshift Bridge. For untold years driftwood tree trunks have served as footbridges across the waters of the Linville River, conveniently joining boulder to boulder—until the next high water swept them away. Now a well-designed Forest Service footbridge crosses the river mid-way between Hawksbill and Table Rock Mountains. Frank W. Bicknell recorded his wife Jessie and friend Turner Vance on one of the "natural bridges" below Bynum's Bluff on October 26, 1910. The flood of 1916 undoubtedly dashed the tree trunk downstream. (Courtesy of the North Carolina State Archives.)

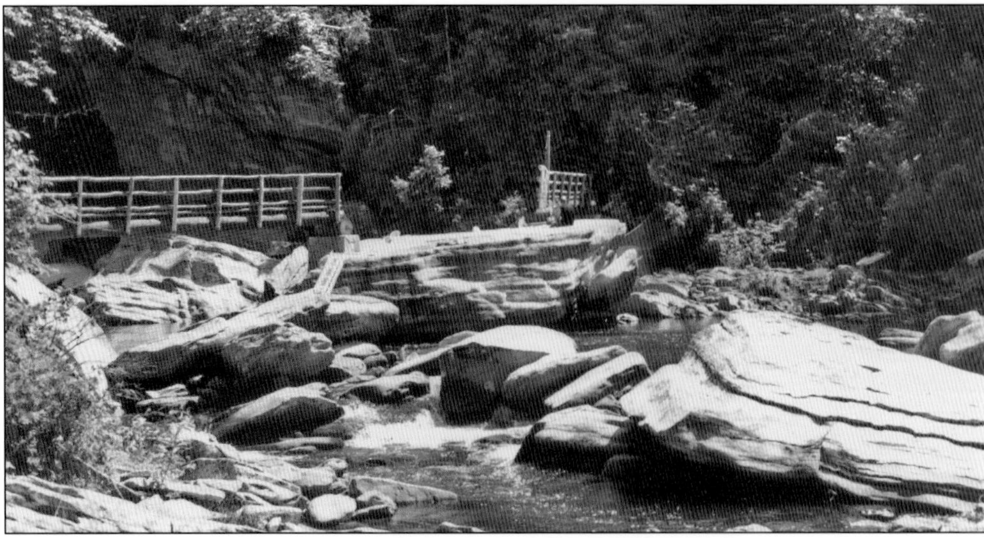

SPENCER RIDGE FOOTBRIDGE. Switchbacks, Inc. of Centerville, Georgia, won the government contract to build the footbridge. Company co-owner Terri Warlick (with husband Charles) sits with her stepson on the large boulder known as "house rock" shortly after the bridge's arrival by helicopter at 9:15 a.m. July 18, 2006. Steps have not yet been installed on the ends of the bridge. The foot logs are made of southern pine from Alabama, and the rails and posts are made of local black locust. The bridge was flown in three sections from a staging area in North Cove on the other side of Linville Mountain. (Courtesy of the author.)

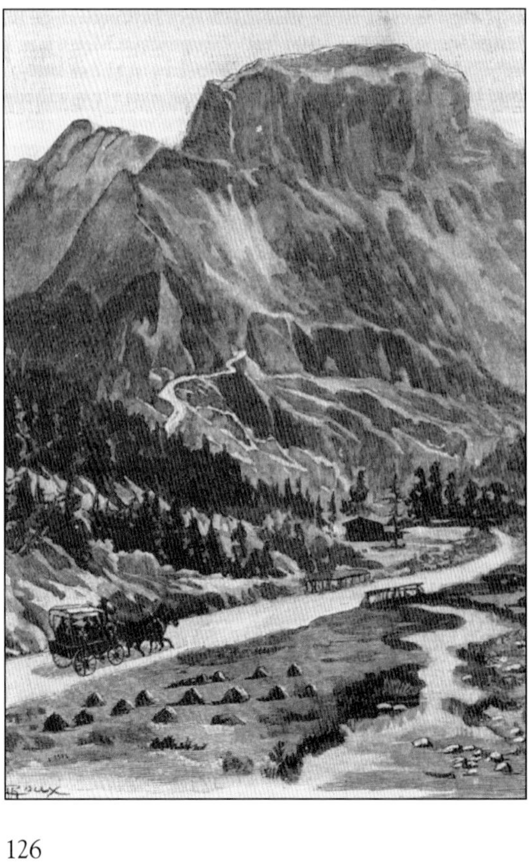

"THE GREAT EYRIE." Table Rock Mountain sets the opening for French science fiction author Jules Verne's 1904 novel, *Master of the World.* It is now conceded that Verne never visited North Carolina; his eight-day visit to America in 1867 did, however, include a trip to Niagara Falls, another location in the novel. Other peaks in the Blue Ridge have been proposed as the origin of Verne's "Great Eerie," namely Pilot Mountain and Mount Airy, but internal evidence in *Master of the World* suggests Table Rock Mountain as the mysteriously rumbling peak in the novel's first chapter. According to Verne authority Jean-Michel Margot, Verne knew no English and probably consulted a 19th-century travel guide written in French. The author was fond of using geographical studies of places he never visited. Margot says that none of Verne's papers have revealed a definite source for the mountain. She adds, "It is still an open question." George Roux illustrated 22 of Verne's novels. (Courtesy of Edward W. Phifer Jr.)

SELECTED BIBLIOGRAPHY

Blake, Christopher. *River of Cliffs: A Linville Gorge Reader.* Boone, NC: Parkway, 2005.

Blake, Christopher and Pete Whehihan. *Common Mushrooms of Linville Gorge.* Linville Falls, NC: Magic Mountain Books, 2006.

Carter, Mark W., Carl E. Merschat, and William F. Wilson. A *Geologic Adventure Along the Blue Ridge Parkway in North Carolina.* Raleigh, NC: North Carolina Geological Survey Section. Department of Environment and Natural Resources, 2001.

Clark, Larry Richard. *Indians of Burke County and Western North Carolina.* Morgantown, NC: TimeSpan Press, 2002.

Draper, Lyman C. *The Life of Daniel Boone.* Ed. With introduction by Ted Franklin Belue. Mechanicsburg, PA: Stackpole, 1998.

Givens, Peter. "Securing Linville Falls." High Vistar. Newsletter of Friends of the Blue Ridge Parkway, Inc. (Fall/Winter 2008): 9.

Hyde, Allen. *The Linville Gorge Hiker's Guide.* Jonas Ridge, NC: Hyde, 2007.

Lambert, Yon and Harrison Shull. *Selected Climbs in North Carolina.* Revised edition. Seattle: The Mountaineers, 2008.

"Linville Falls to Be Made National Park." *The [Morgantown] News-Herald.* January 14, 1952.

Meyer Dan and Diane. *To Know by Experience: Outward Bound, North Carolina.* Photography by Dan Madden. 2nd edition. Morgantown, NC: Artcraft, 1974.

North Carolina State Board of Agriculture. *North Carolina and Its Resources.* Winston: MI& J C Steward, 1896.

Phifer, Edward William Jr. *Burke: The History of a North Carolina County, 1777–1920.* Morgantown, NC: Phifer, 1982.